Mentoring and Coaching in Early Childhood Education

ALSO AVAILABLE FROM BLOOMSBURY

Early Childhood and Neuroscience, Mine Conkbayir
Reflective Teaching in Early Education, Jennifer Colwell
Successful Leadership in the Early Years, June O'Sullivan

Mentoring and Coaching in Early Childhood Education

Edited by Michael Gasper
and Rosie Walker

BLOOMSBURY ACADEMIC
LONDON • NEW YORK • OXFORD • NEW DELHI • SYDNEY

BLOOMSBURY ACADEMIC
Bloomsbury Publishing Plc
50 Bedford Square, London, WC1B 3DP, UK
1385 Broadway, New York, NY 10018, USA

BLOOMSBURY, BLOOMSBURY ACADEMIC and the Diana logo are trademarks of Bloomsbury Publishing Plc

First published in Great Britain 2020

Copyright © Michael Gasper, Rosie Walker and Contributors, 2020

Michael Gasper, Rosie Walker and Contributors have asserted their right under the Copyright, Designs and Patents Act, 1988, to be identified as Authors of this work.

For legal reasons the Acknowledgements on p. xx constitute an extension of this copyright page.

Cover design: Adriana Brioso
Cover images by tunart/Getty Images and RobinOlimb/iStock

All rights reserved. No part of this publication may be reproduced or transmitted in any form or by any means, electronic or mechanical, including photocopying, recording, or any information storage or retrieval system, without prior permission in writing from the publishers.

Bloomsbury Publishing Plc does not have any control over, or responsibility for, any third-party websites referred to or in this book. All internet addresses given in this book were correct at the time of going to press. The author and publisher regret any inconvenience caused if addresses have changed or sites have ceased to exist, but can accept no responsibility for any such changes.

A catalogue record for this book is available from the British Library.

A catalog record for this book is available from the Library of Congress.

ISBN:	HB:	978-1-3501-0073-2
	PB:	978-1-3501-0072-5
	ePDF:	978-1-3501-0075-6
	eBook:	978-1-3501-0074-9

Typeset by Integra Software Services Pvt. Ltd.

To find out more about our authors and books visit www.bloomsbury.com and sign up for our newsletters.

For Alan Chacon

Contents

Tables and Figures x
Contributors xi
Preface xvii
Foreword xviii
Acknowledgements xx
Glossary and Abbreviations xxi

Introduction 1

Part I Mentoring and Coaching Theory

Introduction 5

1 **Theory of Mentoring and Coaching in Early Childhood** *Michael Gasper* 7

2 **The Importance and Value of Mentoring and Coaching in the Early Years Sector** *Michael Reed and Rosie Walker* 17

3 **Mentoring and Coaching and Their Relationship to Management and Leadership in Early Education** *Josephine Bleach* 27

4 **Providing Professional Support to Mentors and Coaches in Early Childhood Education** *Siobhán Keegan* 37

5   **Creating Safe Reflective Spaces for Child Protection Practice** Claire McLoone-Richards

6   **Pedagogic Mediation in the Early Years** Helen Lyndon

7   **A Research-based Approach to Mentoring for Success for Early Years Teachers** Jill Harrison and Diana Harris

8   **Transforming Pedagogy in Early Childhood Education** Naseema Shaik and Hasina Ebrahim

9   **Insights on Mentoring Practices within the Early Childhood Sector in Singapore** Doranna Wong, Manjula Waniganayake and Fay Hadley

10 **Individualized *yet* Standardized Approaches to Coaching in Early Childhood Education** Karrie Snider and Maggie Holley

Part II Appreciative Inquiry: Examples from Practice

Introduction

11 **Appreciative Inquiry Mentoring to Implement the Early Childhood Bicultural Curriculum** Chris Jenkin

12 **Finding Community Through an Induction Support Pilot Project** Laura K. Doan 125

13 **Coaching Teams of Early Years Professionals throughout a County in England** Becky Poulter Jewson 135

14 **Using Collaborative Coaching When Teachers are Experts** Karrie Snider and Maggie Holley 145

15 **Coaching When Teacher Commitment, Confidence and Knowledge are Developing** Karrie Snider and Maggie Holley 154

16 **Cultural Awareness, Narratives and Identity: The Pedagogical Coach as a Facilitator for Quality in ECEC in Belgium** Kaat Verhaeghe and Joke Den Haese 163

17 **Three Key Stages in Mentoring and Coaching** Michael Gasper 180

18 **Using Pre-service Teachers as Mentors to In-service Early Years Teachers to Promote Meaningful Child Participation** Naseema Shaik 188

19 **Critical Reflections on Emerging Themes** Michael Gasper and Rosie Walker 194

Index 200

Tables and Figures

Table

2.1   Type of coaching 23

Figures

7.1   Concentric influences on the Mentor role 76
9.1   Mentoring in the skills framework for EC care and education 91
9.2   Phase 1 participants in PhD study 92
12.1 Induction 127
12.2 Peer mentoring 127
12.3 Gaining confidence 128
12.4 ECE workplace 129
12.5 Beginning ECE 130
13.1 Nursery garden fostering independent learning 136
13.2 Mentoring and coaching template 137
13.3 Interconnecting processes *Impact of Professional Conversations* 140
16.1 Narrative basic attitude 168
16.2 Phase 2: Bringing the story into the here-and-now 168
16.3 Letting the story emerge 173
16.4 Diversattude 176
18.1 Shier's model of participation 191

Contributors

Josephine Bleach is Director of the Early Learning Initiative at the National College of Ireland (NUI). Josephine began her career in primary school teaching. She was involved with national initiatives including: Home School Community, Early Start Pre-School Intervention Programme and the School Development Planning Support Service (Primary) of the Department of Education and Science. She has a PhD in Education (2008) from Trinity College Dublin. Her research interests include: community development using action research; educational disadvantage; parental involvement in children's development and education; professional development for educators; Early Years learning, including literacy and numeracy; policy development and implementation.

Laura K. Doan is an assistant professor in the Faculty of Education and Social Work at Thompson Rivers University in Kamloops, British Columbia, Canada, where she teaches Early Childhood education. Laura's research interests include: how to support new educators as they enter the field, as well as what sustains experienced educators.

Hasina Ebrahim is a professor in Early Childhood education at the University of South Africa. She holds the UNESCO co-chair in Early Childhood education, care and development. Her research is on Early Childhood at the Margins with reference to policy, practice and teacher education. She leads a national project for the European Union and Department of Higher Education on the professionalization of the workforce working with babies and children. She is a key member in the development of the African Based Capacity Development Programme for Early Childhood leaders. She is sector editor of the *South African Journal of Childhood Education*.

Michael Gasper is a self-employed Early Years consultant. After twenty-seven years in teaching he became a research coordinator for Pascal and Bertram's Evaluation of Early Excellence Centres and a tutor, assessor and mentor for the National Professional Qualification in Integrated

Centre Leadership. He has supported and mentored individuals and leadership teams in Children's Centres and schools in England and Ireland. Publications include: *Multiagency working in the early years: challenges and opportunities* (2010); with Kingdon and Gourd, *Flourishing in the early years: contexts, practices and futures* (2017); and with Gibbs, volume 6 of: 'Thinking about pedagogy in early childhood: policy intersecting pedagogy' (2019).

Fay Hadley is a senior lecturer in Early Childhood education and the Director, Initial Teacher Education, in the Department of Educational Studies at Macquarie University, Sydney, Australia. Before becoming an academic, Fay was an Early Childhood teacher, centre director and project manager for Early Childhood organizations in Sydney. Fay's primary area of research examines leadership in Early Childhood education and child and family diversity. Fay is chair of the Publications Advisory Committee for Early Childhood Australia. She is also a member of the editorial board of *Australasian Journal of Early Childhood* and was previously Deputy Editor of this journal.

Joke Den Haese is a lecturer in visual art, intergenerational dialogue and cultural education in the bachelor degree in Early Childhood Education and Care (ECEC) at the Erasmus School, Brussels, Belgium. She has developed a vision about 'growing through art'. In the training of the pedagogical coach, art is a substantial part of the curriculum. Her research aims to discover how art influences (future) professionals. Through experimentation with materials and different art forms, students discover their language (100 languages of Reggio Emilia) to express themselves. She uses 'dialogue and real meeting' between cultures, genders and generations as a mirroring act to confront students with their cultural experiences and background.

Diana Harris has worked as a teacher, lecturer, mentor, facilitator and professional leader across all sectors from nursery classes to Further and Higher Education settings. Her central principles and interests are: individualism, freedom of choice, empowerment and pedagogical practice, alongside her passion for children's literature. Diana strives to spend equal amounts of time reading in the library as weeding in her garden, interspersed with exploration of culture and spaces through travel. She remains a child at heart which is probably why she initially trained as a nursery infant teacher!

Jill Harrison is a principal lecturer and programme leader for Early Years in the Department of Education and Community Studies at the University of Greenwich, England. Jill has worked in the Early Years sector for many years within the private, voluntary, health and social service sectors. She has been the manager of a workplace nursery and of a large Early Years centre for a local authority. She leads on the Bachelor of Arts Hons Early Years and Early Years Initial Teacher Training (ITT) course and is Link Tutor for the Early Years programmes delivered by in SEGi College Malaysia, partners of the University of Greenwich.

Maggie Holley PhD is Adjunct Professor of Early Childhood Education at the University of Missouri–Kansas City (UMKC), USA, where she instructs and coaches teacher candidates. Before working at UMKC, Maggie was the director for twenty-two years of a NAEYC-accredited centre. Her research interests include: teacher beliefs, the classroom daily schedule and teacher resilience.

Chris Jenkin is Senior Lecturer and Ethics Faculty Representative at the Auckland University of Technology, New Zealand. Chris has been involved in education (Early Childhood, primary and tertiary) for more than fifty years. She has particular interests in bicultural development, family and society and issues of equity. She is currently researching the ethics of practitioner research and online learning.

Becky Poulter Jewson is an Early Years lead working with young children in her free-flow setting within the UK. Children's environments are her speciality. She specializes in enabling partnership working, which has led to developing interactive training for parents and practitioners. She has experience as an Early Years lead for Children's Centres, A2YO pilot lead, nursery owner and a nanny.

Siobhán Keegan is a developmental psychologist with special interest in young children's learning and development within Early Childhood Education and Care (ECEC) settings. She works in Ireland as a coordinator with the Better Start Quality Development service, which provides mentoring support to ECEC settings, encouraging them to develop and sustain quality. She has over ten years' experience of leading research projects with children, families and ECEC services in Ireland and has worked as a research consultant, nationally and internationally. Her interests include child-centred approaches to pedagogy and practice and exploiting the potential of mentoring in supporting quality ECEC experiences for children.

Helen Lyndon is Postgraduate Programme Lead for the Centre for Research in Early Childhood in Birmingham, England. She taught initially in primary school education, specializing in mathematics, then took a master's degree in Early Years education while teaching in Children's Centres. She went on to work in higher education on undergraduate and postgraduate courses relating to Early Childhood education. Her doctoral research focuses on pedagogic mediation, including the development of listening methods for daily practice with young children. Helen is the UK Country Coordinator for the European Early Childhood Research Association (EECERA).

Claire McLoone-Richards LL.M is a PhD candidate at the University of Worcester, England. She is a feminist scholar and social scientist whose teaching and research relates to the study and prevention of violence. As a barrister (non-practising) she remains a committed advocate of the rights of children and young people and researches and writes extensively about the rights of the child in the context of child protection, professional practice and integrated working. She has considerable experience of multi-agency partnership working in mental health, substance use and domestic abuse. Claire has been an active member of the Local Safeguarding Children Board.

Michael Reed is an honorary senior fellow in the School of Education at the University of Worcester, England. He is a visiting professor at the University of Ibn Zohr, Morocco. He is a qualified teacher, holding advanced qualifications in Educational Inquiry, Educational Psychology and Special Education. He is a series editor for Routledge and has many publications. These include: *Reflective practice in the early years* (2010), *Quality improvement and change in the early years* (2012), *Work-based research in the early years* (2012), *A critical companion to early childhood* (2015) and *Effective leadership for high quality early years practice* (2016).

Naseema Shaik received her PhD in 2014 and is a senior lecturer in Foundation Phase teaching at the faculty of Education, Cape Peninsula University of Technology in Mowbray, Cape Town, South Africa. She specializes in teaching Grade R and literacy and mathematics in the Foundation Phase. Her research interests are in child participation and participatory pedagogies. She has contributed three chapters to the book, *Teaching Grade R*, published by Juta (2015).

Karrie Snider is Assistant Professor of Early Childhood Education at the University of Central Missouri, USA. She spent over twenty years in Early Childhood education as a teacher, administrator, mentor-coach and teacher educator. Karrie's research interests include: the examination of teacher-child interactions and the ways to strengthen teachers' self-efficacy and instructional capacities. Karrie was the 2018 recipient for the University of Missouri's Faculty Scholar for Application research.

Kaat Verhaeghe is pedagogue for the bachelor degree in Early Childhood Education and Care (ECEC) at Erasmus University College, Brussels, Belgium. She is a researcher for the Knowledge Centre Urban Coaching and Education. Her main subjects – 'identity', 'child and society' and 'good parenting?' – look critically at society and interaction with families and children. Professionals are challenged to contest existing discourses and become more self-aware about their values and concept of the child. Developing personal and professional identity through interaction with others is the central theme of her work. In her research she explores the role of narratives within professionalization.

Rosie Walker is a senior lecturer within the Department for Children and Families, School of Education at the University of Worcester, England. Professionally, she is a qualified social worker, has worked in a variety of social care roles and managed two large Children Centres within the UK. Rosie joined the university in 2010 and has co-written and co-edited a number of books, including *Pedagogies for leading practice* (2019), *A critical companion to early childhood* (2015) and *Success with your early years research project* (2014). She has written several peer-reviewed journal articles.

Manjula Waniganayake is a professor of Early Childhood education at Macquarie University in Sydney, Australia, where she is also the Director of Postgraduate Coursework Studies for the Department of Educational Studies. Manjula has an extensive track record in the Early Childhood sector as: classroom practitioner, parent, policy analyst, advocate, teacher educator, academic writer and researcher. Manjula was awarded an Honorary Doctorate from the University of Tampere, Finland, for her scholarly contributions to Early Childhood Leadership. Manjula's continuing interests in cross-cultural research have been built through collaborations with colleagues from England, Estonia, Finland, Malaysia, Norway, Singapore and South Africa.

Doranna Wong has worked as an Early Childhood teacher, centre director and Early Childhood consultant in Sydney and Singapore since 1994. She is the Early Childhood Teacher Program Manager and Learning Partner for Goodstart NSW/ACT in Australia. She is also currently completing her PhD at Macquarie University, Sydney, Australia. Her thesis research focuses on mentoring in Early Childhood settings in Singapore. Doranna's research interests include exploring perspectives on mentoring practices that shape teacher identity and career development.

Preface

This book has been inspired by the practice we have witnessed, particularly from our experiences as tutors, assessors and mentors on the National Professional Qualification in Integrated Centre Leadership (NPQICL) between 2004 and 2010 and our wider work experience.

We have both experienced the positive impact of mentoring and coaching for those we have supported in developing their reflective practice, validating their self-worth, increasing self-confidence and professional capacity. This is not to say that mentoring and coaching provide a 'magic wand' for instant solutions; rather, they allow practitioners time and space to focus on fundamental values underpinning their practice in Early Childhood education and help them examine and improve their practice.

Early Childhood education is the foundation for the future lives of our youngest children. It is vital that we provide the best quality support for those who dedicate their professional lives to nurture their natural capacities for curiosity, exploration, social and intellectual skills, so that they may flourish.

Michael Gasper and Rosie Walker

Foreword

This book may well become an enduring reference for policy-makers, national and local authority strategists, further and higher educators and especially the professionals and practitioners directly responsible for the provision of Early Childhood education, care and related services for young children and their families. Michael Gasper and Rosie Walker are eminently qualified as editors, having worked as Early Years leaders, researchers, university lecturers, mentors, coaches and authors, with unwavering dedication to developing and sustaining high quality, integrated, community-based services for young children, their families and carers. Their own chapters, together with those of an impressive group of contributors from nine countries, introduce and consider historical and contemporary theories, strategies, systems and research- and practice-based insights that inform mentoring and coaching within Early Years settings. In Part 1, each chapter poses 'reflective questions' with which readers can engage. In Part 2, 'Appreciative Inquiry – Examples from Practice', the chapters describe and analyse in-depth individual and relational processes associated with specific mentoring and coaching stories in and across Early Years settings, with reflective questions helpfully referencing those examples.

It is nearly fifteen years since the beginning of the England-wide National Professional Qualification in Integrated Centre Leadership (NPQICL) pilot and roll-out, through which I led the mentoring component of that year-long, master's level programme. Along with the lead NPQICL developers, Margy Whalley and Patrick Whitaker, Sheila Thorpe and I were gratified that the programme, with mentoring at its heart, survived into 2015, having endured budget cuts from 2010. Reading this book, I feel heartened by the extent to which different forms of mentoring and coaching are being developed, introduced, researched, adapted and embedded in practice. Especially encouraging is the growing evidence of the efficacy of mentoring and coaching in promoting values of social equality and mutual respect that bridge organizational hierarchies, age differences and other social divides. The editors and authors demonstrate their commitment to democratic practices that engender cooperation, cohesiveness and heightened pedagogic awareness and skills within and across teams and settings – including safe, socially responsible, child- and family-centred, reflective, transparent and deeply respectful practice that promotes well-being and learning among young children and their families.

This book provides powerful examples that stress the importance of mentors and coaches not only espousing but *embodying* the values, qualities and attitudes they seek to encourage among Early Years leaders, staff members and trainees. In everyday language, 'walking the talk' is shown to be crucial in the successful promotion of social equality, mutual respect, shifting power dynamics and effective practice within Early Years settings. That is, through providing a reflective, containing and safe space, mentors and coaches listen, empathize and appreciate the needs of each individual, such that these values and qualities are internalized and become apparent in practitioners' relationships and work with young children and their families.

Karen John, PhD
Developmental Psychologist and Adlerian Psychotherapist
Independent Consultant, Researcher, Trainer

Acknowledgements

We would like to extend our warmest thanks to the chapter and case study authors who have been very generous in their willingness to share their knowledge, practice and expertise with us. It has been a pleasure to work with them as they have illustrated how important coaching and mentoring is to quality provision and practice for our youngest children and their families. Together, they have provided a rich international tapestry that will enhance our future thinking about the development of coaching and mentoring.

We hope that all who read this book will be inspired by the possibilities for practice afforded through coaching and mentoring and the vision for the aspiration of the Early Years that can be enriched by successful coaching and mentoring of those who care for and educate children.

Glossary and Abbreviations

Chapter 1

Action Zones Established by the conservative government in England in the 1990s to target identified areas of need in health, education and social services with funding for a set time period. A positive outcome in ECEC was qualified Early Years staff in schools offering expertise to pre-school settings within their catchment areas.

Children's Centres Created by New Labour by merging Early Excellence Centres, Sure Start settings and Neighbourhood Nurseries. They included support for families and, at their peak, provided a wide range of services in partnership with other agencies.

ECEC Early Childhood Care and Education. In the UK this is from babies and children from birth to 8 years of age.

EECs Early Excellence Centres were one of the earliest initiatives introduced by New Labour. Existing nursery schools with recognized good practice and often with a wider community engagement became training centres for Early Years practitioners. They later combined with Sure Start centres and Neighbourhood Nurseries to become Children's Centres.

NPQICL National Professional Qualification in Integrated Centre Leadership. Qualification for Children's Centre Leaders in England between 2005 and 2014.

Neighbourhood Nurseries Under New Labour these settings were created to meet a shortfall in pre-school provision, particularly in areas designated as having high social need.

Sure Start A significant initiative under New Labour in 2007 that established settings to support families with pre-school children. They developed closer multi-agency working which was expanded with the establishment of Children's Centres.

Chapter 3

ELI Early Learning Initiative in the National College of Ireland

First, Second and Third Person Practice First person practice involves taking responsibility for developing skills and practice in your own leadership, management, mentoring and coaching. Second person practice is working with others to improve their practice. Third person practice is about contributing to theory and practice, not just in one's own service, but to a wider network and audience.

Siolta The National Quality Framework for Early Childhood Education in Ireland (2006)

Chapter 5

Safeguarding The term used in the UK to include all aspects of a child's health, safety and well-being at home and in pre-school and school settings.

Child Protection The term used in the UK to include formal procedures to assess risk of harm to children at home and in pre-school and school settings and to decide appropriate action where deemed necessary.

Chapter 6

Pedagogic Mediation This is concerned with the relationship of the 'outsider' with individuals and the organizations they support and the effect of their interaction.

Chapter 7

EYITT Early Years Initial Teacher Training – the current Early Years Teacher qualification.

EYT Early Years Teacher – an earlier teacher training qualification.

Chapter 9

ECCE sector in Singapore (these career tracks range from beginning educators to those with senior roles within each track):
  i) Educarer track – for those working with children aged 2 months to 4 years.
  ii) Teacher track – for those working with children aged 4 to 6 years.
  iii) Leader track for EC educators and reflecting the thirteen occupations in the sector.

Glossary and Abbreviations   xxiii

EC Early Childhood educator – an individual, usually referred to as the 'teacher', who works with children in a kindergarten or childcare centre regardless of their qualifications.
ECCE Skills Framework for Early Childhood Care and Education
ECDA Early Childhood Development Authority
SPARK Singapore's Preschool Accreditation Quality Rating Scale
CPD Continuing Professional Development Framework for EC educators
NQS National Quality Standard (Australian Children's Education and Care Quality Authority, 2018 February)
Childcare Centres Attended by children aged 18 months to 6 years.
EC Centres Refers to both childcare centres (attended by children aged 18 months to 6 years) and kindergartens (attended by children aged 4 to 6 years).
ECDA Early Childhood Development Authority

Chapter 10

ECE Early Childhood Education
CLASS Classroom Assessment Scoring System
The Project Approach An initiative to encourage a more creative and focused curriculum.

Chapter 11

Te Whāriki n[The Woven Mat] New Zealand Early Childhood Provision Template

Chapter 12

ECE Early Childhood Educator
ECEBC Early Childhood Education British Columbia
BCELF British Columbia Early Learning Framework

Chapter 13

EYFS Early Years Foundation Stage
NHS National Health Service

Chapter 14

Head Start Peri-Preschool Project USA
ECPAF Early Childhood Project Approach Fidelity Form
CRT Culturally Responsive Teaching

Chapter 15

CLASS Classroom Assessment Scoring System
ECPAF Early Childhood Project Approach Fidelity Form

Chapter 16

NBA Narrative Basic Attitude (Verhaeghe et al., 2017)
ECEC Early Childhood Education and Care
ECPs Early Childhood Practitioners

Chapter 17

Sure Start and Neighbourhood Nurseries Initiatives of the New Labour government to improve services to children and families.
'Beginnings', 'Middles' and 'Endings' Significant stages in the mentoring relationship.

Chapter 18

Grade R Reception year class (5 and 6 year olds in South Africa). Grade 0 is a pre-reception year for children aged 0 to 4 years.
Grade 1 The year of entry for 7 year olds into main school education in South Africa.

Chapter 19

EYFS UK Early Years Foundation Stage

Introduction

This book was inspired by our work over eighteen years with colleagues in a variety of pre-school and Early Years (birth to 8 years) settings. In our experience, real improvement can be achieved when reflective practice is nurtured and developed in individuals, teams and organizations. The contributors to this book share their experiences of the value and importance of mentoring and coaching, and also supervision, which is often the forum within which they take place.

Context

How is Early Childhood Care and Education (ECEC) perceived?

Although there are exceptions, the Early Years sector internationally is grossly undervalued and is characterized by low pay, limited training and generally poor development opportunities, all of which often conspire to invoke high staff turnover. Early Years tends to be under-resourced at the bottom of the education hierarchy, yet it is a critical time for children as they develop relationships with each other and with the wider world and its exciting possibilities. During these critically important years brain development expands dramatically, even more so where stimuli are high (Gopnick *et al.*, 2001). We would argue that in Early Years settings the young children need the staff caring for them to be confident, well trained in child development and to know how best to stimulate and extend the natural curiosity that children have. This book provides many important and positive aspects of mentoring and coaching programmes shared by the contributing authors representing views from Africa, Asia, Canada, Europe, New Zealand, United Kingdom and United States.

Structure

The book is in two parts: Part I is primarily concerned with theory and how it relates to practice and Part II uses Appreciative Inquiry to explore case study examples from practice. Both parts benefit from international perspectives.

Part I explores mentoring and coaching theory and its rich potential for improving quality in Early Childhood practice. Issues of policy, organizational constraints, top-down pressure and the growing emphasis on quality judgements based on narrow economic values are discussed and challenged. Part II gathers together examples from practice that underline the value of mentoring and coaching for those training and working with Early Years children and the benefits to those staff, children and families. We are passionate about this sector and these approaches to professional development. We hope you will be inspired to be the same.

Part II provides examples of practice from Belgium, Canada, New Zealand, South Africa, United Kingdom and United States of America using an Appreciative Inquiry approach. This explores how the theory of mentoring and coaching are working in practice.

Our final reflection draws together key aspects and questions.

Michael Gasper and Rosie Walker

References

Gopnick, A., Meltzoff, M., and Kuhl, P. (2001) *How babies think.* London, Phoenix.

Oliveira-Formosinho, J. and Formosinho, J. (2012) *Pedagogy-in-participation: childhood association educational perspective.* Porto, Childhood Association and Porto Editoria.

Part I

Mentoring and Coaching Theory

Introduction

Mentoring theory originated in Ancient Greek literature where it related to an older, wiser man supporting a less experienced younger one. Coaching is a more modern construct arising from the needs of sporting personalities and those who support, train and encourage them. The chapters in this section take different aspects of mentoring and coaching in a modern context, exploring their similarities and differences and specifically their value to those working in the context of Early Years education.

Common to all the contributions is the importance of Early Years as a foundation for life itself. Current issues around what mentoring and coaching are and how they can help individuals, groups and settings improve the quality of their reflective practice are reflected upon. The examples provide insights into different political and social contexts, while themes in common emerge from practice shared by many, if not all.

Chapter 1 explores what we mean by mentoring and coaching, their similarities and differences and key features of successful mentoring relationships.

Chapter 2 reflects on the value and importance of mentoring and coaching, including how this supports the leadership of integrated practice.

Chapter 3 is based on the work of the Early Learning Initiative (ELI) in the National College of Ireland since 2007. It considers mentoring and coaching in the context of leading improvements in practice to improve quality in Early Years education.

Chapter 4 examines the value and importance of reflective practice in the training and support of coaches and mentors working in the Better Start teams in the context of a government initiative to improve quality of provision in ECEC settings in Ireland.

Chapter 5 raises issues around safeguarding in ECEC practice in England and the role of mentoring and coaching in supporting practitioners, particularly in supervision sessions.

Chapter 6 explores the concept of 'Pedagogic Mediation' (Oliviera-Formosinho and Formosinho, 2012). This concerns the potential impact of the 'outsider' as a catalyst for positive change.

Chapter 7 draws on research in South Africa and how cognitive coaching can improve teachers' understanding of child participation and encourage and improve it in a system that is traditionally dominated by curriculum- and teacher-led activity.

Chapter 8 shares the approaches and effects of mentoring, which is an integral part of the learning process used with a group of students working towards their Early Years Teacher Status qualification at the University of Greenwich, England.

Chapter 9 is a reflective overview based on the findings of an assessment of mentoring in Singapore within an improvement framework for Early Childhood educators, where mentor support is mandatory for 'beginning teachers', but does not yet extend to those already established and experienced.

Chapter 10 shares perspectives from the USA on the introduction of mentoring and coaching in pre-school settings in supporting increased learning for both teachers and children.

We then step back and reflect on the emerging themes from Part 1 and share the thoughts that these provoke.

1

Theory of Mentoring and Coaching in Early Childhood

Michael Gasper

Chapter Summary

This chapter examines the origins of mentoring and coaching, their attributes, similarities and differences. How they work in practice and their value and importance to practitioners involved in Early Childhood Education and Care (ECEC) practice.

Mentoring and Coaching: Theory in Early Childhood Practice

Mentoring and coaching are approaches to improvement and continuous personal and professional development, recognized as part of current culture and practice in ECEC (McMahon, Dyer and Barker, 2016). Leadership training in these key service areas in England has included both of these approaches as part of senior staff support and development (National Professional Qualification in Integrated Centre Leadership 2005–2014). The generally low levels of funding for training and support, qualification levels and pay of the workforce have contributed to theory and practice being less part of the everyday culture in Early Childhood, particularly for Early Childhood practitioners, until the last decade. Mentoring and coaching, which existed in ECEC practice before then, relied on the initiatives of individual leaders or organizations. The shift towards a universal improvement in pre-school and ECEC services quality began in the UK as part of Conservative Party policy in the late 1990s with the creation of 'Action Zones'. It developed momentum under New Labour, with closer working relationships between education, health and social care through initiatives such as Sure Start (1999–2006) and Early Excellence Centres (1997–2006), which merged to become Children's Centres (1996–).[1] Shared understandings, particularly in terminology, began to emerge between agencies. In the early 2000s mentoring became an integral part of the NPQICL, a qualification for leaders and senior staff in Children's Centres. Professional cultures learned from each other during this period and the growth in awareness of the value and importance of mentoring and coaching in practice was paralleled by the growth of relevant literature. Nevertheless, there remains a specific need for the continuing development of expertise in mentoring and coaching in Early Childhood practice and for literature specifically focused on this area of provision.[2]

What are Mentoring and Coaching?

There is no clear, separate definition of mentoring or coaching. They share similarities in approach. Common usage has blurred historical understanding of what each is and developments in practice have increased the practice elements relevant to both (Garvey, Stokes and Megginson, 2014: 31). Megginson and Clutterbuck recognized the shifts that had occurred in approaches to both coaching and mentoring, between their first edition (2005) and the second (2009), with a broadening interpretation of theory and its conversion to practice. Parsloe and Leedham (2009) echo this, referring to the increase in publications between 1990 and 2009. Both sets of authors also recognized a growing awareness of the links with mentoring and coaching and learning theory and therefore with learning and teaching methods. Parsloe and Leedham's (2009: 11) adoption of the term 'coach-mentors' recognizes the importance of understanding the theories and practice, rather than attempting separation by narrow definition.

---

[1]Since 2017, reductions in funding to local authorities have resulted in the closure of many Children's Centres in England.
[2]See Chapter 2 for a more detailed exploration of the characteristics of the Early Years workforce and sector needs.

Different UK services involved in Early Childhood practice place their own emphasis on mentoring and coaching, who might need them and why. In education, a new member of staff may be 'mentored' by a more experienced colleague. Techniques borrowed from mentoring and coaching may be used in supervision sessions. There is often, however, a negative connotation arising from the pressures to meet education targets when staff may be provided with mentoring or coaching to improve perceived weaknesses. More enlightened settings may well see the beneficial opportunities that mentoring and coaching can provide[3] in building on the positives; in aiming to support individuals or teams as they review and reflect on their work and their perspectives; in assessing progress; in acknowledging successes and considering the challenges; and in improving practice (McMahon *et al.*, 2016: 438). Some supervisees may find security in structure and accountability, but in highly stressful occupations, such as social services, nursing and social care, mentoring and coaching, often in the context of supervision, can provide a 'safe space', allowing an individual to step back from the immediacy of stressful situations to acknowledge and review their own emotional state and reclaim a more objective perspective or identify and set aside the raw emotion of the moment. This can be true of approaches to mentoring or coaching and reinforces the importance of shared understanding of the nature, purpose and practice of each. The nature of the relationship and 'power balance' between mentor and mentee, coach and coachee is critical to establishing confidence in the process and shifts in control: it builds trust that enables an individual to share successes, recognize uncertainties and begin to explore harder areas. A mentor or coach perceived to be an 'imposition' can create an initial barrier that has to be addressed before progress can be made. Mentoring and coaching need not be a hierarchical relationship where the power and control lies with the mentor or coach; it is possible for a colleague in a subordinate position to mentor or coach a senior. While a hierarchical pairing may be supportive as part of a leadership role, it is the antithesis of the shared relationships implicit in the theory of mentoring and coaching. McMahon *et al.* (2016) suggest that developmental support should also include emotional support, recognizing the stressful nature of Early Childhood professional practice (2016: 439). The approach to practice, therefore, is highly dependent on the prevailing culture of an organization, the style of the organization's

---

[3]See Chapter 4 for examples.

leadership and the purpose for which they are used, all of which will colour the balance and defining detail for each.

In terms of mentoring, Starr proposes that: 'A mentor is someone who takes on the role of a trusted adviser, supporter, teacher and wise counsel to another person' (2014: 3), but this could also apply to a coach and is certainly part of many leadership roles. Clutterbuck suggests that the defining feature of mentoring, '... is the holistic nature of the mentoring role that distinguishes it from other learning or support roles, such as coaching and counselling' (2004: 3). But he also quotes a range of definitions (12), each of which is subtly, but importantly, different. The suggestion that it is more important to consider the context, purpose and parameters of the relationship, which will require different strategies and approaches to achieve effective support, is more helpful than attempting a hard and fast definition.

The view of a mentor as an older or wiser person supporting another who is not is based in ancient Greek culture and suggests a hierarchy of knowledge and the passing of knowledge from the 'knower' (the mentor) to the 'not knowing other' (the mentee). However, even here the definition is blurred by process and practice, for example, with Socrates *not* providing answers, but asking questions to encourage his listeners to think, reflect and shift towards a better understanding of what they already knew, or towards their own new knowledge, through dialogue, debate and reflection. This approach is still widely used[4] and could also be argued as being the origin of coaching. This takes us closer to reflecting on the process of learning. Garvey, Stokes and Megginson reflect further on the connections with Greek philosophy (2014: 12), describing Aristotle's philosophy of learning, the earliest recorded, which involves three aspects:

> the practical (as associated with political life); the theoretical (the seeking of truth through thought, observation, consideration and the achievement of knowledge for its own sake); and the productive (making something) ... Arguably a mentor may engage the mentee in discussions of the practical, theoretical and the productive in order to develop holistic and all-round wisdom. (2014: 14)

Their detailed historical perspectives on the emergence of a common understanding of mentoring and coaching examine the *processes* of each

---

[4]See Chapter 4 for more information about the use of Socratic questioning.

as separate disciplines, concluding that there is no single 'one best way' in mentoring or coaching 'and therefore no one definition' (2014: 31).[5] Garvey (in Bachkirova, Cox and Clutterbuck, 2014) reflects on 'mentoring in a coaching world' (2014: 361–374), providing further historical perspectives on mentoring, supporting the view that definitions are less helpful than reflection on the processes and practices of mentoring and coaching in differing contexts. Garvey quotes Geertz's (1971) suggestion that 'thick description' is more helpful and offers four characteristic features of mentoring that involves: a shared trusting relationship; listening, questioning and associated skills; grounding in the mentee's perspective, hopes, fears and often linking to transitions; and a shared process of learning and development (2014: 364). I suggest that, in the context of Early Years, the dynamics of all these are important but the first, *trust*, and last, *mutuality*, underpin everything else.

Bachkirova, Cox and Clutterbuck (2014) define coaching as: 'a human development process that involves structured, focused interaction and the use of appropriate strategies, tools and techniques to promote desirable and sustainable change for the benefit of the coachee and potentially for other stakeholders', and refer to coaching as: 'a powerful vehicle for increasing performance, achieving results and optimizing personal effectiveness' (2014: 1).

While there is an emphasis on improvement, this suggests a more specific focus and a more particular structure than mentoring, but with aims that are focused on outcomes while acknowledging personal dimensions. Their book is a rich resource providing a detailed overview of thirteen separate coaching approaches including, inter alia: psycho-dynamic, cognitive behavioural, solution-focused, person-centred, Gestalt and Existential approaches, as well as twenty-five different genres and contexts for coaching. These approaches represent specific areas of psychology that can be applied equally to techniques of mentoring. Understanding what these are, how they work, their relative strengths and limitations and when and with whom to use them (Parsloe and Leedham, 2009: 10) is arguably much more important than attempting to provide narrow definitions which cannot do justice to the practice of mentoring and coaching.

---

[5]Bachkirova, Cox and Clutterbuck (2014: 361–362) explore historical origins in more detail.

The Underlying Psychology of Mentoring and Coaching

A powerful influence and theoretical grounding for the process and practice of all three is *positive psychology*. The theory is based on the work of Alfred Adler, whose work underpinned the approaches used in the NPQICL mentoring programme that was led by Karen John. Being positive does not mean ignoring negatives where they exist or things that have not happened as they should or at all. It does mean exploring the individual's feelings and the underlying causes of anxiety and their reaction to their feelings. Adlerian psychology is to do with 'the profoundly social nature of human existence and ... that social inequality and the discouragement it engenders is at the root of most mental health problems' (John, 2009: 56). The theory was further developed by Martin Seligman (see also Garvey *et al.*, 2014: 102). Seligman (2011: 26–27) lists five 'core features': 'positive emotions, engagement, interest, meaning, purpose', all of which need to be present, as well as three of the six 'additional features': 'self-esteem, optimism, resilience, vitality, self-determination' for an individual to 'flourish'. These resonate with the ethos of Early Childhood practitioners and embody fundamental aspects, reflective attitudes and characteristics that are at the heart of ECEC programmes and essential grounding for secure Early Childhood development. John points to the importance of 'social interest or community feeling' and refers to '... the deep satisfaction gained from co-operation and helping others' (2013: 56) both in terms of those working in Early Years and the process of mentoring. She also warns of the dangers inherent in mentoring and coaching, '... within psychotherapy, counselling and social work it is well understood that those who work with distress and discouragement are at risk of becoming distressed and discouraged', and stresses the importance of supervision 'which helps us to look at how our work is affecting us and to maintain, or regain, a healthier life perspective and helpful distance' (2013). Therefore, those undertaking roles as mentor or coach focus as much as possible on positives, rather than dwelling on negatives, even if the initial reason for their input is due to underperformance on the part of the individual they are supporting in order to restore or to maintain a balance.

Common Core Characteristics and Differences of Mentoring and Coaching

Mentoring and coaching each involve a mutual relationship that needs trust to work well. Establishing the structure and purpose of sessions, setting clear boundaries and acknowledging the two-way process will help. In mentoring, particularly, which may well include much more about the person themselves, the basis of trust is made clear with shared ground rules and agreed principles negotiated from the start and regularly reviewed and adjusted if necessary. This process reinforces mutual respect and indicates that the mentee is valued by the mentor in a partnership of equals. However, Starr underscores the need to avoid dependency (2014: 166ff) pointing to the danger of the mentee seeing the mentor as a 'help', which infers that the mentee is 'helpless'. This applies equally to coaching.

Each session is time limited and meetings are regular. However, coaching aims to assist an individual in improving specific areas or aspects, whereas the improvement in mentoring is seen to be more holistic and includes nurturing the inner person rather than anticipating a particular outcome. In each case there is a starting point, a progression and an end point, but the length of each and the sequence of sessions are context- and purpose-dependent: both involve regular meetings where progress will be reviewed, issues discussed and new aims set.

The location for each session is important and can help or hinder the process. Sessions may take place inside or outside the workplace, but a setting that puts each person in a mind frame to want to participate, with a degree of comfort, while ensuring that no interruptions, a comfortable temperature, calm lighting and minimal external distractions, should aid the processes involved. Trying to mentor or coach a nursery or pre-school practitioner in a busy room full of the children in their care is not recommended.

In mentoring and coaching the relationship is critical, though subtly different. Mentoring is a mutual process and the motivation of the individual is critical: without this the process cannot begin. A reluctant mentee (Watling and Gasper, 2012) presents a challenge to a mentor in finding a way of winning their trust and willing engagement. In coaching there is a parallel in the sense that little or no progress can be achieved without the willingness and motivation of the coachee/supervisee. However, the power relationship and dynamics are usually different in these two cases: while a coach may well show empathy, encourage the individual and be equally challenged by a reluctant coachee, they are fundamentally unequal[6] and usually have the organizational structure supporting their role. For each, the relationship will have a starting point, a middle and an end within an overall timeframe. Where there is some prior knowledge of the individual, the skill of the mentor or coach is to ensure this works positively, supporting trust rather than the reverse.

The skills involved overlap considerably. Each require the ability to listen actively: this mean reflecting on how what they hear relates to what has gone before while listening; noticing confidence or deviation, hesitation, repetition of words, names or phrases; observing body language, eye contact and facial expression; questioning; being comfortable with silence; summarizing; pausing and allowing space and time to think. In each case the listener needs to operate at different levels simultaneously, listening, keeping track of emerging themes and of the time and progress of the session. However, a mentor will try to maintain a non-judgemental attitude, where a coach or supervisor may not, depending on the context and circumstances of the session. Each may be role models, but the coach may need to maintain professional distance where a mentor may offer professional friendship. Each may need to say things that the individual will find hard to hear and be able to do so without them disengaging or 'switching off'. Equally, each may have to listen to things that are hard or unpleasant and maintain calmness and clarity. How they deal with what they hear will depend on their role, the nature of the disclosure and overall context of the session.

While there are differences between mentoring and coaching focused on context and involving different kinds of relationships, they have a great deal in common. They each usually involve a partnership between two individuals, focused on one individual supporting another to overcome challenges and to improve their practice. They can involve groups, but for the purposes of this chapter it is assumed that a group is made up of individuals and is essentially a shared activity, implying a two-way process and suggesting equal respect between participants. When mentoring or coaching takes place within supervision there is a difference: it suggests a hierarchical relationship with a person who is more senior or more experienced supervising a junior or

---

[6]There is an interesting variation to be found in Chapter 6 exploring 'pedagogic mediation'.

less experienced colleague, though this could possibly be true of mentoring or coaching in certain situations. A supervisor may use some of the same skills and techniques as in mentoring and coaching, such as active listening, reflection and Socratic questioning, but with a different focus, aim and kind of professional relationship and responsibility, including directing the supervisee and a focus on the aims of the organization. Mentoring support is more holistic and less outcomes-focused or directive than coaching or supervision. However, what is essential in each case is that those involved understand and agree the purpose, scope and expectations, whatever name they may give to the process.

Conclusion

The increasing use of these approaches in Early Childhood practice[7] indicates a shift towards a more professional and reflective approach in all kinds of provision since the start of the twenty-first century. The benefits of mentoring and coaching in UK Early Childhood settings were evident in the evaluations of the NPQICL mentoring programme conducted by Karen John (2009) and Isaacs and Trodd (2010). Later chapters will provide examples from practice and explore the degree to which these practices are becoming embedded.

Reflective Questions

1 How might mentoring and coaching help to bridge gaps in ECEC practitioners' confidence and formal training?
2 How important is it for those supporting others to experience training as mentors or coaches?

References

Bachkirova, T., Cox, E., and Clutterbuck, D. (2014) 2nd edn. *The complete handbook of coaching*. London, Sage.

---

[7] See Part II for examples from practice in different countries.

Clutterbuck, D. (2004) 4th edn. *Everyone needs a mentor: fostering talent in your organisation*. London, Chartered Institute of Personnel and Development.

Garvey, B. (2014) 2nd edn. Mentoring in a coaching world. In Bachkirova, T., Cox, E., and Clutterbuck, D. (eds) *The complete handbook of coaching*. London, Sage. pp. 351–375.

Garvey, B., Stokes, P., and Megginson, D. (eds) (2014) 2nd edn. *Coaching and mentoring: theory and practice*. London, Sage.

Isaac, S. and Trodd, L. (2009) *Sustaining leadership learning: the tutor and mentor voice on NPQICL*. Available online: https://www.tandfonline.com/doi/full/10.1080/13502930801896972 (Accessed 11 December 2018).

John, K. (2009) Sustaining the leaders of children's centres: the role of leadership mentoring. *European Early Childhood Education Research Journal*, 16 (1): 53–66. DOI: 10.1080/13502930801897012.

McMahon, C., Dyer, M., and Barker, C. (2016) Mentoring, coaching and supervision. In Trodd, L. (ed.) *The early years handbook for students and practitioners*. London, Routledge. pp. 433–447.

Megginson, D. and Clutterbuck, D. (2009) *Further techniques for coaching and mentoring*, London, Butterworth-Heinemann.

Parsloe, E. and Leedham, M. (2009) *Coaching and mentoring: practical conversations to improve learning*. London, Kogan Page.

Seligman, M. (2011) *Flourish: a new understanding of happiness and well-being and how to achieve them*. London, Nicholas Brearley Publishing.

Starr, J. (2014) *The mentoring manual: your step by step guide to being a mentor*. Harlow, Pearson.

Watling, P. and Gasper, M. (2012) Centre for Research in Early Childhood, Leadership MA, Mentoring and Coaching module, unpublished.

2

The Importance and Value of Mentoring and Coaching in the Early Years Sector

Michael Reed and Rosie Walker

Chapter Summary

This chapter examines the way in which policies, systems and actions on the ground can be integrated to promote quality professional learning. It provides a broad view of the international field with regard to coaching and mentorship and examines how systems, policy and government initiatives drive and move forward strategies that involve mentorship and coaching.

Introduction

In countries around the world, those who promote and protect the welfare of children expect practitioners to become professionally competent. This involves the workforce developing the professional skills necessary to operate within complex systems and demanding not only qualifications and experience, but also the ability to listen, reflect and solve problems. This is a point echoed by Pascal and Bertram (2018) in findings from a comparative international study of eight different countries across the world. They recognize that developing effective integrated Early Childhood policies is a formative part of educational and social support for children and families. For this to happen requires an investment in services, the promotion of workforce integration and professional accountability that is wider than just adhering to a series of regulations. Equally essential is a sound and effective process of professional development, allowing experienced leaders to foster innate skills and reflective development with others and to develop professional learning in practice; for example, by adopting effective professional development through mentoring and coaching.

Terminology and Definitions

In Chapter 1, Mike Gasper offers definitions of coaching and mentoring and their relationship to one another. He presents differing views but concludes that the definitions for each have similar elements across the international arena. **Mentoring** involves meeting developmental needs for advice and guidance and is usually provided by a more senior experienced person who supports the professional development of the mentee. It can be a formal or informal arrangement.

Coaching offers a more personal approach to an individual and the issue under discussion. It requires having a particular goal or vision in mind and uses an appreciative approach to empower development and make the most of the potential of the person receiving the coaching. This makes it a uniquely person-centred experience which, in order to be successful, needs to be sensitive to the culture and context in which the coaching is operating.

The differences between coaching and mentoring are therefore perhaps subtler and less distinct that might be assumed. Both aim to ensure that personal and professional outcomes are for the benefit of the individual and the organization. Research indicates that both are highly successful in their own right (Passmore, Brown and Csigas, 2017). Coaching and mentoring interconnect at the point where both depend for success on the **relationship** between the parties involved being based on trust, commitment and respect in order to maximize impact. Both require strong ethical frameworks, including the consideration of confidentiality issues. They also utilize strategies, such as developing the ability to engage in reflective practice, through a process of sensitive, pertinent questioning as well as by recognizing the importance of supportive, collaborative feedback and evaluation.

Mentorship and Coaching: Policy and Systems

Governments around the world are increasingly focused on the design and development of integrated Early Childhood systems (Pascal and Bertram, 2016; OECD, 2017), a term meaning the design and development of national policies and operational systems to connect Early Childhood Education and Care (ECEC) services one with another. The rationale is to ensure that public policy should support the development of effective systems which ensure that young children and their families have access to high quality services from birth to the start of primary schooling. The value of the integrated systems approach is in allowing a practitioner from a particular field to understand and be critically aware of what different agencies do, 'which in turn enables practitioners [to] work more efficiently with individuals from different professional backgrounds' (Ang, 2012: 295).

Children and families will clearly benefit from such an approach. Moreover, in terms of mentoring and coaching strategies, if integrated systems are to work, then those systems must rely on a cross-fertilization of professional skills and an interface between different agencies for the benefit of children and families. Therefore, a key question should be: where is the evidence that shows cross-sectoral mentoring happens and is there evidence to show how skills from one agency or sector are devolved, shared and transposed with another? There is also evidence that professionals find this difficult; as the research work of Payler and Georgenson (2013) found, there is a variation in working practices between professions. Their findings suggest the need to tailor training to individual contexts, arguing for securing space for practitioners to gain experience of inter-professional working through mentored opportunities. These should be viewed as a positive force for change rather than the solving of organizational problems.

Another challenge is finding ways for professional groups to develop a shared language, understanding and meaning of what integrated systems look like and what this means in practice. A useful starting point is to explore key internationally recognized descriptors used by researchers, policy-makers and academic commentators to describe integrated systems and to see how mentoring and coaching works within this.

Integrated Systems is a term used to describe developed or developing systems where coordinated policies and procedures support children and families across sectors such as health, education, social services and the voluntary sector. These have emerged as legislators and policy formers access research, which suggests that integrated ECEC systems are part of a national investment that generates returns in terms of children's life chances and provides the economic benefits of lessening of pressures on social welfare (Levitt, 2009; Garcia et al., 2016). The systems are increasingly applied by governments around the world (Pascal and Bertram, 2016; 2018) and recognize the interplay of environmental, social and economic factors throughout a person's life and the way in which these impact on their learning and development. The ECEC sector represents one strand of that life course; other strands come into play as the child moves through primary and secondary education and into adulthood to continue his/her life cycle into old age. It is therefore important to see the ECEC sector as one part of a 'life course approach', where formal systems, stemming from policies that are underpinned by legal and statutory entitlements for young children and their families, provide access to welfare services, education and care before primary schooling takes place.

These systems require a coordinated professional strategy that requires those in the Early Years education sector to act together across government policies and systems in supporting the health and well-being of children. In effect, they operate the service delivery or systems delivery of an integrated system. This, in turn, needs a coordinated approach, which involves implementing a legislative framework that meets regulatory requirements and follows professional standards. The way children and families receive these services can vary. The many examples of how multi-agency services are accessed reveal frequent differences in practice. Resolving this will involve the interpretation of national policies into local practices, prompting professionals to work together. For example, policies and procedures to safeguard and protect the welfare of children are followed by all professional services locally, all conforming to national guidelines.

Although mentoring and coaching are key elements underpinning these requirements, it may be unsustainable to provide mentoring and coaching for every person within an organization. A more effective model may be to provide this for the leader who can then support colleagues and staff. This necessitates the development of a culture through mentoring where there is an understanding of the structural regulatory requirements of working with other professions, as well as a willingness to practically engage with other professionals, families and children, and it means placing the child at the centre of provision while being able to cross professional boundaries.

The aim is to arrive at system integration as a 'set of methods, processes and tools to support the alignment and coordination of services' (Rosen *et al.*, 2011: 10). This implies the need for leaders, educators and practitioners to coordinate and collaborate in the setting up and the implementation of high quality and economic services within and across agencies. There is evidence to suggest that fully integrated systems do lead to high performance. Rosen *et al.* (2011) present findings from four case studies from Carolina, New York, Denmark and Scotland and conclude that successful integration is more than a one-off event; rather, it is an ongoing process that needs continual refinement, adaptation and development of shared values. This particularly lends itself to mentoring and coaching as an ongoing process that can be adapted to the circumstances as required.

It can develop skilled, trusted leaders with excellent communication skills, who can act as agents of change within practice, as well as educators working at ground level. Although external drivers for change may be in place, such as financial and policy arrangements, it is the people on the ground who make this work. This is why mentoring and coaching are so important in gaining positive outcomes when professional development in real world systems is adopted.

Research evidence tells us that integrated systems have a positive and pronounced impact on children and families. It tells us less about navigating a way though those systems and what energy and skills are required to do that, which is where coaching and mentoring have an essential part to play.

How Coaching and Mentoring Supports Effective Leadership in ECEC

Integrated practice is an essential component of a life-course approach to intervention and support for children and families. This means changing to the adoption of a professional approach, driven by professionally challenging systems that are failing those they purport to support, rather than simply meeting regulations. Otherwise, there is a danger that the system can become immune to failure and is not fully accountable to those who enact policy in the workplace. This is an important part of leading practice.

Research has indicated the complexity and fast-paced movement of change within ECEC systems internationally. There is a systemic change taking place across nations and the need for Early Childhood systems to respond to the current thinking and to ever-increasing regulation (Pascal and Bertram, 2018). As Urban *et al.* (2012) assert, for contemporary initiatives such as integrated working to be successful they need to be 'embedded in a coherent system of continuous professional development that is focused on transformative practice' (2012: 515). This includes a professional approach, such as mentoring, which recognizes and builds on educators' prior and everyday experience. The process aspects of practice that are determined by a leader and those who work within these systems (Reed, 2017) are what cements the elements of the systems and regulatory requirements together. Mentoring and coaching are the bedrock of quality practice within these contexts.

Pascal and Bertram (2018) have developed the notion of 'Pedagogic system leadership' as a dynamic approach to meet developing and future needs of organizations and to take account of their role within systemic change, as well as working with educators to develop practice accordingly. A key role of this new leader is to provide an 'open and vibrant' learning culture, which we suggest includes the development of mentorship and coaching to provide not only transformational, pedagogic, collaborative leadership but to equip educators with the means to meet the challenges of collective, locality-wide integrated systems that address the impact of social and economic inequities. Urban *et al.* (2012) discuss the development of 'competent' systems that support educators in developing responsive and ethical practices that meet the changing needs of children and families and that foster the ability not only to 'build on a body of professional *knowledge* and *practice* and develop professional values' (2012: 515), but for all staff to critically reflect on and engage in joint learning. The leader, supported by both coaching and mentoring for themselves and others, is at the heart of this.

This is where mentoring becomes of paramount importance in the role it can play in developing leaders and educators within organizations. An example of this can be found in Chapter 3, where mentoring and coaching and their relationship to management and leadership in the Early Years is examined in detail. Leaders require ther own personal coaching and mentoring to become successful. They need training and support to be able to provide coaching and mentoring appropriate to the organizational values, culture and language of the workforce and their values, vision and aspirations to create the conditions where all children can flourish.

Key Debates/Discussion

We have highlighted the need for coordinated integrated services within ECEC to maximize life chances for children and families. As Nores and Fernandez (2018) assert, in order to achieve this a number of factors need to be in place in building the capacity of organizations to meet new agendas. These include: leadership, innovation, evidence-based intervention models and effective partnerships, all of which help make such interventions more culturally relevant, financially stable and institutionally sustainable through long-term support. Mentoring and coaching are key to supporting professional capacity in these areas.

Identifying vertical and horizontal alignment within systems is critical. Vertical alignment includes coordination, partnership and participation across all levels from national to local provision. Horizontal alignment includes collaboration across sectors. Britto *et al.* (2014) suggest horizontal and vertical coordination are needed at national, regional and local levels of government.

Coaching and mentoring are important in helping leaders to develop the 'competent system' (Urban *et al.*, 2012) and 'collaborative professionalism' (Norres and Fernandez, 2018) that such ECEC organizations require. The traditional picture of coaching and mentoring, as defined in Chapter 1, suggests that the coach or the mentor is usually more experienced and knowledgeable than those with whom they are working. This calls into question the power dynamics between the participants and whether there can be an equal contribution and learning from the process, given that it may be considered a vertical approach to mentoring and coaching. Does it always need to be the case that this type of coaching or mentoring within an integrated, collaborative system is the most useful way forward? Conversely, a horizontal system where both parties take responsibility for the learning may also be a useful approach. Table 2.1 shows the differences between the

Table 2.1 Type of Coaching

Type of Coaching/ Mentoring	Reflective Factors	Impact
Vertical	Imparts work-based knowledge, skills, technical aspects	Roles and responsibilities are clear within the relationship
	Concentrated focus on the coachee/mentee and developing practice/potential	Coach/mentor holds power which could be disempowering for participant
	Allows the leader to draw up expectations, vision, culture	Both parties may feel more secure

Type of Coaching/ Mentoring	Reflective Factors	Impact
Horizontal	Two-way process Power is shared Potential for peer mentoring	Organization may benefit from a fresh pair of eyes in the case of new staff or sharing of multiple perspectives Careful setting out of boundaries needed Improved communication as more perspectives involved Deeper and more honest discussions may take place

different types of coaching in terms of issues to be considered when deciding which type to adopt and the impact of each.

Conclusion

Mentorship, coaching and supervision are interconnected – they share the same skills set as the coach or mentor. We are entering an era where more research into the importance and impact of mentoring is being undertaken. The field of mentoring and coaching is, according to Clutterbuck (2013), under-researched, but we are entering an era of mentoring research in order to bring about positive changes for children and families. This book and chapter are contributing to some of the current debates and new models of practice needed to meet global policy agendas.

Reflective Questions

1 What is your experience of coaching and mentoring? Do the vertical and horizontal models play a part in your organization and how effective are they?
2 Can you see a use for a blend of both models within your setting and, if so, how can they be used to the best effect?

References

Ang, L. (2012) Leading and managing in the early years: a study of the impact of a NCSL programme on children's centre leaders' perceptions of leadership and practice. *Educational Management Administration and Leadership*, 40 (3): 289–304.

Britto, P., Yoshikawa, H., Van Ravens, J., Ponguta, L. A., Reyes, M., Nieto, A. M., and Seder, R. (2014) Integrating nutrition and early childhood development interventions strengthening systems for integrated early childhood development services: a cross-national analysis of governance. *Annals of the New York Academy of Science*. 1308: 245–255. ISSN 0077-8923.

Clutterbuck, D. (2013) 'Where next with research on mentoring?' *International Journal of Mentoring and Coaching in Education*, 2 (3). Available online: https://www.emeraldinsight.com/doi/full/10.1108/IJMCE-09-2013-0048 (Accessed 1 January 2019).

García, J. L., Heckman, J. J., Ermini, D., María, L., and Prados, J. (2016) *The life cycle benefits of an influential early childhood programme*. National Bureau of Economic Research. Working Paper 22993. Available online: http://www.nber.org/papers/w22993 (Accessed 1 January 2019).

Levitt C. A. (2009), *From best practices to breakthrough impacts: a science-based approach to building a more promising future for young children and families*. Cambridge, MA, Center on the Developing Child, Harvard University. Available online: http://developingchild.harvard.edu/wp-content/uploads/2016/05/From_Best_Practices_to_Breakthrough_Impacts-3.pdf (Accessed 30 March 2019).

Nores, M. and Fernandez, C. (2018) Building capacity in health and education systems to deliver interventions that strengthen early child development. Towards competent systems in early childhood education and care. Implications for policy and practice. *Annals of the New York Academy of Sciences* –Wiley Online Library. Available online: https://nyaspubs.onlinelibrary.wiley.com/doi/full/10.1111/nyas.13682 (Accessed 1 November 2018).

OECD (2017) *Starting strong: key OECD indicators on early childhood education and care. Towards competent systems in early childhood education and care. Implications for policy and practice*. Available online: http://dx.doi.org/10.1787/9789264276116-en (Accessed 1 November 2018).

Pascal, C. and Bertram, T. (2016) *Early childhood policies and systems in eight countries: findings from IEAs early childhood education study*. Hamburg, The International Association for the Evaluation of Educational Achievements.

Pascal, C. and Bertram, T. (2018) Pedagogic system leadership within complex and changing ECEC systems. In Cheeseman, S. and Walker, R. (eds) *Pedagogies for leading practice*. Oxon, Routledge. pp. 182–203.

Passmore, J., Brown, H., and Csigas, Z. (2017) *The state of play in European coaching and mentoring.* Oxon, University of Reading. Available online: https://assets.henley.ac.uk/defaultUploads/The-State-of-Play-in-European-Coaching-Mentoring-Executive-Report-2017.pdf?mtime=20171204192802 (Accessed 3 April 2019).

Payler, J. and Georgeson, J. (2013), 'Multiagency working in the early years: confidence, competence and context', *Early Years*, 33 (4): 380–397.

Reed, M. (2017) *Effective Leadership for high quality early years practice.* London, Pre-school Learning Alliance.

Rosen, R., Mountford, J., Lewis, G., Lewis, R., Shand, J., and Shaw, S. (2011) *Integration in action: four international case studies.* London, Nuffield Trust. Available online: https://www.nuffieldtrust.org.uk/files/2017-01/integration-in-action-research-summary-web-final.pdf (Accessed 3 April 2019).

Urban, M., Vandenbroeck, M., Van Laere, K., Lazzari, A., and Peeters, J. (2012) Towards competent systems in early childhood education and care. Implications for policy and practice. *European Journal of Education*, 47 (4): 508–526.

3

Mentoring and Coaching and Their Relationship to Management and Leadership in Early Education

Josephine Bleach

Chapter Summary

Improving practice is essential to the provision of quality Early Years education. This chapter will review leadership and management theories and their relationship to mentoring and coaching using the framework of first, second and third person practice (Torbert, 2001). First person practice focuses on reflective practice and individual skill development. Second person practice examines the mentoring and coaching skills needed to build collaborative knowledge-creating relationships within a setting. Third person practice considers the development of theory and practice in both individual services and wider networks.

Much of this chapter is based on the work of the Early Learning Initiative (ELI) in the National College of Ireland. Since 2007, ELI has worked with Early Years educators to improve the quality of teaching and learning in their centres. Coaching and mentoring, which embeds learning and allows for the dissemination of knowledge among practitioners and parents, is a critical element of ELI's work (Bleach, 2013). Evaluations highlight the importance of managers' support for the implementation of agreed changes.

Leadership and Management Theories

In the literature, the terms manager and leader are often used interchangeably, with similar definitions and characteristics used to describe both roles. Tuohy (1997: 12) contends that: 'Good leadership requires good management to put the vision into practice. Good management also needs the vision of good leadership to ensure the organization not only 'does the thing right, but also, "does the right thing".' In this chapter, we assert that leadership involves vision, purpose and overall direction, while management is concerned with working effectively with people to ensure that correct structures and processes are in place. One cannot function without the other. However, while anyone can play a leadership role, management is usually defined as a designated position of authority with a clear mandate and responsibility for the well-being of children and staff. However, when we talk about good managers and leaders, a moral sense is assumed, particularly as their actions can have such long-term consequences for children, families and practitioners.

Management is demanding, particularly in times of frequent changes and new policy initiatives (John, 2008). Managers must balance the often conflicting roles of change agents, 'centres of gravity' (Shamir, 1999: 63) and agents of continuity. Providing temporary stability and emotional reassurance while people are adapting to change is a key aspect of the role. Competent managers who are 'guardians of stability' (Shamir, 1999: 60) may be preferable to transformative visionary leaders. Many factors – including the community, culture and socio-political context – can work as powerful constraints, with a well-organized service taking precedence over the improvement of teaching methodologies and curriculum development (Bleach, 2002).

The Leadership Styles Framework (Lewin *et al.*, 1939) describes three types of leaders: authoritarian, democratic and laissez-faire. The authoritarian leader makes decisions without consulting anyone else, while the laissez-faire leader has little or no involvement in the decisions made. The democratic leader, considered the most effective (John, 2008) and most ethical, involves others in decision-making processes. There are many variations on the democratic leadership style. All foster relational approaches where multiple individuals assume leadership roles and collectively share duties. While decision-making processes may take longer and are more convoluted, participants were found to be happier in the long term with the decisions made and more likely to implement them (Lewin *et al.*, 1939).

However, Blanchard, Zigarmi and Zigarmi (2004: 27) argue that managers need to be 'situational leaders', those who change their styles depending on the person and situation. Inexperienced or new staff benefit from being given direction and coaching. Competent staff require support or mentoring, while delegating is more appropriate for highly experienced skilled staff. Knowing your staff and what they need is the key to situational leadership (Blanchard *et al.*, 2004). Identifying leaders who have the confidence and skills to support others will lessen the burden on the manager and increase the commitment of the stakeholders. However, managers need to be able to trust these leaders to safeguard the participants and facilitate high quality coaching and mentoring interactions.

Mentoring and Coaching

While the use of coaching and mentoring is increasing, the terms, like leadership and management, are often used interchangeably (Morgan and Rochford, 2017) and confused with other forms of professional development. In this chapter, coaching is defined as a short-term collaborative relationship, which is focused on working in a systematic way towards agreed goals (Morgan and Rochford, 2017). Aimed at enhancing professional performance, it is most useful when new practices are being implemented or someone is new to a role. Mentoring typically involves an ongoing relationship of support for significant transitions in knowledge, thinking and skills to enable professional growth and career development (Morgan and Rochford, 2017). While both coaching and mentoring are important in enhancing workplace well-being, research indicates that they are most effective in organizations where there is a highly motivated supportive culture.

Planning when to use coaching and mentoring is a key management task, as is the establishment of clearly defined professional development needs, goals and relationships characterized by trust, empathy, respect and confidentiality. Strategies are needed to address the complex ethical issues that may arise, including potential and actual conflicts of interest, professional standards, service users' best interests, legislative requirements and performance management (Morgan and Rochford, 2017).

First, Second and Third Person Practice

In this section, the framework of first, second and third person practice (Torbert, 2001) is used to discuss mentoring and coaching and their relationship to management and leadership. First person practice involves taking responsibility for developing your own leadership, management, mentoring and coaching skills. Second person practice is working with others to improve one's practice. Third person practice is about contributing to theory and practice, not just in one's own service, but to a wider network and audience.

First Person Practice

First person practice is about leading and managing oneself (Torbert, 2001). Reflective practice, which involves critically evaluating the impact of one's actions on others, is essential. All managers have a responsibility to critically reflect on and address how their service supports quality practice, professional development and individual well-being. Discouragement is common among Early Years educators, particularly those who work with vulnerable children and families (John, 2008). Required to be both the agents and managers of change, they face constant challenges with their ability to deal with these challenges influencing their effectiveness. As Alder (1995: 14) states:

> Being in control is largely a matter of perception – one person feels in control, acts accordingly and achieves a lot in a limited time. Another person might have far fewer actual external demands, but quickly caves in and can do no more than fire fight. This is not so much a matter of tools and techniques, as a state of mind and belief.

Productive educational change at its core is not 'the capacity to implement the latest policy, but rather the ability to survive the vicissitudes of planned and unplanned change while growing and developing' (Fullan, 1993: 5). Not only do managers have to know how to cope with change, they need to be one step ahead of it. They also need 'the skills to manage organizations and people in a way that buffers them against, and challenges them with, the imperatives of change' (MacBeath, Moos and Riley 1998: 21). This requires them to reflect on, rather than react to, the needs of their service and their stakeholders (John, 2008) as well as seeking support from others, both inside and outside their organization.

Defining and implementing a shared educational vision, while developing one's own deeply held philosophy, is a vital aspect of leadership (Sergiovanni, 1992). It enables leaders to resist the fads of popular culture and to withstand the disapproval of others when their sense of integrity is at stake (Starratt, 1996: 108). First person practice helps leaders develop their intrapersonal intelligence, thereby helping them to know their own mind, including their thoughts, values and strategies (Gardner and Laskin, 1996: 36). This self-knowledge allows leaders to communicate their thoughts, feelings and understandings to others effectively, thereby enabling them to mentor and coach others successfully.

Second Person Practice

Second person practice occurs through engagement with others. This section will examine the skills and processes needed to build and sustain collaborative relationships that support quality. Early Years education services are social systems, where understanding resistance and developing a strategy of motivation is a key leadership task (Tuohy, 1997: 22). Managers need to be skilled enough to understand and manage the context and the community in which they operate along with the various dilemmas created by new initiatives, stakeholders' concerns, curriculum planning and policy formation. This can only be achieved through effective first person practice, positive supportive working relationships and astute communication. Individual and organizational needs have to be addressed. Encouraging engagement in coaching and mentoring is not easy. Many practitioners have low levels of education and lack confidence, not only in their own practice, but also in their basic communication and literacy skills (Share et al., 2011). ELI believes a social, collaborative and dialogic approach (Wong, 2009) to be most effective, particularly if action research and dynamic conversations (Schön, 1983) are integral elements of a coaching and mentoring programme (Bleach, 2013).

Dynamic conversations (Schön, 1983) enable participants to learn from each other. By critiquing perspectives and actions, existing philosophies and norms are challenged. Taking part in discussions can be difficult, particularly if practitioners are unfamiliar with the language and concepts being used. Initial coaching may be required, including translating jargon and providing participants with the 'words' or language to express their opinions and make their practice explicit (Bleach, 2013): 'Again we got chatting … about numeracy week. … said that she didn't really understand how you could "teach babies numeracy". We explained the concept and talked about language related to capacity' (ELI, 2017). Listening to practitioners describe their practice, translating it into the official technical-rational discourse (McNiff and Whitehead, 2006) and then supporting them to speak confidently in public is a vital element of second person leadership practice.

Action research, a powerful tool for change and improvement (Cohen et al., 2000), is closely related to the Síolta Standard 8: Planning and Evaluation, which Irish ECEC settings are expected to implement: 'Enriching and informing all aspects of practice within the settings requires cycles of observation, planning, action and evaluation, undertaken on a regular basis' (CECDE, 2006). This process begins by creating a learning community that works together to 'nurture and sustain a knowledge-creating system', based on valuing each other equally (Senge and Scharmer, 2001: 238–250). Managers have the responsibility of creating this community of learners with the capacity to model quality practice and collaboratively improve children's outcomes.

Stage one of each action research cycle and second person practice begins with collective first person practice, i.e. by reflecting on the quality of existing practice. This allows the manager to identify priorities and devise a programme that addresses the needs of whole organization as well as individual staff. Managing the pace of change will be important to avoid overload: the implementation dip described by Fullan (2005). Preparation for coaching and mentoring sessions is important. Finding the right balance of challenge and support is critical. Opportunities, whether one-to-one or in a small group, for practitioners to discuss and tease out practice implications need to be organized. Focusing on issues chosen by the practitioners will support implementation. For many, the demands of their management role often leave them with little time or energy to get involved in mentoring or coaching (Bleach, 2013). Therefore, they need to identify others capable of second person leadership practice.

Mentoring works best when arrangements are made for mentees to have non-contact time with their mentor, whereas coaching sessions *can* take place with children present. By engaging with the children, the coach can model best practice, thereby enabling the practitioner to better understand the methodology:

> We met with one of the staff who was so enthusiastic and was asking lots of questions. She asked if it was ok to set up the sand tray for our capacity activity as she had lots of different sized containers for the sand tray. We spent almost an hour with the staff member and the children, modelling the interactions and relevant language relating to capacity. The children did not want the activity to end! (ELI, 2017)

ELI has found regular short visits to be more effective (Bleach, 2013). Flexibility is also required as sessions sometimes must be rescheduled due to staff absenteeism and/or other unforeseen factors. Structuring the visits around a theme is particularly effective.

An integral part of ELI's programme was the one-to-one mentoring of the managers and team leaders, who led and managed change within their settings (Bleach, 2013). Having the opportunity to talk to the ELI team about the dilemmas they faced encouraged and supported them throughout the process. It enabled them to resolve many of the implementation issues and maintain their commitment, motivation and energy levels (John, 2008).

Third Person Practice

Third person practice will consider how a leader contributes to the development of theory and practice (Torbert, 2001). First and second person practices are essential to third person practice as they support the development of the personal and interpersonal skills needed to communicate with different audiences. Exposure to the ideas of academic, professional and political elites provides a benchmark against which their practice can be measured and helps them to conceptualize the professional roles and norms of an Early Years educator (Bleach, 2014).

ELI's relationship with Early Years education services has fostered the development of a structured 'learning community' where all participants can engage in a collaborative construction of knowledge (ELI, 2017). At its core is the Early Numeracy Working Group, which is responsible for developing, planning and implementing the programme. Consisting of nominees from each service, this group provides a valuable networking opportunity with nominees sharing practice and learning from others. It has developed a repertoire of experiences, stories, tools and perspectives, with their growing knowledge improving educational outcomes for children.

Conclusion

This chapter, using the framework of first, second and third person practice (Torbert, 2001), has explored how Early Years education managers and leaders can manage change and support ongoing quality improvement through an integrated mentoring and coaching programme. Promoting quality practice, professional development, leadership and ongoing networking is important. Only by engaging in self-transformation through first person practice can ECEC managers and leaders encourage transformation in others (Torbert, 2001). Critical reflection on theories, practice and interactions with others is a central component. Knowing who you are and how others see you is essential, as is identifying and addressing your own coaching and mentoring needs.

Second person practice involves ECEC managers developing a coaching and mentoring programme in their service, which enables staff to reflect on past experiences, monitor the present and envision the future through dynamic conversations (Schön, 1983) and action research (Bleach, 2013). Managing the power dynamics will be important if the programme is to meet individual and organizational needs appropriately. This requires managers to use first person practice to critically reflect on and address how their service is supporting quality practice and individual well-being.

Third person practice is about engagement with external networks. It enables leaders and managers to develop their own individual professional identities and skills, along with providing them with the opportunity to contribute to theory and practice. Third person leadership practice involves continually using first and second person leadership practices to first understand one's philosophy and then to implement a mentoring and coaching programme that supports high quality Early Years education.

Reflective Questions

1 Are first, second and third person practices apparent within your organization? If not, how can this be developed?
2 What is your philosophy of coaching and mentoring?

References

Alder, H. Dr. (1995) *The right brain manager*. London, Judy Piatkus.
Blanchard, K., Zigarmi, P., and Zigarmi, D. (2004) *Leadership and the one minute manager, increasing effectiveness by being a good leader*. London, HarperCollins.

Bleach, J. (2013) Using action research to support quality early years practice. *European Early Childhood Education Research Journal*, 21 (3): 370–379.

Bleach, J. (2014) Developing professionalism through reflective practice and ongoing professional development. *European Early Childhood Education Research Journal*, 22 (2): 185–197.

Bleach, M. J. (2002) The use of release days by teaching principals, Master of Studies thesis. Dublin, University of Dublin, Trinity College (unpublished).

Centre for Early Childhood Development and Education (CECDE) (2006) *Síolta: the national quality framework for early childhood education*. Dublin, User Manuals Dublin, CECDE.

Cohen, L., Manion, L., and Morrison, K. (2011) 7th edn. *Research methods in education*. Oxford, Routledge.

Early Learning Initiative (ELI) (2017) Annual Report 2016–17. Dublin, National College of Ireland (unpublished).

Fullan, M. (1993) *Change forces: probing the depths of educational reform*. London, Falmer Press.

Fullan, M. (2005) Education in motion. Leading in a culture of change. UK and Ireland Workshop Tour.

Gardner, H. and Laskin, E. (1996) *Leading minds. An anatomy of leadership*. London, HarperCollins.

John, K. (2008) Sustaining the leaders of children's centres: the role of leadership mentoring. *European Early Childhood Education Research Journal*, 16 (1): 53–66.

Lewin, K., Lippitt, R., and White, R. K. (1939) Patterns of aggressive behavior in experimentally created social climates. *Journal of Social Psychology*, 10: 271–301.

MacBeath, J., Moos, L., and Riley, K. A. (1998) Time for a change. In MacBeath, J. (ed.) *Effective school leadership: responding to change*. London, Paul Chapman. pp. 20–30.

McNiff, J. and Whitehead, J. (2006) *All you need to know about action research*. London, Sage Publications.

Morgan, M. and Rochford, S. (2017) *Coaching and mentoring for frontline practitioners*. Dublin, Centre for Effective Services.

Schön, D. (1983) *The reflective practitioner: How professionals think in action*. London, Temple Smith.

Senge, P. and Scharmer, O. (2001) Community action research: learning as a community of practitioners, consultants and researchers. In Reason, P. and Bradbury, H. (eds) *Handbook of action research, participative inquiry and practice*. London, Sage. pp. 238–250.

Sergiovanni, T. J. (1992) *Moral leadership: getting to the heart of school improvement*. San Francisco, CA, Jossey-Bass.

Shamir, B. (1999) Leadership in boundaryless organisations: disposable or indispensable? *Work and Organizational Psychology*, 8 (9): 49–71.

Share, M., Kerrins, L., and Greene, S. (2011) *Developing early professionalism. Evaluation of the early learning initiative's professional development programme in community childcare centres in the Dublin docklands.* Dublin, National College of Ireland.

Starratt, R. J. (1996) *Transforming educational administration.* New York, NY, McGraw-Hill.

Torbert, W. R. (2001) The practice of action inquiry. In Reason, P. and Bradbury, H. (eds) *Handbook of action research, participative inquiry and practice.* London, Sage. pp. 250–261.

Tuohy, D. (1997) *School leadership and strategic planning.* Dublin, Association of Secondary Teachers in Ireland.

Wong, A. C. Y. (2009, Fall/Autumn) Dialogue engagements: professional development using pedagogical documentation. *Canadian Children*, 34 (2): 25–30.

the right approach to take based on their own experience or be guided by the approach of a mentor who may have previously supported them. While it can be important for the credibility of a mentor that they understand and have experience of the working environment of those they are mentoring (Elliot *et al.*, 2000), having too overt a focus on the previous experience of a mentor can negatively affect the mentoring process by risking a shift of focus from the mentee's concerns to those of the mentor (Clutterbuck, 2014). Effective mentoring training or education courses need to address key aspects of mentoring theory and practice (Achinstein and Athanases, 2006; Carver and Feiman-Nemser, 2009; Evertson and Smithey, 2000; Schwille and Dynak, 2000). Specifically, knowledge on the theory and practice of adult learning (Knowles, 1970; Ozuah, 2005), mentor and mentee roles (Garvey, Stokes and Megginson, 2014), communication (Bokeno and Gantt, 2000) and reflective practice (Schön, 1987; Mezirow, 1985) are important for mentors working with those in Early Childhood education and care settings.

As well as learning classroom-based content, it is important that mentors are given opportunities to implement their own work in practice at an initial training stage and as an ongoing aspect of their continuous professional development (Earl and Timperley, 2008; Langdon, 2014; Robinson and Lai, 2005). These practice sessions provide opportunities for mentees to construct their own learning (Bruner, 1966) and consider the social (Lave and Wenger, 1991) and contextual applications of their work (Fullan, 2008). This practice can contain an additional layer of support if it allows opportunities for mentors to come together in communities of practice, adding a peer learning and support dimension to the process (Galinsky, 2012). Research has indicated that peer groups can support those in leadership or mentoring roles in educational settings and enable them to have a reduced sense of professional isolation and an increased sense of self-efficacy, buoyed up by a sharing of experience and access to new strategies based on the learning of others (Ambrosetti, Knight and Dekkers, 2013; Langelotz, 2013: Thornton, 2010). Some studies that have examined the transferability of peer mentoring approaches to Early Childhood education have found that it leads to personal growth through increasing self-efficacy and acts as a catalyst for change in pedagogical leadership and practice through interaction and peer influence (Cherrington and Thornton, 2015; Penman and O'Connell Sutherland, 2015). Critically, the fact that peer groups alone are insufficient to affect and sustain change was emphasized, underlining the importance of organizational ethos and the provision of structural resources to processes such as mentoring.

Reflective Supervision with Mentors in Early Childhood Education and Care

While the term supervision has traditionally implied a hierarchical relationship often associated with performance management, salary and human relations practice, there has been a move in many professions to recognize the need for professional supports that have developmental, relationship-based and person-centred roots. There has been a tradition of providing supervision in the helping professions, such as counselling, social work and psychotherapy, particularly, emphasizing the well-being of both the professional and the client. Mentors working in Early Childhood education increasingly take on the role of supporting others as they engage in reflective practice. Hawkins and Shohet (2012) describe a formative/educative supervisory role for the supervisor of a developing mentor that focuses on supporting the mentor to identify a mentoring process that is effective for them, with a focus on dynamic relationships, boundaries and skills development. Rouse (2015) posits that, unless a mentor is able to reflect on their own behaviours, values and assumptions, their capacity to support others to develop those skills is inhibited. The importance of providing a protected space to discuss and reflect upon mentoring practice with a 'mentoring mentor' is key as it offers an opportunity for mentors to receive guidance and support so that they, in turn, can effectively support their mentees.

The tradition of 'reflective supervision' (Chu, 2014: 150) is already established and has been articulated by those who work with children in the birth to 3 years of age programme area in the United States, in particular (Eggbeer, Mann and Seibel, 2007; Parlakian, 2001; 2002; Weatherston, Weigand and Weigand, 2010). Chu (2014) proposes this term as being an appropriate workplace support element for those who mentor in ECEC, given that it emphasizes empathy, support and facilitated reflection. She suggests that it has 'the power to promote increased competence in Early Childhood professionals while providing a process for respectful partnership and open communication among staff on the same program [sic]', Chu, 2014: 149). Moreover, it appropriately mirrors the structural leadership supports that are increasingly acknowledged as being key to high quality Early Childhood education systems internationally (Urban et al.,

4

Providing Professional Support to Mentors and Coaches in Early Childhood Education

Siobhán Keegan

Chapter Summary

Mentoring centres on the application of knowledge to practice, which is regarded as critical to ensuring effective and lasting professional development (Isner *et al.*, 2011; Peeters and Vandenbroeck, 2010; Vujičić, 2008). Research indicates that mentoring is an effective form of professional development in Early Childhood Education and Care (ECEC) settings (Howe and Jacobs, 2014; Peterson *et al.*, 2010; Ramey and Ramey, 2008). The OECD's (2012) Quality Toolbox for Early Childhood Education and Care states that mentoring is widely regarded as one of several mechanisms to ensure that educators remain aware of appropriate research, methods and knowledge to inform their curriculum and practice. This chapter discusses how mentors can be supported so that they can develop their skills and effectively support others to work effectively in ECEC settings.

Introduction

The role of a mentor in Early Childhood education is an important and diverse one, with many mentoring programmes in ECEC settings developing in an organic way, in response to local and targeted needs or when pockets of funding become available for pilot schemes. As such, mentoring in Early Childhood education has evolved as a flexible and open-ended process, which has meant that less has been written or even considered regarding the mechanism by which a mentor in Early Childhood education is provided with professional support opportunities. There is an increasing focus on topics such as how a mentor builds relationships, uses mentoring and coaching strategies and supports those in ECEC settings to develop their practice.

It is not sufficient that mentors are good teachers or educators, rather, 'Mentors need mentoring, and this facility must be found in the workplace, however it is defined, as well as through continuing training' (Callan, 2006: 15). There is growing recognition of the need for mentors and coaches, including those working in ECEC settings, to participate in formal as well as informal professional support structures. In a general sense, professional development for those working in ECEC should involve opportunities for observation, reflection, planning, teamwork and cooperation as outlined in the proposed European Union Quality Framework for Early Childhood Education and Care (European Union Commission, 2014). Similarly, Early Childhood education and care mentors require professional development and support structures that underline the importance of the role they play in the Early Childhood education sector.

Training and Education that Focuses on Mentoring and Coaching Skills

Training or preparation for mentoring that focuses on mentoring in and of itself, appears to be limited (Ambrosetti, 2014: Watson *et al.*, 2014). This is perhaps related to the fact that mentors traditionally assumed their roles to be based on their experience, age or perceived proficiency in their 'day job'. Less consideration was made of the need for mentors to possess key mentoring and coaching skills, perhaps with an assumption that the mentor would know the right approach to take based on their own experience or be guided by the approach of a mentor who may have previously supported them. While it can be important for the credibility of a mentor that they understand and have experience of the working environment of those they are mentoring (Elliot *et al.*, 2000), having too overt a focus on the previous experience of a mentor can negatively affect the mentoring process by risking a shift of focus from the mentee's concerns to those of the mentor (Clutterbuck, 2014). Effective mentoring training or education courses need to address key aspects of mentoring theory and practice (Achinstein and Athanases, 2006; Carver and Feiman-Nemser, 2009; Evertson and Smithey, 2000; Schwille and Dynak, 2000). Specifically, knowledge on the theory and practice of adult learning (Knowles, 1970; Ozuah, 2005), mentor and mentee roles (Garvey, Stokes and Megginson, 2014), communication (Bokeno and Gantt, 2000) and reflective practice (Schön, 1987; Mezirow, 1985) are important for mentors working with those in Early Childhood education and care settings.

As well as learning classroom-based content, it is important that mentors are given opportunities to implement their own work in practice at an initial training stage and as an ongoing aspect of their continuous professional development (Earl and Timperley, 2008; Langdon, 2014; Robinson and Lai, 2005). These practice sessions provide opportunities for mentees to construct their own learning (Bruner, 1966) and consider the social (Lave and Wenger, 1991) and contextual applications of their work (Fullan, 2008). This practice can contain an additional layer of support if it allows opportunities for mentors to come together in communities of practice, adding a peer learning and support dimension to the process (Galinsky, 2012). Research has indicated that peer groups can support those in leadership or mentoring roles in educational settings and enable them to have a reduced sense of professional isolation and an increased sense of self-efficacy, buoyed up by a sharing of experience and access to new strategies based on the learning of others (Ambrosetti, Knight and Dekkers, 2013; Langelotz, 2013: Thornton, 2010). Some studies that have examined the transferability of peer mentoring approaches to Early Childhood education have found that it leads to personal growth through increasing self-efficacy and acts as a catalyst for change in pedagogical leadership and practice through interaction and peer influence (Cherrington and Thornton, 2015; Penman and O'Connell Sutherland, 2015). Critically, the fact that peer groups alone are insufficient to affect and sustain change was emphasized, underlining the importance of organizational ethos and the provision of structural resources to processes such as mentoring.

Reflective Supervision with Mentors in Early Childhood Education and Care

While the term supervision has traditionally implied a hierarchical relationship often associated with performance management, salary and human relations practice, there has been a move in many professions to recognize the need for professional supports that have developmental, relationship-based and person-centred roots. There has been a tradition of providing supervision in the helping professions, such as counselling, social work and psychotherapy, particularly, emphasizing the well-being of both the professional and the client. Mentors working in Early Childhood education increasingly take on the role of supporting others as they engage in reflective practice. Hawkins and Shohet (2012) describe a formative/educative supervisory role for the supervisor of a developing mentor that focuses on supporting the mentor to identify a mentoring process that is effective for them, with a focus on dynamic relationships, boundaries and skills development. Rouse (2015) posits that, unless a mentor is able to reflect on their own behaviours, values and assumptions, their capacity to support others to develop those skills is inhibited. The importance of providing a protected space to discuss and reflect upon mentoring practice with a 'mentoring mentor' is key as it offers an opportunity for mentors to receive guidance and support so that they, in turn, can effectively support their mentees.

The tradition of 'reflective supervision' (Chu, 2014: 150) is already established and has been articulated by those who work with children in the birth to 3 years of age programme area in the United States, in particular (Eggbeer, Mann and Seibel, 2007; Parlakian, 2001; 2002; Weatherston, Weigand and Weigand, 2010). Chu (2014) proposes this term as being an appropriate workplace support element for those who mentor in ECEC, given that it emphasizes empathy, support and facilitated reflection. She suggests that it has 'the power to promote increased competence in Early Childhood professionals while providing a process for respectful partnership and open communication among staff on the same program [*sic*]', Chu, 2014: 149). Moreover, it appropriately mirrors the structural leadership supports that are increasingly acknowledged as being key to high quality Early Childhood education systems internationally (Urban *et al.*,

2012). This cascading of reflective and reflexive practice (see below) through the different roles in an organization ensures that learning can happen through meaningful partnership, the outcomes of which are strengthened as a result of collaboration. It provides opportunities for the consideration of the complexities of mentoring work as jumping off points for new and innovative approaches rather than mere problems that must be solved.

Characteristics of a Reflective Supervision Relationship

In the concept of reflective supervision there is a reliance on the facilitation skills of the supervisor, who should possess the relevant professional competencies to encourage a mentor to reflect on, and learn from, experience; exploring relationship dynamics; the establishment of boundaries; and the development of skills in response to the mentoring conversation. While they may be concerned with broader or bigger picture organizational goals, they must valorize the support and learning needs of the mentor above other more day-to-day concerns when assuming a reflective supervision role. Organizations can help to set up reflective supervision for success by resourcing and establishing adequate structural supports for mentors (Watson *et al.*, 2014) such as daily check-in meetings, regular staff meetings (including communities of practice) and one-to-one reflective supervision sessions that are timetabled, protected and rescheduled by agreement as necessary.

The functions of supervision (Hawkins and Shohet, 2012) should be clearly discussed and mutually agreed, perhaps through the negotiation and signing of a supervision contract, which can be renegotiated as required. Acknowledgement and open discussion of the fact that different hats may be worn by a reflective supervisor is key to the success of the process and imperative in acknowledging the existence of power dynamics in the relationship and how they might influence the discussion. This helps to dispel difficulties that might arise if managers also adopt a reflective supervision role. While it is important that reflective supervisors are willing to guide mentors' decision-making (Scott-Heller and Gilkerson, 2009), it is equally important that they are aware of when to step back and ensure that mentors are directing their own learning, problem-solving and decision-making.

They should model a learning disposition for the mentors by openly and honestly acknowledging when they do not have the answers and be willing to work together to reach conclusions through experimentation and reflection. Strategies such as the use of open-ended questions or Socratic questioning (John, 2008) can be used by a reflective supervisor to encourage the mentor into an educative space, echoed in Kolb's (1984) experiential learning cycle. The use of open-ended questions by a reflective supervisor can lead to a challenging of the assumptions behind the mentor's account and is considered a key feature of both effective mentoring and supervision (Clutterbuck, 2014).

Traditionally, mentoring in Early Childhood education has been associated with the professional development of Early Childhood teachers as part of efforts to strengthen the pedagogical expertise of staff working in Early Childhood education settings or to help bridge the experience gap of newly qualified teachers and educators. However, there are increasing numbers of mentoring programmes and models being developed in Early Childhood education, which take differing approaches to the process of supporting others to change and develop their practice.

Conclusion

This chapter argues that, regardless of approach or focus, it is imperative that mentors in Early Childhood education are provided with necessary professional guidance to enable them to support those who work in ECEC settings in a meaningful way.

In addition to receiving education and training that provides content knowledge on how to be an effective mentor, mentors must be enabled and encouraged continuously to practise their mentoring skills. The mentee must also be given protected and supportive reflective supervision, which will empower them as they learn from practice and enable them to implement plans based on that learning. The fact that the support structures required by mentors in ECEC settings are multi-faceted and complex indicates the importance of the role in the context of the ECEC systems around the world. Mentors fulfil a key role in ensuring quality Early Childhood educational experiences for children and parents; therefore, it is imperative that the professional support provided is robust enough to engender sustained and meaningful change.

> **Reflective Questions**
>
> **1** What professional supports are there in place for mentors and leaders within your setting?
> **2** How effective are these? Can they be improved?

References

Achinstein, B. and Athanases, S. Z. (2006) *Mentors in the making: developing new leaders for new teachers*. New York, NY, Teachers College Press.

Ambrosetti, A. (2014) Are you ready to be a mentor? Preparing teachers for mentoring pre-service teachers. *Australian Journal of Teacher Education*, 39 (6): 3.

Ambrosetti, A., Knight, B. A., and Dekkers, J. (2013) Perceptions and experiences of peer mentoring in pre-service teacher education. In Shaughnessy, M. F. (ed.) *Mentoring: practices, potential challenges and benefits*. New York, NY, Nova Science Publishers. pp. 125–144.

Bokeno, R. M. and Gantt, V. W. (2000) Dialogic mentoring: core relationships for organizational learning. *Management Communication Quarterly*, 14 (2): 237–270.

Bruner, J. S. (1966) *Toward a theory of instruction*. Cambridge, Harvard University Press.

Callan, S. (2006) What is Mentoring? In Robbins, A. (ed.) *Mentoring in the early years*. London, Sage. pp. 5–17.

Carver, C. L. and Feiman-Nemser, S. (2009) Using policy to improve teacher induction: critical elements and missing pieces. *Educational Policy*, 23 (2): 295–328.

Cherrington, S. and Thornton, K. (2015) The nature of professional learning communities. New Zealand early childhood education: an exploratory study. *Professional Development in Education*, 41 (2): 310–328.

Chu, M. (2014) *Developing mentoring and coaching relationships in early care and education: a reflective approach*. Boston, MA, Pearson.

Clutterbuck, D. (2014) *Everyone needs a mentor: fostering talent in your organisation*. London, CIPD Publishing.

Earl, L. M. and Timperley, H. (2008) *Professional learning conversations: challenges in using evidence for Improvement* (Vol. 1). New York, NY, Springer Science and Business Media.

Eggbeer, L., Mann, T., and Seibel, N. (2007) Reflective supervision: past, present, and future. *Zero to Three Journal*, 28 (2): 5–9.

Elliott, K., Farris, M., Alvarado, C., Peters, C., Surr, W., Genser, A., and Chin, E. (2000) *The power of mentoring. Taking the lead: investing in early childhood leadership for the 21st century*. Boston, MA, Center for Career Development in Early Care and Education.

European Commission (2014) *Proposal for reflective principles of a quality framework for early childhood education and care: report of the working group on early childhood education and care*. Brussels, Belgium, European Commission.

Evertson, C. M. and Smithey, M. W. (2000) Mentoring effects on proteges' classroom practice: an experimental field study. *The Journal of Educational Research*, 93 (5): 294–304.

Fullan, M. (2008) *The six secrets of change*. San Francisco, CA, Jossey-Bass.

Galinsky, E. (2012) Learning communities: an emerging phenomenon. *YC Young Children*, 67 (1): 20.

Garvey, R., Stokes, P., and Megginson, D. (2014) 2nd edn. *Coaching and mentoring: theory and practice*. London, Sage.

Hawkins, P. and Shohet, R. (2012) *Supervision in the helping professions*. London, McGraw-Hill Education (UK).

Howe, N. and Jacobs, E. (2014) Mentors' perceptions of factors associated with change in early childhood classrooms. *Alberta Journal of Educational Research*, 59 (4): 591–612.

Isner, T., Tout, K., Zaslow, M., Soli, M., Quinn, K., Rothenberg, L., and Burkhauser, M. (2011) Coaching in early care and education programs and Quality Rating and Improvement Systems (QRIS): identifying promising features. *Child Trends*. Available online: https://www.childtrends.org/wp-content/uploads/2013/05/2011-35CoachingQualityImprovement1.pdf (Accessed 17 July 2019).

John, K. (2008) Sustaining the leaders of children's centres: the role of leadership mentoring. *European Early Childhood Education Research Journal*, 16 (1): 53–66.

Knowles, M. S. (1970) *The modern practice of adult education: andragogy versus pedagogy*. New York, NY, New York Association.

Kolb, D. A. (1984) *Experiential learning*. Englewood Cliffs, NJ, Prentice Hall.

Langdon, F. J. (2014) Evidence of mentor learning and development: an analysis of New Zealand mentor/mentee professional conversations. *Professional Development in Education*, 40 (1): 36–55.

Langelotz, L. (2013) Teachers' peer group mentoring – nine steps to heaven? *Education Inquiry*, 4 (2): 375–394.

Lave, J. and Wenger, E. (1991) *Situated learning: legitimate peripheral participation*. Cambridge, Cambridge University Press.

Mezirow, J. (1985) A critical theory of self-directed learning. *New Directions for Adult and Continuing Education*, 25: 17–30.

OECD (2012) *Starting strong III – a quality toolbox for early childhood education and care*. Paris, OECD.

Ozuah, P. O. (2005) First, there was pedagogy and then came andragogy. *Einstein Journal of Biology and Medicine*, 21: 83–87.

Parlakian, R. (2001) *Look, listen, and learn: reflective supervision and relationship-based work*. Washington DC, WA, Zero to Three Center for Program Excellence.

Parlakian, R. (2002) *Reflective supervision in practice: Stories from the field*. Washington DC, WA, Zero to Three Center for Program Excellence.

Peeters, J. and Vandenbroeck, M. (2010) Childcare practitioners and the process of professionalization. In Miller, L. and Cable, C. (eds) *Professionalization, leadership and management in the early years*. London, Sage. pp. 62–77.

Penman, R. and O'Connell-Sutherland, K. (2015) Fostering pedagogical leadership through peer mentoring groups. In Murphy, C. and Thornton, K. (eds) *Mentoring in early childhood education: a compilation of thinking, pedagogy and practice*. Wellington, New Zealand, New Zealand Council for Educational Research Press. pp. 51–66.

Peterson, S. M., Valk, C., Baker, A. C., Brugger, L., and Hightower, A. D. (2010) We're not just interested in the work: social and emotional aspects of early educator mentoring relationships. *Mentoring and Tutoring: Partnership in Learning*, 18 (2): 155–175.

Ramey, S. L. and Ramey, C. T. (2008) Establishing a science of professional development for early education programs: the knowledge application information systems theory of professional development. In Justice, L. and Vukelich, C. (eds) *Achieving excellence in preschool literacy instruction*. New York, NY, Guilford Press. pp. 41–64.

Robinson, V. and Lai, M. K. (2005) *Practitioner research for educators: a guide to improving classrooms and schools*. Thousand Oaks, CA, Corwin Press.

Rouse, E. (2015) Mentoring and reflective practice: transforming practice through reflexive thinking. In Murphy, C. and Thornton, K. (eds) *Mentoring in early childhood education: a compilation of thinking, pedagogy and practice*. Wellington, New Zealand, NZCER Press. pp. 25–38.

Schön, D. (1987) *Educating the reflective practitioner*. San Francisco, CA, Jossey-Bass, Publishers.

Schwille, S. A. and Dynak, J. (2000). Mentor preparation and development. In Odell, S. J. and Huling, L. (eds), *Quality mentoring for novice teachers*. Indianapolis, IN, Association of Teacher Educators & Kappa Delta Pi. pp. 67–76.

Scott-Heller, S. and Gilkerson, L. (2009) *A practical guide to reflective supervision*. Washington DC, WA, Zero to Three.

Thornton, K. (2010) Developing leadership through blended action learning. *Early Childhood Folio*, 14 (1): 7–12.

Urban, M., Vandenbroeck, M., Van Laere, K., Lazzari, A., and Peeters, J. (2012) Towards competent systems in early childhood education and care. Implications for policy and practice. *European Journal of Education*, 47 (4): 508–526.

Vujičić, L. (2008) Research and improvement of one's own practice – way to development of teachers'/preschool teachers' practical competence. Paper in the proceedings of the Association for Teacher Education in Europe Spring University. In *Teacher of the 21st century: quality education for quality teaching*. Riga, University of Latvia Press.

Watson, C., Neilsen Gatti, S., Cox, M., Harrison, M., and Hennes, J. (2014) Reflective supervision and its impact on early childhood intervention. *Early Childhood and Special Education (Advances in Early Education and Care)*, 18: 1–26.

Weatherston, D., Weigand, R. F., and Weigand, B. (2010) Reflective supervision: supporting reflection as a cornerstone for competency. *Zero to Three Journal*, 31 (2): 22–30.

5

Creating Safe Reflective Spaces for Child Protection Practice

Claire McLoone-Richards

Chapter Summary

Organizational cultures imbued with calm and compassion are noted for being conducive to effectively supporting the practice of safeguarding children. Having safe spaces for practitioners is considered vital for fostering quality supervision, staff mentoring and the nurturing of practitioners' advocacy skills in protecting the rights of children. The effect of past trauma and abuse of practitioners is examined, together with the possible impact on responses and decision-making in the protection of children. The chapter considers Pierre Bourdieu's concept of 'Habitus' (Bourdieu and Wacquant, 1992) and how its application may have meaning for child protection practice. A fictitious case scenario based on domestic violence and abuse aims to represent important issues related to mentoring and coaching in the supervision and child protection practice. Any resemblance of the case study to a past or present case is entirely coincidental.

Introduction

The protection of children is undoubtedly one of the most challenging and complex practice issues for any individual working with children and their families. There is a need for effectively trained practitioners who are supported and nurtured in their various work contexts while they undertake their daily child safeguarding responsibilities. Good quality supervision, and the coaching and mentoring of less experienced practitioners and students, are all part and parcel of supporting each individual involved in child protection. There has been a significant change on an international scale in the Early Years profession, with a more prominent recognition of the importance of reflective practice and quality supervision in the care and education of children. These factors go some way to nurturing the advocacy skills of the practitioner in augmenting the rights of the child. A crucial relationship with 'the self' is integral to the practitioner, while the emotionality and vicarious trauma experienced by practitioners in child protection work needs to be acknowledged as conscious links are made to practitioner narratives and their own histories of abuse. The personal narratives of previous or current trauma can impact directly or indirectly on our work with children, families and colleagues (Bradbury-Jones, 2013 and Conti O' Hare, 2002). These are issues that will be explored further in the chapter.

Critical Questions

1 How does your child protection practice 'feel' when you reflect on your role and responsibilities within your professional spaces?
2 What is your experience of mentoring, coaching and supervision in your workplace and what might you do to improve this experience?

The Meaning of 'Safeguarding and Protecting Children' and the Relationship to Supervision, Mentoring and Coaching

Definitions and theories of mentoring, coaching and supervision have been introduced in Chapter 1 of this book, which seek to promote a shared understanding of what we mean by these terms. This chapter will offer definitions for consideration in the context of safeguarding and protecting young children. The 'discovery' of child abuse has beleaguered many professional disciplines (notably frontline social work), public inquiries, survivor testimonies, research and literature over the last 100 years or more. While there is recognition that the term 'safeguarding' is more familiar in a UK context, the concept does translate fluently across nations and cultures when considering the principles of early intervention and prevention for a child's welfare and safety. The terms safeguarding and child protection will be used throughout this chapter when exploring both concepts. Firstly, in referring to child protection there is the recognition of a child's safety and how their welfare and safety is of paramount importance to all concerned within their world. I have described 'safeguarding' children as 'the processes of supporting families and empowering children. It is about early intervention and preventative strategies to ensure better outcomes for children. Being safer, more resilient and to grow in confidence, fulfilling their potential' (Richards, 2009: 73).

The concept of professional advocacy is an essential component of professional skills and practice in promoting the rights of children. Anderson, Chitwood and Hayden (1997) helpfully describe an advocate as someone who speaks on behalf of another person or persons in order to bring about change. Advocacy for others is arguably more difficult and stressful when challenging poor practice: the ability or willingness of a novice student or seasoned practitioner to question the prevailing judgement or opinion of what is or is not in the interests of a child's safety and welfare. Lord Laming referred to supervision as 'the cornerstone of good social work practice' (2003: 14) and Helm (2017) describes more innovative approaches in supervision practice where colleagues are encouraged to engage with those aspects of uncertainty in child protection work and to extract meaning, rather than seek solutions, within unhurried professional encounters. Harlow (2016) suggests that the terms mentoring and coaching can become intertwined and blurred in terms of meaning and application, but she succinctly describes a mentor as someone who offers assistance to a less experienced colleague, while a coach is more typically appointed as an external facilitator to the organization to support the improvement of role performance. In terms of good practice in supporting students and new colleagues as they begin their placement or work in a childcare setting, the norm should be to allocate a mentor as part of the induction process. The mentor will also oversee and foster their long-term development within the new environment. This is an exemplar of good practice and should readily ease any apprehensions the new student or colleague may have as they settle into their new professional environment.

Critical Questions

1 Why is it important to advocate for the rights of the child as part of your safeguarding and child protection practice?
2 What would you suggest is important in supporting the needs of new students or staff in the context of their child protection role and responsibilities?

An Organizational Culture of Calm and Compassion

The sounds or noise of our workplace can sharpen or dull our senses to what is happening around us, and we may find ourselves having difficulty in finding a quiet space to be calm and to reflect on our practice. Whether or not we work within a large or small team, our workplace, at times, can be a stressful place. How we manage this depends on the culture and the leadership within our workplace. Helm (2017) asserts that it is important for practitioners to have a 'secure base' (2017: 395), and activities such as making coffee or sharing food with each other give them the opportunities to communicate and express emotion. In my own experience, I have found that such practices lead to a calm and compassionate culture in any workplace. Ruch (2007) stresses the importance of 'emotionally informed thinking spaces' (2007: 372) as being critical for effective child protection practice, and this concept parallels the provision of supervision for practitioners by their immersion within collaborative and inclusive communications.

Peshkin (2002) makes thoughtful reference to the power of silence within our reflective practice as it alerts us to the less visible or invisible, the silenced and the unheard within organizations and institutions. The silencing of others as an injustice may trouble us, and there is recognition of how children are silenced by their abusers, just as practitioners may also be silenced for speaking out and advocating for the rights of the child (Ferguson, 2005; Goddard and Hunt, 2011; Richards, 2015). Bourdieu's conceptual triad of 'field', 'habitus' and 'capital' (Bourdieu and Wacquant, 1992) offers an illuminating perspective of how power is acquired by individuals or groups and how power within institutions is exercised. This includes how power is used and abused by those in positions of dominance and higher status over those who have less power and status. For the purpose of the chapter, the primary focus is on the concept of Habitus, but students are encouraged to read further to acquire a fuller appreciation of the connectivity of these triadic concepts.

Pierre Bourdieu (1930–2002) was a French sociologist who had an immense interest in researching and writing about how society works, including the subtle dynamics of relationships between people and institutions and their influences and status within wider society. He has written extensively on concepts and realities of power and culture that perpetuate the dominance of individuals and groups over those who are dominated. Bourdieu suggests that Habitus is acquired over time in how we are shaped and influenced by our life experiences and knowledge. The Habitus becomes a series of mental and physical dispositions (or blueprints) within us, determining who we are, how we perceive ourselves in our family, community, culture and wider society. Habitus informs and influences our positioning in society and evokes the dispositions that we have acquired. However, Bourdieu suggests that Habitus is not fixed: 'Being the product of history, it is an open system of dispositions that is constantly subjected to experiences' (1992: 133) and hence open to change.

In applying the concept of Habitus to your experience, you may see that your disposition/s as a child, adolescent, student or professional is acquired over time and through a range of experiences in your lifespan. These life experiences can inform your perceptions of who you are and of your place in the world; the same applies to your professional contexts. An awareness of a sense of place or 'knowing one's place' is thought-provoking, particularly when we apply this notion to 'the structures of organisational cultures and the status and power taken or given to professionals in the context of their expert position in child welfare' (Richards and Gallagher, 2018: 88). The student who sees themselves as 'less worthy' or uninformed to question or challenge poor practice in relation to the welfare of a child, in contrast to their more knowledgeable and experienced colleagues, is something that I suspect is familiar to many students across a range of professional disciplines. However, as we are open to learning experiences, and challenge and reflexivity in research and practice, then the Habitus, whether individually or collectively, may be open to positive transformation. Additionally, an organizational culture that is calm and compassionate and which gives all practitioners an equal voice benefits all those who work within the institution and, ultimately, the children and families who use the service.

Critical Questions

1 In your experience, what factors do you think contribute to a calm and compassionate culture within a workplace and service for children and their families?
2 How does Bourdieu's concept of Habitus relate to you as a student or practitioner? How might the meaning of Habitus inform and develop your role in advocating for children within your organization and working with other professionals?

Domestic Violence and Abuse as a Practitioner Narrative

There is a wealth of literature and research that reminds us of the impact of domestic violence and abuse (DVA) on women's health and well-being, in pregnancy and on women in their role as mothers (Barlow, 2016; Douglas and Walsh, 2010; Humphreys, 2010; Moulding et al., 2015; Morrison, 2015). Goodard and Hunt (2011) highlight the gendered perspective of the social work profession which tends to be female dominated; this point also relates to the Early Years profession. Douglas and Walsh (2010) highlight how mothers as victims of DVA can be viewed as unprotective of their children, especially when caught in a violent relationship. However, there is much evidence that shows the protectiveness of mothers where DVA is a feature of family life. Her coping and survival strategies include responding to the emotional needs of her children after they witness abuse, avoiding situations where her children are left alone with her partner, or trying to reassure her partner that she is not leaving them (Moulding et al., 2015). This last tactic is possibly one of the safest strategies for her and her children, as the point of leaving or having left an abusive relationship is the most dangerous time of all (Fleury et al., 2000; Kim and Gray, 2008). In the context of past trauma and abuse, the following fictitious case scenario attempts to illustrate the complex dynamics and perspectives when the personal and professional worlds of the practitioner collide.

Case Study Scenario

Jacqui is an Early Years Professional in a pre-school and she is a key worker to 4-year-old Jacob, who is currently in foster care. His mother was seriously injured by her partner and there was a history of domestic violence in the family before Jacob was born. His mother remained with her violent partner and Jacob was removed from his home by the Local Authority as it is no longer a safe place for him. Jacqui experiences Jacob as a very anxious child who is reluctant to participate in any of the daily activities with his peers. He is distrustful of adults in the pre-school, avoids eye contact with others and is almost mute, communicating non-verbally to Jacqui and her colleagues. Jacob has become attached to Jacqui and is reluctant to be away from her side during his pre-school sessions. He follows her and wants to sit close to her, which makes Jacqui's interactions with other children and colleagues quite difficult. Jacqui feels very protective towards him and is aware that she feels sad. She is concerned about his welfare if he is to return home to his mother. In fact, she acknowledges that she is feeling angry about the child's circumstances.

Jacqui is herself a survivor of domestic violence. She grew up in a household where she witnessed and experienced violence and the threats of violence to her mother, herself and her younger siblings. She once stayed in a refuge when her mother fled the violence, but returned home again because her younger sister was missing their pet dog. Jacqui remembers how frightened she felt and she is reminded of her own childhood trauma when she thinks about Jacob.

Critical Questions

1. What might some of the challenges be for Jacqui as a key worker for Jacob?
2. How can safe and supportive supervision enable Jacqui to be effective in her role with Jacob, while acknowledging her own feelings about her traumatic childhood?
3. How might the experience of mentoring and coaching be useful to Jacqui?

Hurt and Pain as Histories of Practitioners in Practice

It is important to consider the impact of the trauma of child abuse on the individual practitioner who themselves had an abusive childhood, and especially those who are still living with trauma as adults, such as domestic violence, and who may witness their own children being affected by this experience of abuse. These issues are complex and undoubtedly have implications for how the 'personal and professional being' of a practitioner are intertwined and connected to the everyday interactions with children, families and colleagues. The mess that troubles a child's world, the mire where professionals can become stuck and the feelings that resurface when faced with the trauma of children's narratives of violence, pain and hurt, evoke a re-traumatization for hurt practitioners as they recollect past histories of their own abuse as children. Meadors *et al.* (2010) reflect on the concern of secondary traumatization of healthcare professionals as their study highlights the emotional challenges for practitioners in meeting the needs of patients because of their Secondary Traumatisation Syndrome (STS). Goddard and Hunt (2011) emphasize the concern of vicarious trauma and post-traumatic stress within the discipline of social work, including secondary traumatization.

The emotional impact of child protection work is increasingly recognized in the literature. Good supervision and mentoring enable a practitioner to express their anxieties, hopes and doubts for a child based on their relationship with them and what they know, or do not know, about the child's world. Bradbury-Jones (2013) adds that this point highlights ethical issues vis-à-vis the 'protection of practitioners' (2013: 261), suggesting that a willingness for some disclosure is required and that this should be in the domain of safe and supportive supervisory structures and practice in a setting.

The Reflective Practitioner

Ferguson (2005) reminds us of the expressive element of child protection and it is this expressiveness that is called upon in your advocacy in promoting the rights of the child, their needs and wishes, within every aspect of your practice. This, critically, includes your inter-professional discussions and your voice within supervision. I have described the possible benefits of calm and compassionate workplaces for the benefit of you and your colleagues, and most importantly for the children who attend your setting. This environment is not representative of every workplace. However, it is something every professional working with children should strive for, recognizing, fostering and promoting their safety and well-being. In determining a cooperative approach to child protection and safeguarding practice, each student and staff member should be provided with the safeguarding policy of the setting, introduced to the designated leader for safeguarding children, and given access to appropriate training and to regular supervision, which specifies the joint responsibility of the supervisee and the supervisor.

Relating these factors to the above case scenario prompts a reflection on the role of supervision, which would allow Jacqui the opportunity to acknowledge the vicarious trauma that she experiences in working with Jacob and the secondary trauma she experiences as her past childhood trauma resurfaces. The Peshkin Approach to Reflection (1988) as mentioned previously merits consideration as it places vital emphasis on the subjective role of reflective practice in acknowledging Jacqui's past history and memory of childhood trauma. This approach enables her to reflect on this self-awareness and insight and to consider the implications for her safeguarding practice.

Conclusion

The chapter has sought to address pertinent issues in the context of the role of supervision, mentoring and coaching and safeguarding children. It is important to acknowledge the emotional component of safeguarding and protecting children and to acknowledge that these emotions of anxiety, sadness or anger are valid. This means you are emotionally connected to those children in your care. You are a caring practitioner and you have a developing disposition for the advocacy of children. The availability of safe, sound supervision is important to your developing professionalism and includes the space for you to acknowledge and check out your thoughts and feelings of concern for a child, in addition to how you are working effectively with others in your safeguarding role. By acknowledging the emotionality of our safeguarding and child protection practice, and the importance of safe and sound supervision, mentoring and coaching, we may begin to appreciate the benefits of calm and compassion in our work settings as we, who do the caring, feel cared for in caring for those who need our care, too.

> **Reflective Question**
>
> How can vicarious or secondary trauma of students and practitioners be addressed as part of holistic approaches in good safeguarding and child protection practice?

References

Anderson, W., Chitwood, S., and Hayden, D. (1997). *Negotiating the special education maze: a guide for parents and teachers*. Bethesda, MD, Woodbine House.

Barlow, J. (2016) The effects of emotional neglect during the first two years of life. In Gardner, R. (ed.), *Tackling child neglect. Research, policy and evidence-based practice*. London, Jessica Kingsley Publishers. pp. 23–44.

Bourdieu, P. and Wacquant, L. J. D. (1992) *An invitation to reflexive sociology*. Chicago, MI, University Chicago Press.

Bradbury-Jones, C. (2013) Refocusing child protection supervision: an innovative approach to supporting practitioners. *Child Care in Practice*, 19 (3): 253–266.

Conti-O'Hare, M. (2002) *The nurse as wounded healer: from trauma to transcendence*. Toronto, ON, Jones and Bartlett Publishers International.

Douglas, H. and Walsh, T. (2010) Mothers, domestic violence, and child protection. *Violence Against Women*, 16 (5): 489–508.

Ferguson, H. (2005) Working with violence, the emotions and the psycho-social dynamics of child protection: reflections on the Victoria Climbié case. *Social Work Education*, 24 (7): 781–795.

Fleury, R. E., Sullivan, C. M., and Bybee, D. I. (2000) When ending the relationship does not end the violence: Women's experience of violence by former partners. *Violence Against Women*, 6 (12): 1363–1383.

Goodard, C. and Hunt, S. (2011) The complexities of caring for child protection workers: the contexts of practice and supervision. *Journal of Social Work Practice*, 25 (4): 413–432.

Harlow, E. (2016) The management of children and family social workers in England: reflecting upon the meaning and provision of support. *Journal of Social Work*, 16 (6): 674–687.

Helm, D. (2017) Can I have a word? Social worker interaction and sense-making. *Child Abuse Review*, 26: 388–398.

Humphreys, C. (2010) Crossing the great divide: response to Douglas and Walsh. *Violence Against Women*, 16 (5): 509–515.

Kim, J. and Gray, K. A. (2008) Leave or stay? Battered women's decisions after intimate partner violence. *Journal of Interpersonal Violence*, 23 (10): 1465–1482.

Lord Laming (2003) *The Victoria Climbié inquiry*. London, The Stationery Office.

Meadors, P., Lamson, A., Swanson, M., White. M., and Sira, N. (2010) Secondary traumatization in paediatric healthcare providers: compassion fatigue, burnout and secondary traumatic stress. *Omega*, 60 (2): 103–128.

Morrison, A. (2015) 'All over now?' The ongoing relational consequences of domestic abuse through children's contact arrangements. *Child Abuse Review*, 24: 274–284.

Moulding, N., Buchanan, F., and Wendt, S. (2015) Untangling self-blame and mother-blame in women's and children's perspectives on maternal protectiveness in domestic violence: implications for practice. *Child Abuse Review*, 24: 249–260.

Peshkin, A. (2002) Angles of vision: enhancing perception in qualitative research. *Qualitative Inquiry*, 7 (2): 238–253.

Richards, C. M. (2009) Safeguarding children: every child matters so everybody matters! In Reed, M. and Canning, N. (eds) *Reflective practice in the early years*. London, Sage. pp. 69–83.

Richards, C. M. (2015) Taking a holistic view: critically examining complex professional issues. In Reed, M. and Walker, R. (eds) *A critical companion to early childhood*. London, Sage Publications. pp. 154–164.

Richards, C. M. and Gallagher, S. (2018) Common vigilance: a perspective on the role of the community in safeguarding children. In Brown, Z. and Ward, S. (eds) *Contemporary issues in childhood, a bio-ecological approach*. London, Routledge. pp. 84–93.

Ruch, G. (2007) 'Thoughtful' practice: childcare social work and the role of case discussion. *Child and Family Social Work*, 12: 370–379.

6

Pedagogic Mediation in the Early Years

Helen Lyndon

Chapter Summary

This chapter introduces and explores pedagogic mediation, a new concept encompassing the notion of the 'external agent of change' and the nature and possibilities of associated relationships, focused on improving practice. The concept includes skills and techniques that resonate with those associated with mentoring and coaching.

Introducing a New Concept

Pedagogic mediation offers a new perspective on developing pedagogic practice, which stems from a rich theoretical and research base. It is a mechanism for continued professional development through which pedagogic mediators and practitioners work in partnership to develop pedagogy. Pedagogic mediation extends the traditional mentor/mentee relationship as there is a specific pedagogical context and professional standards that guide both parties. While coaching and mentoring have broad application beyond education, this approach offers sector-specific development and support.

Pedagogic mediation is centred on the relationship between the pedagogical mediator and the practitioner. This relationship provides time, space and support for deep reflection, which facilitates the development of pedagogy. While it has been commonplace to have advisors working with practitioners in education historically, this approach offers recognition of the hierarchies that exist while allowing the practitioner to develop at their own pace, appreciating that lasting change needs to come from the individual practitioner.

Pedagogic mediation was conceived by the Childhood Association, Portugal, through Pedagogy-in-Participation (Oliviera-Formosinho and Formosinho, 2012) and is an approach to context-based teacher education. Within this specific pedagogy is a participatory framework through which the children are involved in the construction of knowledge and learn through continuous interactive experience. Pedagogy-in-Participation has democracy as its heart and this influences all elements of practice: educational outcomes, spaces, staff development and research (Oliviera-Formosinho and Formosinho, 2012: 12).

Communication is at the centre of Pedagogy-in-Participation and the role of the pedagogic mediator. Children, educators and parents discuss everyday events and participate in the processes of meaning-making and decision-making (Oliveira-Formosinho, 2009). At the heart of this communication are the four pedagogical pillars (Oliveira-Formosinho, 2009: 235–236):

- the pedagogy of being represents a commitment to the basic rights and needs of children;
- the pedagogy of belonging and participation represents a right to be connected and fosters an understanding of those links;
- the pedagogy of experiential learning represents experience and communication;
- the pedagogy of meaning represents situated activity that allows children to develop their own narratives.

In the Childhood Association's approach, pedagogical mediators are employed to support practice development in these four areas and are engaged in research at a postgraduate level which informs such development. They share the underpinning philosophies of Pedagogy-in-Participation and their work facilitates the embodiment of such values.

Pedagogic mediation has also been utilized in England for Early Years practice development, specifically through the work of Pascal and Bertram (2016). Here, pedagogic mediation has taken place within the parameters of a national framework (DfE, 2017) and practitioners have been able to develop practice while maintaining statutory requirements. Through this framework the unique child is placed centrally and positive relationships and enabling environments facilitate the areas of learning and development. The UK context is such that the Early Years workforce does not require graduate qualification and traditionally educational professional development has consisted of externally provided courses or in-service training in which the provider delivers a predetermined set of outcomes.

Underpinning Theory

While providing a new approach to context-based professional development, pedagogic mediation is underpinned by seminal theorists. Mediation comes primarily from Vygotskian terminology and in its simplest form means something that facilitates the relationship between the learner and the subject (Smidt, 2009). In this case, the pedagogic mediator facilitates the relationship between the practitioner and enhanced pedagogical practice. Wertsch (1985: 15) describes mediation as Vygotsky's 'most important and unique contribution', as part of an integrated approach that ties human development to the culture in which it is situated; fundamental to this is the assumption that learning is facilitated in a social and cultural context.

Mediation was proposed by Vygotsky to support an understanding of the development of higher mental functions and to explore concepts such as memory and language development (Vygotsky, 1978). Mediation takes place through communication using cultural tools such as language (Vygotsky, 1978). Vygotsky largely focused on the child's developing cognition in his exploration of mediation and explained that children's learning experiences are mediated by the adults around them. This has become commonplace in our current educational philosophy and has influenced practice worldwide. Vygotsky believed that learning was not concerned with the direct transmission of information but involves both guidance and personal agency; this can be seen in the zone of proximal development through which the learner can achieve more with assistance (Vygotsky, 1978).

While Vygotsky did not write specifically about adult development and learning, there are those who believe the process to be the same. Eun (2008) argues that what is applicable to students in the classroom is also appropriate for teachers, and Shabani (2016) links Vygotsky's zones of proximal development to current mentoring practices where a facilitator provides support in the development of practices. Due to the social and cultural nature of learning, as described by Vygotsky, mediation becomes inevitable as interactions inform individual's pedagogical approaches. In recognizing this, the pedagogic mediator can embrace shared values and philosophies and help the practitioner work towards common goals in a participatory manner.

The participatory prerequisite of pedagogic mediation is influenced by the work of Freire and the deconstruction of traditional, transmissive pedagogy, described as a 'banking model' through which educators can deposit knowledge to ensure that learning has taken place (1996: 53). Freire encourages a consciousness (1996: 49) through which those who are oppressed by a transmissive approach can take control of their own learning and through reflecting and acting upon this they transform their experiences. The assumption that individuals take control of their own learning is at the centre of pedagogic mediation and there is an understanding that time is required. The pedagogic mediator does not dictate the pace of progress, as the practitioner must be ready to undertake change. Freire (1996) recognizes the need for a problem-posing education system in which dialogue and communication are key; these elements are also central to pedagogic mediation, which is underpinned by the relationship between the practitioner and the mediator.

A further socio-cultural and participatory influence comes from Communities of Practice (Wenger, 1999), which recognizes that groups and networks informally support our daily existence at work, home, school and in the community. Wenger (1999) considers the impact that learning has on an individual, community and organization. He considers learning to be lifelong, social and embedded in the practices of everyday life. Pedagogic mediation offers a pathway to the creation of a Community of Practice. Furthermore, Wenger's influence on pedagogic mediation can be seen through the emphasis on relationships and the recognition that interpersonal engagement can generate tension and conflict (Wenger, 1999: 77); the elements of pedagogic mediation (outlined below) recognize this.

How Does It Work?

The four elements of pedagogic mediation are bound by the context of the setting and are situated within time, thus highlighting the socio-cultural nature of the approach. It is important to recognize that pedagogic development will be different depending on setting, situation and staffing. The four elements are:

Openness – this is the first of the four elements and represents the approach of the pedagogic mediator to the whole setting. It is essential that time is spent in the setting so that the ethos and pedagogical approach of the practitioners is understood. This initial element lays the foundation for positive relationships to be built between the pedagogic mediator and the practitioners, children and parents. Power becomes a central consideration: the role of the pedagogic mediator is not to be the expert; the practitioners themselves are the experts of their own pedagogical space. This first element reflects the liberating approach of transformative pedagogy as outlined by Freire (1996); the practitioners must be the ones to liberate themselves from unhelpful elements of their current pedagogical practice.

Listening – this represents the second stage of pedagogic mediation through which the pedagogic mediator helps to raise the level of critical consciousness for practitioners. This provides a reflexive approach and is afforded through openness. At this stage the pedagogic mediator listens to practitioners through informal dialogue, tour-setting, observations and staff meetings. Listening will increase the pedagogical mediator's understanding of the setting and will also reinforce the notion that practitioners are experts within their own context.

Suspending – as the pedagogic mediator spends time within the setting they gain an understanding of the nature of pedagogy in the setting and can begin to co-develop processes and practice. Daily problems become the focus for development and attitude change. Throughout this time the pedagogic mediator will need to suspend some of their own pedagogical beliefs and allow the practitioners to change at their own pace. There will be times when the pedagogical mediator would pursue things differently, but this needs to be set aside as the transformation can only occur from within the practitioner.

Finally, pedagogic mediation reaches an **encountering** phase, which represents a pedagogy of consciousness (Freire, 1996). Through the relationships built over time, the pedagogical mediator can question and provoke the practitioners. Here the practitioners can explore a breadth of pedagogical notions and develop a responsive pedagogy that reflects the context of children and families who use the setting. At this level there is transformation as the practitioners shift to a practice that is based on their own pedagogic awakening.

A facilitating process within pedagogic mediation is that of isomorphism. 'Pedagogical isomorphism is a metaphor borrowed from the natural sciences to express the same equivalence of mode of development between adult learning mode and children learning mode' (Formosinho and Formosinho, 2016: 103). This recognizes that all stakeholders are learning and developing together, with an equivalency between child and adult learning and a participatory approach embedded throughout. There is an understanding that in affording the practitioners learning opportunities that are respectful – thereby ensuring their agency and participation – there is a hope that they will create similar opportunities for children (Souza and Formosinho, 2014). This engenders a participatory and democratic approach to professional development through which the pedagogic mediators work to diminish power relationships and allow the practitioners to develop at their own pace. In established Childhood Association settings, the results of this isomorphic relationship are evident as children's needs and interests drive the development of pedagogic intentions.

Pedagogic mediation can be evidenced in different ways and the pedagogic mediator should ensure that documentation suits the context. As settings embark upon a journey of change, the pedagogic mediator captures observations in a variety of ways: through written narrative or visually; by recording extracts of dialogue and through documenting the transformative journey chronologically. This pedagogic documentation then forms part of the reflective process and provides a stimulus for dialogue. Reflections can then also be captured and documented accordingly, demonstrating specific areas which show evidence of pedagogic change. Both the mediator and the practitioners should be encouraged to keep a personal journal evidencing their reflections. While personal privacy should be respected, extracts from the journal contribute towards the setting's overall documentation.

Pedagogic mediation also offers a useful methodological framework through which participatory research can be undertaken. Pedagogic mediation sits somewhere between action research and case study and offers a participatory and transformative hybrid which focuses specifically on the development of pedagogic practices and the relationships which drive these. Action research, from the work of Lewin (1946), is participatory and transformative but can often put the researcher in a position of power, driving the change. On the other hand, case study seeks not to disturb the normal patterns of behaviour (Stake, 1995), which does not account for the impact a researcher could have on practitioners in a setting. This leaves pedagogic mediation as an ethical and praxis-driven alternative within educational research, which enables the researcher to recognize their professional heritage and previous experience, while contributing in an ethical manner to practice development.

Recent Research Findings

Pedagogic mediation was used to develop listening practices in three different settings in England as part of a doctoral research project (Lyndon, 2016). The elements of pedagogic mediation could be identified within the interactions that were recorded. The following are non-chronological extracts from the research diary, along with the element of mediation that was demonstrated:

> Openness: 'I spent time with the practitioners helping them to pack away at the end of the session … Whilst packing away there was a rich reflective dialogue as practitioners reviewed the session and discussed the next steps for children in coming days.'
>
> Listening: 'Having been invited into the setting at the weekend to review the wider environment the discussion turned to the effectiveness of the planning and how it was linked to documenting assessments. The practitioners articulated frustration with the amount of paperwork they were completing and wanted to ask about my previous experiences with this pedagogical aspect.'
>
> Suspending: 'When the manager asked for my thoughts on the session, I felt very uncomfortable. The session has not worked for me at all and I knew that the children were not participating well either. Rather than discussing my opinion of the session I asked questions about the layout of the room and how this dictated some elements of the session.'
>
> Encountering: 'I really thought about our discussion and I've tried to make sure there is time and space to listen to the children's ideas. It is definitely something we can do more of!'
> (Researcher Reflections, June 2018)

This research concluded that the elements of pedagogic mediation are as fluid as the relationships within which they exist. Progress through the mediation process varied amongst staff, with certain practitioners rarely engaging in encountering interactions with the mediator throughout a two-year research cycle. Where an encountering relationship was developed and maintained there were shifts across many pedagogical aspects, some of which were intentional and part of the research focus and others that were unintentional.

Another key finding of the research was the reciprocal nature of pedagogic mediation. Each of the elements also exists in terms of the setting's relationship with the researcher. This is testament to the ethical and participatory nature of pedagogic mediation. This can be illustrated by the following extract from the research diary:

> *Practitioner S really pushed me today for other ways we can listen to the children. We talked of reading I had done around Elden's concentric circles of closeness (Elden, 2012) and how we might approach the idea of a graduated consultancy with the pre-school children. We discussed that many of the children were young within the academic year and I queried their capacity to fully understand the task. Practitioner S felt that the children would be able to participate and that we could talk to them about their understanding of the task. She insisted that we look to developing that over the next week and I was pleased that she felt confident and able to request this of me.* (Researcher Reflections, July 2016)

This extract demonstrates that the practitioner was taking the lead on further developments with the research project and challenging the researcher's assumptions; here the researcher encounters by drawing upon academic research materials and the practitioner encounters by drawing upon her detailed knowledge of the children. Lasting change was documented in the settings, which engaged in more practitioner encounters across the whole research process.

Advantages and Limitations

Pedagogic mediation offers an ethically sound way of working to develop practice. The flattened hierarchy provides practitioners with a safe space within which they can review their pedagogical assumptions and consider new ways of working. It also offers a unique approach for both practitioners and settings, rather than following a predetermined, outcome-driven programme, i.e. a problem-posing rather than passive approach to education (Freire, 1996). This flexibility enables development to take the pace and form that best suits the individual. The unique approach and flexibility also ensure that changes can reflect the needs of the individual setting.

Pedagogic mediation requires time and a long-term commitment to enable practitioners to work at their own pace within the normal routine of the setting for such reflective discussions to take place. A commitment of this duration is not without cost, and Early Years education does not receive equal funding or commitment when comparing with international situations. A further limitation for international contexts would be the level of study required of the pedagogical mediator. Not all countries require practitioners to obtain a postgraduate qualification in order for them to lead pedagogy, and yet a deeper understanding from research would be afforded if this was the case.

> **Reflective Questions**
>
> 1 How can pedagogic mediation contribute to mentoring and coaching at your setting?
> 2 What would be the benefits for your setting?

References

DfE (2017) The Early Years Foundation Stage Statutory Framework. Available online: https://www.gov.uk/government/uploads/system/uploads/attachment_data/file/596629/EYFS_STATUTORY_FRAMEWORK_2017.pdf (Accessed 20 September 2018).

Elden, S. (2012) Inviting the messy: drawing methods and children's voices. *Childhood*, 20 (1): 66–81.

Eun, B. (2008) Making connections: grounding professional development in the developmental theories of Vygotsky. *The Teacher Educator*, 43 (2): 134–155.

Formosinho, J. and Formosinho, J. (2016) The search for a holistic approach to evaluation. In Formosinho, J. and Pascal, C. (eds) *Assessment and evaluation for transformation in early childhood*. Abingdon, Routledge. pp. 93–106.

Freire, P. (1996) *Pedagogy of the oppressed*. London, Penguin.

Lewin, K. (1946) Action research and minority problems. In K. Lewin (ed.) *Resolving social conflicts*. New York, NY, Harper and Row.

Lyndon, H. (2016, 30 June–1 July) Pedagogic mediation as a developmental tool for lasting change? Paper presented to The 12th Annual Conference of the British Education Studies Association (BESA). Available online: https://educationstudies.org.uk/abstract/pedagogic-mediation-as-a-developmental-tool-for-lasting-change/ (Accessed 10 July 2019).

Oliveira-Formosinho, J. (2009) Togetherness and play under the same roof: children's perceptions about families. *European Early Childhood Research Association Journal*, 17 (2): 233–248.

Oliveira-Formosinho, J., and Formosinho, J. (2012) *Pedagogy-in-participation: childhood association educational perspective*. Porto, Childhood Association and Porto Editoria.

Pascal, C. and Bertram, T. (2016) Pedagogic Mediation EDU7157/7159 MA Education, Birmingham City University.

Shabani, K. (2016) Applications of Vygotsky's sociocultural approach for teachers' professional development, *Cogent Education*, 3 (1). DOI: 10.1080/2331186X.2016.1252177.

Smidt, S. (2009) *Introducing Vygotsky. A guide for practitioners and students in early education*. Abingdon, Routledge.

Souza, J. and Oliveira-Formosinho, J. (2014) *The pedagogical mediator: a case study on pedagogical transformation*. Crete, European Early Childhood Education Research Association.

Stake, R. (1995) *The art of case study research*. London, Sage.

Vygotsky, L. S. (1978) *Mind in society. The development of higher mental processes*. London, Harvard University Press.

Wenger, E. (1999). *Communities of practice*. Cambridge, Cambridge University Press.

Wertsch, J. G. (1985) *Vygotsky and the social formation of the mind*. London, Harvard University Press.

7

A Research-based Approach to Mentoring for Success for Early Years Teachers

Jill Harrison and Diana Harris

Chapter Summary

In 2017 the University of Greenwich was awarded a research grant from London Providers to explore an effective model for mentoring trainees on the Early Years Initial Teacher Training (EYITT) programmes. An outcome of this research was to provide a best practice guide that could be used to support competency-based training. The voice of the trainees was included, which gave them opportunity to share and develop high quality practice. This chapter focuses on the findings from the interpretive-style research carried out with a small group of mentors and mentees on the Early Years Teachers Status pathways.

Introduction

Since the inception of the Early Years Teacher (EYT) status qualification, mentoring has been integral to and required for implementation of this programme (CWDC, 2008; NCTL, 2014). Its underlying aim was to develop the workforce from within using transformational leadership (Bush and

Middlewood, 2013). Bass (1985) describes the key reflective aspects of transformational leadership as follows:

- Integrity and fairness;
- Having high expectations;
- Encouraging others;
- Supporting recognition;
- Stirring emotion;
- Looking beyond self-interest;
- Inspiring others to reach their potential.

Therefore, those involved with leading development need to have a deep connection with, commitment to and understanding of the requirements of the role of the Early Years practitioner and of the importance of developing positive outcomes for children and their families.

There are many definitions of coaching and mentoring, as discussed in Chapter 1. All strive to enable and empower a person to develop their skills and mindset. Each method takes a different perspective that informs the approach taken by the mentor or coach. Coaching is described as task-orientated, working on a specific agenda and breaking tasks down into small targets. It is an immediate, short-term solution and usually involves management in goal-setting for measurable impact (Robins, 2009). Mentoring is a longer-term relationship that is planned. It is described as a relationship between two people, with a focus on the individual, where the mentee together with the mentor sets professional goals.

Context

Mentoring within education and specifically in an Early Years context is a nascent research area (Kupila *et al.*, 2017). Mentoring has a long history of being associated with learning and as a tool for self-development (Doherty and Jarvis, 2016). The development of mentoring is important as part of the wider recognition of the need for a high quality workforce able to contribute to and enhance the lives of young children and their families.[1] Balduzzi and Lazzarri (2015) identify mentoring as an essential part of the continuing development of an Early Years professional. Froebel (Tovey,

---

[1] See Chapters 1 and 2.

2012) recognized and advocated for the distinct phase of early childhood and the kindergarten, so this would also need to be explored in relation to mentoring when considering this model for Early Years teachers. Callan (2006) would endorse this, emphasizing that mentoring does not emerge from a vacuum but is situated in the political and social context.

The theoretical framework for the model used to support Early Years teachers at the University of Greenwich derives from reflection and a dialogic approach. In this chapter we will draw on the narratives of four mentors and four mentees who were on the EYITT programmes during 2017. These storytellers were from random sampling groups from both the graduate entry programme (those new to Early Years) and the mainstream programme (those already graduated in Early Years and employed in early childhood settings). They were culturally and economically diverse and reflective of the London South East area. The listeners were lecturers employed in the Early Years team as mentors.

The Beginning of the Story

At the beginning of the mentoring process it was important to ensure that mentors and mentees understood the organization, the expectations and the boundaries. This meant that both partners participated in the induction together and in ongoing training sessions to understand the expectations and competencies involved in order to receive the same information. This ensured consistency of training and steered outcomes. Expectations were made clear to both parties as construction of knowledge is identified as important.

Mentor 2a commented: *'There wasn't one part of the course we didn't get training on'*, and Mentor 4a stated: *'I was never left in any doubt when I left the sessions what I needed to do. What was expected and what the university expected.'* This deliberate strategy helps in the formation of professional relationships, as often the trainee does not choose the mentors, nor are they based in their settings.

We also have a mixed model whereby some mentors are settings-based and others are employed by the university to carry out the role. This model does not rely on leadership involvement in the mentoring process. The University of Greenwich recognizes that there is a variation in Early Years providers from the private, voluntary and independent settings.

This non-statutory approach to Early Years provision enables those with experience to be leaders in these settings, but they are always required to hold Level Six qualifications. The mentor needs to have ethical responsibility for the organization and to realize that the mentee does not function as an island but as part of a multi-faceted team.

Mentor A1 exemplifies this.

> You [mentees] need to understand [that] the mentor's role is a tricky role as it is about sometimes being your best friend and being your main point of contact when you are in need, but it is also about being given feedback, setting targets and sometimes, where necessary, for the greater good having a conversation that always isn't the most pleasant conversation but as a mentor I know that is going to help my mentee develop or improve or reach their goal. Then I have the confidence to have that conversation.

The mentor and the mentee at the very beginning of this relationship identify boundaries, encourage clarity and share information. Aspirations are set, with the expectation that trainees will achieve high standards. This is working from a positive viewpoint that fosters a shared vision and commitment and gives participants knowledge about what they are aiming for. Mentor 2a vocalizes this: 'I have high expectations, I expect you to aim for that grade 1 outstanding. We'll set our goals. I will be there for you, but you have got to give me the same amount of commitment.'

The Essence of the Story

'Someone actually believes, so really gave me confidence.' Mentee 3B

As part of this model there is a requirement for trainees and mentors to meet on a three-weekly basis and have regular contact with each other in between throughout the duration of the programme. This helps in developing strong professional reciprocal relationships built on trust and encouraging honesty within the feedback and assessment process. The mentor acts as a critical friend, basing their feedback on observation of practice. The emphasis is on increasing people's work performance capacity and developing their skills using the GROW model (Whitmoor, 2002), which is about setting **GOALS**, observing the current **REALITY** of their practice, formulating the **OPTIONS** for the development of skills and finding solutions for a way **FORWARD**. This method encourages purposeful dialogue that includes effective listening and questioning and taking participants through a logical sequence to achieve their goals (Atkins et al., 2017b).

Mentee 1B describes this process:

> Feedback is really important to help you develop yourself further and in the fact [that] they have given you an email contact, the fact that you can, even though you can't speak to them about this point right now but at least email them, so opening up the lines of communication.

It is important that the assessment process is robust to ensure that mentors track trainees' progress carefully. Independent moderators review this assessment on a regular basis so that the quality and consistency of mentoring is evident across the programme. A clear assessment framework is presented at the beginning of the programme to ensure that mentors and mentees are working towards common goals and expectations.

At this point, we may discover through the moderation process that difficulties are arising; for example, the relationship is not working effectively, or neither of the partners are engaged fully with the process, or trust is not established to facilitate constructive reflective thought. In such circumstances the relationship may need to end and a new mentor assigned. This process is transparent, with clear guidelines set to highlight these processes (Atkins et al., 2017a). It also enables tutors to set targets for both mentors and mentees to facilitate and reflect upon progress. This is acknowledged by two of the participating mentors: Mentor 2A: 'It needs to be two way; you need to give as much as you wish to receive, you need to be open and honest' and Mentor 3A: 'If you don't assess, if you don't know how they are doing you can't set them targets, achievable SMART targets; you can't help them to move forward and they're therefore at risk of not passing.'

This cyclical process of observation, assessment and reflection enables the partners to work together in developing strategies to improve skills. This process supports the development of trust and inspires confidence in the trainees, enabling them to try out new ideas and initiate new practices. For this process to fully develop the mentor needs to be highly skilled and knowledgeable and both parties need to feel secure within this relationship and in the processes involved (Atkins et al., 2017a).

Mentee 4B discusses the importance of feedback: 'She would ask me questions knowing that somebody is putting time into it. It makes you realize that somebody believes in me; [it] really gives me confidence.' Mentee 2B notes that the mentor relationship helps to *'bring practice and theory together'*, while Mentee 1B explains the benefits of the relationship: *'I have gained how to be more effective as a practitioner, how to improve my knowledge and the theory side of things. Looking at what kind of resources would work. I was given the freedom to use my own initiative and apply my own creativity.'*

Nolan and Molla (2016) claim that an essential part of mentoring is to challenge assumptions, values and beliefs. Therefore, in the study face-to-face contact was the most important means of communication to facilitate successful mentoring. However, emails were most frequently used to engender a quick response to any questions that arose. Having boundaries was paramount in supporting this mode of communication. As Mentee 3A reported, *'With the email she [the mentor] was open to it* [email communication], *if we ever had a problem just to email her. So it was quite nice to have that.'* Mentor 4A observed: *'I was at the end of the phone 24/7 if she needed me and eventually that became a bit like "I can't do this anymore" so there is the boundary [that] we don't text past or you don't contact me past this time, because that's my home lifetime.'* Mentor 1A reported that face-to-face meetings took longer: *'Because I am spending more time with them more frequently now we are sitting face-to-face having a chat and that I think is a much improved way of working.'*

Moving the Story On

The relationship needs to evolve over time and as it does, mentees become less dependent on their mentors as they develop self-confidence and professional competency. Mentors and mentees have a clear ending to their relationship as it finishes with the final assessment of the programme. It is essential that there is an agreed ending as mentoring can continue in a variety of forms over extensive periods. Some of these relationships may continue but become much less formal. We recognize that closure is important for both partners. A graduation is a deliberate strategy to acknowledge the ending of the relationship, so that these relationships can be celebrated and reflected upon. A three-stage process has been introduced to help facilitate this. Mentor 1A reflects: *'I don't think your relationship is as strong at the end as you have started to let them go, but I feel that is the role of the mentor, just making them understand that. Yeah sometimes that especially in teaching things change so quickly. Things are forever evolving, things are forever moving on.'*

Transition into Practice

Stage 1

At the end of the training programme each trainee is given an exit interview and they complete a transition document in which they evaluate and reflect on their progress, identify the areas where they feel they need further development and support to enable them to feel confident and competent in their Early Years Teacher roles. Training is offered to give mentees the ability to transfer their experiences and to become mentors in the future. Mentor 4a shows how mentoring can support intrinsic motivation: *'It is satisfying being on someone's journey. It is fantastic watching someone learn.'*

Stage 2

Trainees move into pedagogical leadership roles, a strategy introduced to support mentees further after completion to ensure that one mentor oversees the transitions of the newly qualified Early Years teachers into employment or change of role in the setting. This requires a less formal approach to mentoring through continual professional development and it supports transformational leadership – this means that they can change settings from within. Most of the mentees in this research showed that they would like to become a mentor in the future. This perpetuates change and quality improvement from within the organization.

Stage 3

The continuous professional development that is provided is based on the transition document. Collegiate relationships are developed further, with employers to encourage communities of practice and the sharing of expertise through networking and conferences. Reciprocal relationships are key to effective delivery of this strategy. The relationship needs to benefit the mentee, the mentor and training providers/university. This is achieved by offering ongoing professional development opportunities. Mentee 4B expresses salient thoughts at the end of the programme: *'I would love to be that person that helps somebody else achieve their dreams.'*

Discussion

A model of learning has been carefully planned and developed through distribution and enactment, based on the sharing of skills. This model has a clear intentionality for learning with robust procedural systems requiring careful management. This is a complex process, which involves reflection and reflexivity. Drawing on the work of Argyris and Schon (1974), the underlying aims are to develop outstanding practitioners who are not only technocrats but Early Years professionals who can critically reflect on organizational and personal assumptions, values, polices and principles to ensure the best possible outcomes for children and their families.

There are two strands to reflection: single loop and double loop (Argyris and Schon, 1974). Single loop reflection is based on the practitioner reflecting on the now and what, i.e. reflecting on effective strategies to meet competency-based agendas. Double loop is regarded as a deeper reflection that is centred on questioning and co-researching to inform, challenge and initiate new practice. In the model researched, the single loop reflection is very apparent, but the double loop is little identified and we wonder if this is possible in this goal-structured framework. The next area of development in this process is to challenge mentors and mentees to reflect on the political discourse around Early Years, which continues to raise the profile, validity and necessity of a reflective graduate-based workforce.

A key aspect of this model's success was the reciprocal relationships that were created through the processes that were put into place (Wenger, 1998). These provided both partners with a sense of self-worth as they developed their own professionalism and professional identity. The impact and outcome of this relationship was success for the mentees who all achieved EYT Status with 'Outstanding' or 'Good with outstanding features'. The positive impact on quality within settings is implicit in this.

This is a transferable model that can be used for all trainees within Early Years, regardless of the level of study. It has shown to be a transformational leadership model of practice through creating shared vision and 'Building ever stronger, trust-based relationships' (Bass, 1985: 9). A model that has impact requires time and commitment, by all parties, but the relatively low cost ensures that it is a sustainable model to use within the Early Years workforce. Henshall *et al.* (2018) report that those undertaking this type of programme had a sense of pride, felt secure in their professional knowledge and aspired to use that knowledge in developing quality services across the sector.

Conclusion

We believe that mentoring is a key leadership strategy that supports collaborative working. It is important that mentoring relationships are planned, with clear intentions to support learning through a constructive and meaningful way. Reflection is an essential ingredient to ensuring that an effective, successful, reciprocal relationship is developed, leading to the highest outcomes.

> ### Reflective Questions
>
> As discussed earlier in this chapter, within Early Years settings the mentee does not stand alone – teamwork is essential, along with the socio-political climate in which they work and the impact of the wider environment.
>
> 1 Consider how this climate impacts on you as a mentor or mentee?
> 2 Reflect on how Figure 7.1 relates to you and your own situation.
>
> (Concentric circles diagram with labels, from outer to inner:)
> - Government, policy and international influences
> - Cultural and external environment
> - Mentor and mentee relationship
> - You and your role
>
> **Figure 7.1** Concentric influences on the Mentor role
>
> (Adapted from Bronfenbrenner 1979)

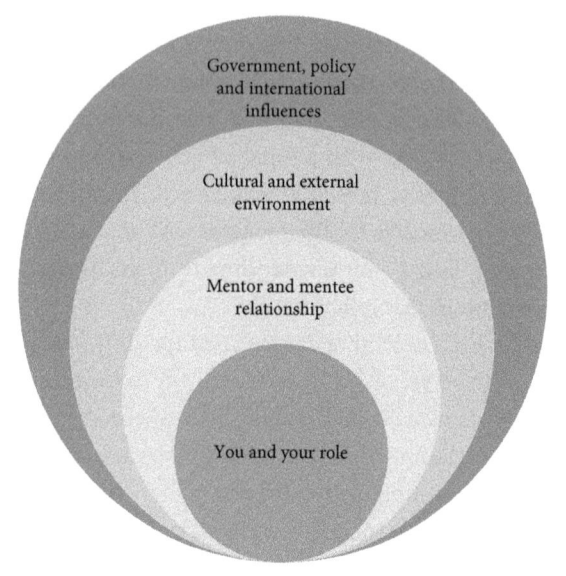

3. How do you overcome challenges in your workplace?
4. How can mentors support mentees to become more creative in their thinking, effectively developing double loop reflection on practice?
5. How do we ensure equity in mentoring practice?

References

Argyris, M. and Schon, D. (1974) *Theory and practice: increasing professional effectiveness.* San Francisco, CA, Jossey-Bass.

Atkins, L., Bolan, R., Chaplin, D., Harris, D., Harrison, J., Henshall, A., Munn, H., and Whale, L. (2017a) *Best practice guide supporting early years teachers status initial teachers training.* London, University of Greenwich.

Atkins, L., Bolan, R., Chaplin, D., Harris, D., Harrison, J., Henshall, A., Munn, H., and Whale, L. (2017b) *Mentoring in early years initial teachers training. A report for the London providers.* London, University of Greenwich.

Balduzzi, L. and Lazzari, A. (2015) Mentoring practices in workplace-based professional preparation: a critical analysis of policy developments in the Italian context. *Early Years: An International Journal of Research and Development,* 35 (2): 124–138.

Bass, B. (1985) *Leadership and performance beyond expectations.* New York, NY, Free Press.

Brofenbrenner, U. (1979) *Ecology of human development.* Cambridge, MA, Harvard University Press.

Bush, T. and Middlewood, D. (2013) 3rd edn. *Leading and managing people in education.* London, Sage.

Callan, S. (2006) What is mentoring? In Robins, A. (ed.) *Mentoring in the early years.* London, Sage. pp. 5–17.

Children's Workforce Development Council (2008) *Introduction and information guide: early years professionals creating brighter futures.* London, CWDC.

Doherty, J. and Jarvis, P. (2016) 3rd edn. Continuing professional development. In *The complete companion for teaching and leading practice in the early years.* London, Routledge. pp. 215–243.

Henshall, A., Atkins, L., Bolan, R., Harrison, J., and Munn, H. (2018) Certified to make a difference: perceptions of newly qualified early years teachers in England. *Journal of Vocational Education and Training,* 70 (3). Available online: https://www.tandfonline.com/doi/full/10.1080/13636820.2018.1437063 (Accessed 10 December 2018).

Kupila, P., Ukkonen-Mikkola, T., and Rantala, K. (2017) Interpretations of mentoring during early childhood education mentor training. *Australian Journal of Teacher Education*, 42 (10). Available online: http://dx.doi.org/10.14221/ajte.2017v42n10.3 (Accessed 10 December 2018).

National College of Teaching and Learning (2014) *Early years initial teachers training requirements supporting advice.* London, HMSO.

Nolan, A. and Molla, T. (2016) Teacher professional learning in early childhood education: insights from a mentoring programme. *Early Years and International Research Journal.* 8 (12–16): 1–13.

Robins, A. (2009) 2nd edn. *Mentoring in the early years.* London, Sage Publications.

Tovey, H. (2012) *Bringing the Froebel approach to your early years practice.* London, Routledge.

Wenger, E. (1998) *Communities of practice: learning meaning and identity.* Cambridge, Cambridge University Press.

Whitmoor, J. (2002) 3rd edn. *Coaching for performance: growing people, performance and purpose.* London, Nicholas Brealey.

8

Transforming Pedagogy in Early Childhood Education

Naseema Shaik and Hasina Ebrahim

Chapter Summary

Twelve Foundation Phase pre-service teachers participated in a qualitative study focusing on cognitive coaching, which provides opportunities for understanding child participation in Grade R. Data was collected through a number of different means: the reflections of pre-service teachers, face-to-face sessions, learning conversations and a focus group interview. The findings show that cognitive coaching aimed at accessing prior knowledge and shaping different states of mind creates opportunities for practitioners to expand their views on child participation.

Introduction

Coaching has been adopted across many disciplines, but there has been limited research on the value of coaching in the field of education, both in the South African context (Rutgers, 2012) and internationally (Fillery-Travis and Lane, 2006; Kampa and White, 2002). Child participation is thought of as a multi-dimensional issue: teachers play a pivotal role in supporting active child participation in Early Years education (Venninen, Lipponen and Ojala, 2014). Many South African teachers and educators adhere to teacher-centred customs dating back to the authoritarian structures evident in apartheid in

South Africa and which retain a deficit model of children as incompetent (Bae, 2009). This model counteracts Ebrahim's (2011) argument that children in early childhood act as agents who are purposeful, deliberate and intentional. For teachers to acknowledge and embrace this new perspective, it means that they must let go of control (Shaik and Ebrahim, 2015) and prioritize and engage in active listening so that young children's voices are heard (Venninen, Lipponen and Ojala, 2014). Currently, children are only listened to within the parameters of planned learning goals and few teachers consider involving children in decision-making. This aspect is seldom taken seriously while the dominant view is that young children lack the cognitive capacities that shape early learning.

Cognitive coaching is a means of reshaping the mindsets of pre-service teachers towards the concept of child participation. This must be understood within the context of a highly prescriptive curriculum environment inherited from the past. Currently, children's participation is focused on achieving academic goals and targets vis-à-vis term-by-term outcomes. The chapter shows that, by using cognitive coaching, opportunities are created that allow for the introduction of alternative teaching methods.

Understanding Grade R Pedagogy in South Africa

Grade R in South Africa is the entry point for basic education, is part of the Foundation Phase and is the first year of primary school for learners aged 5 and 6 (South Africa: Curriculum Assessment Policy Statement, 2011). This educational ethos has emerged from the development of a prescribed curriculum and the location of most Grade R classes within schools. Many Grade R classes are characterized by a strong teacher-directed environment whereby teaching is implemented in transmissive ways, leaving little or no room for child participation.

Oliviera-Formosinho (2007) shows that transmissive pedagogy focuses on the acquisition of pre-academic skills, acceleration of learning and a deficit compensation model. Teachers who adopt a transmissive pedagogy shape behaviour and assess results solely by these criteria. Children often expect the teacher to correct their mistakes after feedback and make changes to their behaviour through the teacher's instruction. In this model of teaching, child pedagogy conforms to what Formosinho (1987) terms a civic passivity through pedagogic passivity. The Grade R curriculum is designed to balance teacher-directed and child-initiated activities. However, in practice most Grade R contexts are dominated by teacher-directed activities that place children in passive roles (Shaik and Ebrahim, 2015). In a rapidly changing Early Childhood educational environment, not only in South Africa but internationally, it is critical to explore how pre-service teachers are educated to elicit a paradigm shift to learner-centred education in Grade R.

Conceptual Framework

Two concepts informed the analysis of this study: cognitive coaching and child participation. Both concepts are understood from a social constructionist perspective where social reality is shaped through experiences and interactions with others (Berger and Luckmann, 1991).

Coaching and Cognitive Coaching

Coaching has been considered an essential process in improving job performance. As a multi-dimensional approach, it is practical and inclusive of a psychological process that involves behavioural change (Stefan *et al.*, 2015). Coaching is directed at an individual's self-knowledge and re-evaluation and aims at correcting an individual's behaviour. Coaching is considered to be a social process in which a working relationship is formed between a coach and student. Through this relationship a change in behaviour, or change in how a skill is implemented, might occur (Taylor, 2007).

Cognitive coaching was deployed in this study to shape the understanding that pre-service teachers had of child participation. Cognitive coaching is a method of instruction to enhance independent learning that comes through metacognition, that is, helping adults to think about their thinking (Costa and Garmston, 1994; Schon, 1987). Coaches support the teacher through a three-step process (Ellison and Hayes, 2009). Dialogue is key: the coach facilitates conversations and questioning strategies, while taking the role of facilitator. At the heart of cognitive coaching is the application of five states of mind: efficacy, flexibility, consciousness, craftsmanship and interdependence.

The Five States of Mind in Cognitive Coaching

Efficacy relates to an individual knowing that s/he can make a difference and is willing to do so (Costa and Garmston, 1994). **Flexibility** refers to coaching the pre-service teacher to help them see situations from another perspective and not just maintain their own views. **Consciousness** is the capacity to monitor and reflect on oneself (Costa *et al.*, 2003). Conscious individuals are self-directed and are aware of their thoughts, feelings and surroundings. They can 'direct their course' while in a state of metacognitive consciousness (Costa and Garmston, 1994). Conscious people progress towards their goals by monitoring their own thoughts and behaviours (Costa and Garmston, 1994). **Craftsmanship** focuses more on quality than perfection. Individuals take pride in their work and strive for precision and they seek elegance, refinement and specificity, similar to that of a performer (Ellison and Hayes, 2009). The final state of mind is **interdependence**, which refers to the ability to learn from others and to contribute to a common good (Costa and Garmston, 1994; Costa *et al.*, 2003).

Child Participation

Child participation is best understood by unpacking the the notions of 'child' and 'participation'. Traditional conceptions of children emerged from developmental psychology; children were seen as adults-in-the-making, with full human status only granted to them in adulthood (James, Jenks and Prout, 1998). Pascal and Bertram (2009) urge us to recognize children as active citizens in the here and now, participating in a democratic life where they have full rights and responsibilities. It is through the sociology of childhood that children have been recognized as agents in their lives (Ebrahim, 2011). Children's comments or suggestions are often met with reservation. The thought of participation often brings doubt into the minds of adults, especially those who maintain teacher-centred models of tuition.

This study is an entry point for pre-service teachers to learn about cognitive coaching and view child participation as a socially constructed and active process where both teachers and children are positioned as agents.

Methodology

The ethics committee of the Cape Peninsula University of Technology obtained consent from pre-service teachers who each signed a consent letter. The ages of the participants ranged from 22 to 26 and their mother tongue was English and isiXhosa. In their fourth year of study, pre-service teachers are required to study Grade R pedagogy, including participatory pedagogy. This is where active child participation receives optimal attention. Pre-service teachers were cognitively coached about child participation. The data that was obtained came from a number of sources: the reflections of the teacher educator, the learning conversations, face-to-face sessions and interviews with pre-service teachers, which were undertaken through a qualitative approach.

Findings and Discussions

Two themes are presented: accessing prior knowledge and shaping states of mind. Both show processes and techniques that were adopted to enable pre-service teachers to make some shifts in their thinking about child participation.

Accessing Prior Knowledge

Taking into account the fact that cognitive coaching is concerned with shaping states of mind, it was necessary to find an entry point for allowing pre-service teachers to share their preconceived ideas about child participation. Initially, it was important to help pre-service teachers feel confident as they positioned themselves as 'knowers' and 'speaking subjects' on a topic where many assumptions are hidden or taken for granted. The teacher educator's time was invested in making the classroom a co-constructive space where pre-service teachers could see themselves less as 'knowers' and more as 'learners' and open to acquiring new knowledge. The study environment created a safe space for participants to explore thoughts and ideas. The pre-service teachers gradually warmed to the idea that knowledge is socially constructed and that children have valuable perspectives to share.

Techniques were chosen to find out about the prior knowledge of the pre-service teachers. This was important, bearing in mind that they came from different racial, linguistic, cultural and socio-economic backgrounds. It was observed that they used different techniques to record their answers relating to their understanding of child participation. This freedom encouraged them to construct their own meaning-making. Some drew mind maps while others took up particular postures that indicated they were thinking about the question. The following are examples of how pre-service teachers understood child participation.

> 'Child participation ... the child is taking part by doing the action to the rhyme and answering the questions on the mat, yes, and doing an activity with the teacher when it involves the teacher.'
>
> '... that is my knowledge of what child participation was ... interactive, taking part in the lesson.'
>
> 'The stuff is there that the teacher has put out, okay, so the teacher actually chose [sic] what she wants them to play with and they just can choose from that.'
>
> 'Yeah I saw it as being basically anything other than [using] a worksheet .... So ... doing a rhyme ... or going outside ... if they're learning about pollution to pick up the paper, I thought that was child participation. I saw participation as being free play and the drama and fantasy play.'

The first three examples show that the pre-service teaches viewed child participation as being framed within a teacher-directed and teacher-prepared environment. Initiative for learning is taken by the teachers. The children 'take part' in what the teacher has prepared for them. In the last excerpt, child participation is viewed as being outside the dominant learning culture of completing worksheets, instead allowing the children to engage with alternative learning opportunities that go beyond desk work and into different indoor and outdoor spaces. This type of response is more associated with approaches such as Montessori and Reggio Emilia. It was clear that pre-service teachers had particular conceptions of child participation, but they needed expanding through cognitive coaching, which would broaden their thinking.

Shaping States of Mind

The most pressing issue was that pre-service teachers felt they were not capable of making a difference in a powerful system where they saw themselves as a guest to a host culture during their practicum (i.e. practical course of study). Hence, from an efficacy point of view, there was a sense of disempowerment. In the learning conversations and interviews, it was clear that the pre-service teachers still felt challenged about their ability to make changes regarding child participation in the Grade R programme. In the face-to-face sessions, pre-service teachers were given opportunities to articulate their teaching practice experiences by identifying aspects where they could effect some control and gain a sense of ownership. One commented: *'It's about setting up the right environment for the children to explore what they want to do in the classroom.'*

In the face-to-face sessions, pre-service teachers were exposed to different pedagogical approaches to enable them to build a repertoire of options for use with child participation strategies. The goal was to allow them to go beyond the dominant transmissive practice through adopting cognitive flexibility. This was motivated by the idea that a teacher who is flexible is open to multiple perspectives and can shift perspectives quickly and use a wide range of thinking and processing skills (Ellison and Hayes, 2009). Flexible teachers are also creative (Perkins 1983) and can balance a variety of activities all happening at once (Costa and Garmston, 1994).

The consciousness state of mind allows for self-monitoring and reflection to guide the learning process. The following statement illustrates consciousness and a shift in thinking: *'Previously my understanding was that participation meant children taking part; now I see it as listening to children's voices.'*

The interdependence state of mind came to the fore when pre-service teachers were asked to share how they worked together to arrive at a shared position. The expression of individual perspectives, the identification of commonalities and the agreement for taking a shared stance indicated the level of interdependence, tensions and group cohesion.

Pre-service teachers were obtaining the tools to refine their pedagogies that supported a high degree of child participation. The expanded visions and alternatives to which they were being exposed obviously needs further substantive work. Nonetheless, this study shows that the seeds for new craftsmanship were sown through cognitive coaching and specifically through a focus on other states of mind.

Discussion

The main aim of this study was to explore how cognitive coaching was used to influence pre-service teachers' understanding of child participation in Grade R in the context of formal didactic teacher-centred teaching. The findings show that cognitive coaching can change pre-service teachers' understanding of child participation. The pre-service teachers were subjected to learning experiences that afforded them opportunities to access their prior knowledge and to enable them to experience different states of mind that encouraged more affirmative thoughts about child participation and that translated into positive action.

This gives the pre-service teacher greater confidence as they increase child participation in learning opportunities. The emotional dimension that contributes to the states of mind must be taken into account in any reform process. Reflective practice is valuable so that pre-service teachers can document their feelings and thoughts as they move to new ways of thinking in their work practice.

Conclusion

Cognitive coaching and other forms of coaching can be highly beneficial in strengthening pre-service teachers' understanding of child participation. Future research would therefore contribute immensely to the education of pre-service teachers, inform their thinking and attitudes towards child participation, influence their actions and, at a more theoretical level, engender participatory pedagogies.

Reflective Questions

1 To what extent does your setting facilitate opportunities for child participation in their learning in order to give children the knowledge and cultural capital they need to succeed?
2 What would you look for within coaching strategies that strengthens this within your practice?

References

Bae, B. (2009) Children's right to participate – challenges in everyday interaction. *European Early Childhood Education Research Journal*, 17 (3): 391–406.

Berger, P. and Luckmann, T. (1991) *The social construction of reality*. London, Penguin Books.

Costa, A. L. and Garmston, R. J. (1994) *Cognitive coaching: a foundation for renaissance schools*. Norwood, MA, Christopher-Gordon Publishers, Inc.

Costa, A. L., Garmston, R. J., Saban, J., Battaglia, A., and Brubaker, B. (2003) Designing and constructing the holonomous school. In Ellison, J. and Hayes, C. (eds) *Cognitive coaching: weaving threads of learning and change into the culture of an organization*. Norwood, MA, Christopher-Gordon Publishers, Inc. pp. 125–135.

Ebrahim, H. B. (2011) Children as agents in early childhood education. *Education as Change*, 15 (1): 121–131.

Ellison, J. and Hayes, C. (2009) Cognitive coaching. In Knight, J. (ed.) *Coaching approaches and perspectives*. Thousand Oaks, CA, Corwin Press. pp. 70–91.

Fillery-Travis, A. and Lane, D. (2006) Does coaching work or are we asking the wrong question? *International Coaching Psychology Review*, 1: 23–36.

Formosinho, J. (1987) Educating for passivity: a study of Portuguese education. PhD dissertation, London, University of London. Institute of Education.

James, A., Jenks, C., and Prout, A. (1998) *Theorizing childhood*. London, Polity Press.

Kampa, S. and White, R. P. (2002) The effectiveness of executive coaching: what we know and what we still need to know. In Lowman, R. L. (ed.) *The California School of Organisational Studies: handbook of organisational consulting psychology: a comprehensive guide to theory, skills, and techniques*. San Francisco, CA, Jossey-Bass. pp. 139–158.

Oliviera-Formosinho, J. (2007) Pedagogia(s) da infancia: Reconstruindo uma praxis de participacao. In Oliviera-Formosinho, T., Kishimoto, M., and Pinazza, M. (eds) *Pedagogicas(s) da Infancia. Dialogando com o passado, construindo o future*. Sao Paulo, Artmed Editora. pp. 13–16.

Pascal, C. and Bertram, T. (2009) Listening to young citizens: the struggle to make real a participatory paradigm in research with young children. *European Early Childhood Education Research Journal*, 17 (2): 249–262.

Perkins, D. (1983) *The mind's best work: a new psychology of creative thinking*. Cambridge, MA, Harvard University Press.

Rutgers, L. (2012) Coaching Foundation Phase teachers as leaders in a school in the Western Cape Province. A professional development strategy. PhD dissertation (Curriculum Studies), Stellenbosch, Stellenbosch University.

Schon, D. (1987) *Educating the reflective practitioner*. San Francisco, CA, Jossey-Bass.

Shaik, N. and Ebrahim, H. (2015) Child participation in Grade R: a case for a child participation focus. *South African Journal of Childhood Education*, 35 (2): 1–8.

South Africa (2011) *Curriculum Assessment Policy Statement*. Pretoria, Government Printer.

Stefan, D., Orboi, M. D., Gavrilla, C., and Savescu, J. (2015) Theoretical aspects regarding specific techniques of stimulating activities of training in coaching pedagogic practice. *Research Journal of Agricultural Science*, 47 (4): 147–150.

Taylor, J. (2007) Instructional coaching: the state of the art. In Mangin, M. and Stoelinga, S. (eds) *Effective teacher leadership: using research to inform and reform*. New York, NY, Teachers College Press. pp. 10–36.

Vennin, T., Leinonen, J., Lipponen, L., and Ojala, M. (2014) Supporting children's participation in Finnish child care centres. *Early Childhood Education Journal*, 42 (3): 211–218.

9

Insights on Mentoring Practices within the Early Childhood Sector in Singapore

Doranna Wong, Manjula Waniganayake and Fay Hadley

Chapter Summary

Mentoring of Early Childhood (EC) educators[1] in Singapore has been aligned with government initiatives since the introduction of the Childcare Masterplan in 2008. Since then, such mentoring has been linked with several national policy frameworks. Analysis of data collected during interviews for a small-scale exploratory study with eight key EC professionals provides insights into the positioning of mentoring within the EC sector in this country. The discussion of key findings shows how mentoring of EC educators are influenced by national policy frameworks, such as the Skills Framework for Early Childhood Care and Education (ECCE), Singapore's Preschool Accreditation Quality Rating Scale (SPARK) and the Continuing Professional Development (CPD) Framework

---

[1] An individual, usually referred to as the 'teacher', who works with children in a kindergarten or childcare centre regardless of their qualifications.

for EC educators. In this chapter, we examine current practices that indicate how mentoring in EC is perceived in Singapore, and this includes a discussion of the impact it has had on leading and managing EC centres.

Introduction

'Mentoring' for professional purposes can be seen as a dynamic interpersonal relationship involving two or more people, where professional development and/or personal support form the basis of the relationship. Mentoring in EC centres is often perceived as a leadership development strategy (Rodd, 2013; Waniganayake et al., 2012; Wong and Waniganayake, 2013). In the last decade, mentoring has been used with both in-service as well as pre-service teachers to overcome day-to-day challenges within EC centres and to enhance pedagogical practice (Izadinia, 2016; Nolan, 2017; Schatz-Oppenheimer, 2017). Mentoring has been a developing phenomenon in recent years, with governments considering its presence to be an indicator of an EC setting's capacity to deliver quality programmes. This is evident in Australia and Singapore where staff mentoring is identified in the National Quality Standard (NQS) (Australian Children's Education and Care Quality Authority, 2018) and in the Singapore Pre-school Accreditation Framework (SPARK) Quality Rating Scale (Ministry of Education Singapore, 2010).

Singapore's Childcare Masterplan (2008)

Singapore's Childcare Masterplan (2008) focused on improving access to childcare centres[2] and the development of professional pathways for EC educators working with young children to encourage their professional growth and learning through various short courses. In October 2016,

---

[2] Attended by children aged 18 months to 6 years.

the Skills Framework for ECCE (2016b) was established by SkillsFuture Singapore. This framework outlined three career pathways for the ECCE sector in Singapore: 1. Educarer track – working with children aged 2 months to 4 years; 2. Teacher track – working with children aged 4 to 6 years; and 3. the Leader track, which identifies thirteen occupations[3] in the sector. These career tracks range from beginning to senior roles within each track. According to the ECCE Skills Map (2016a), the mentoring of educarers, teachers and leaders is part of the role in six of these occupations: senior educarer, senior pre-school teacher, lead teacher, centre leader, senior centre leader and the pinnacle leader (see Figure 9.1). Mentoring as part of the Skills Map is considered to be a leadership activity solely for senior EC

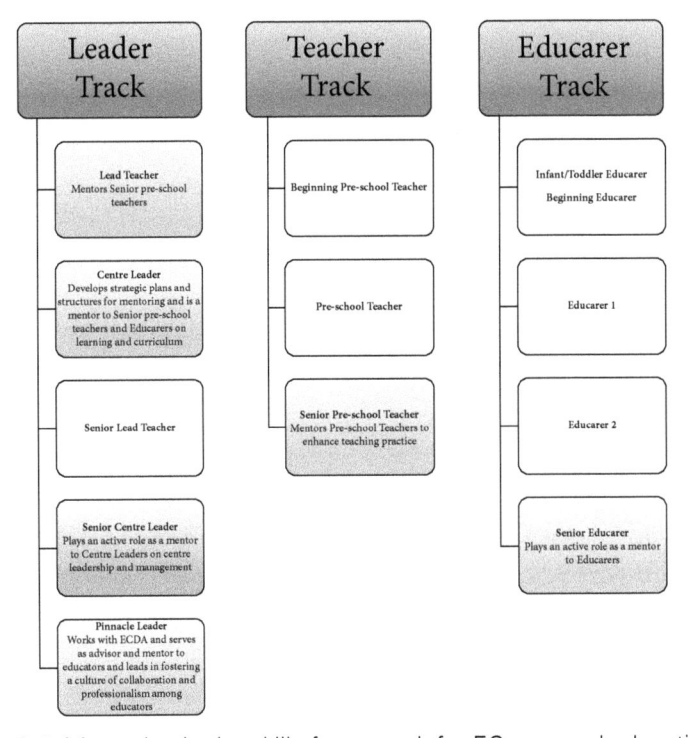

Figure 9.1 Mentoring in the skills framework for EC care and education

(adapted from the Singapore ECCE Skills Map 2016a)

---

[3]Beginning Educarer, Infant/Toddler Educarer, Educarer 1, Educarer 2, Senior Educarer, Beginning Pre-school Teacher, Pre-school Teacher, Senior-Pre-school Teacher, Lead Teacher, Centre Leader, Senior Lead Teacher, Senior Centre Leader and Pinnacle Leader.

educators. Educarers work with children aged 2 months to 4 years. Teachers work with children aged 4 to 6 years.

While mentoring is expected as part of the six occupations, it is generally associated with an induction programme in EC centres.[4] The availability of a mentor for a new teacher is seen as a quality indicator of staff management. This is reflected in the SPARK Quality Rating Scale (Ministry of Education Singapore, 2010) that provides benchmarks with the aim of raising the quality of pre-schools. For the purpose of SPARK, the term 'pre-schools' is used to mean the programme for children aged 4 to 6, regardless of the type of EC centre. SPARK for babies and children aged from birth to 3 has yet to be implemented. The focus on mentoring as a quality indicator assessed at emerging, performing and mastering levels is primarily relevant

Participant	Organisation	Role
Phase 1-1	Kindergarten	Senior Principal
Phase 1-2	Training Organisation	Deputy Director
Phase 1-3	Kindergarten	Academic Head Head of Centre
Phase 1-4	Child Care Centre	Principal
Phase 1-5	Child Care Centre	Principal
Phase 1-6	Partner Operator Child Care Centre	Principal
Phase 1-7	Anchor Operator Child Care Centre	Principal
Phase 1-8	Child Care Centre	Principal

Figure 9.2 Phase 1 participants in PhD study

---

[4]Refers to both childcare centres (attended by children aged 18 months to 6 years) and kindergartens (attended by children aged 4 to 6 years).

to beginning teachers, with no mention of mentoring for existing teachers in the sector. Mentoring is considered a 'leadership-related activity' and regarded as a competency in the following areas: family and community engagement, and management, administration and leadership in the CPD Framework for EC educators (Ministry of Social and Family Development Singapore, 2012: 83). As such, this approach is considered relatively narrow in scope as it targets only novice EC educators at entry.

In-depth interviews with eight stakeholders of EC organizations were conducted during the exploratory phase of a PhD thesis that studied mentoring practice and policy in Singapore. The majority of interviewees were principals (also known as centre leaders) and they reflected on the mentoring practices of EC educators, anchor operators, partner operators and an EC training institute (see Figure 9.2).

Perceptions and Practice of Mentoring

The classical description of mentoring based on Greek mythology was evident in the interviews conducted in this study. Interviewees believed that mentoring was defined as 'handholding' an individual, usually a pre-service teacher, trainee teacher, a novice teacher or a teacher new to the organization. Such 'handholding' was explained by one participant as '[I will] teach you and show you the ropes' (Phase 1-6). This involved guiding teachers in what to do, observing how teachers performed their daily work, providing teachers with feedback, showing them what was expected in that organization and developing the goals for mentoring.

The main purpose of mentoring is to introduce the teacher to the environment, the programme and the culture of that organization. This might include: informing and orienting the mentee to the organization's vision, mission, philosophy and curriculum beliefs; giving them access to teacher and child resources; explaining the organizational hierarchy, introducing them to the people in charge to whom they could go; and explaining the standard operating procedures (SOPs), such as the dress code for the organization. Taken together, this forms a common set of information given to mentees at the point of entry to the organization, regardless of their position as pre-service teachers, trainee teachers, novice or experienced teachers. While this was commonly described as mentoring, it can be argued that the information shared in these instances is better defined as part of the processes of induction to an organization or induction to a role within an organization (Athanases *et al.*, 2008; Ingersoll and Strong, 2011). These could have occurred outside the context of an ongoing professional relationship and within the staff management function of employment (Bryant and Gibbs, 2013), and with a mentor who did not have any EC expertise.

Curriculum implementation was also a significant aspect of mentoring evident in the data. As each organization had different educational beliefs and philosophy, mentoring about the curriculum occurred with a view to orientating teachers to the specific approach adopted by the employing organization. Analysis showed that this could mean a specific curriculum approach like the project approach, '*training for our curriculum because our curriculum is on project approach*', or a set of beliefs that were transferrable to other similar centres within the organization: '*we train them to our curriculum so if the person is deployed to "centre x" at least she grows up with that culture*' (Phase 1-6). It can be argued here that curriculum implementation training as presented here is defined as coaching rather than mentoring as learning is uni-directional where the focus is intentionally on 'training' the less experienced individual how to teach young children (Elek and Page, 2018). Here, the less experienced individual is seen as someone who is unfamiliar with the organization's curriculum methodologies and may or may not be inexperienced in the EC sector.

This misconception is further amplified where mentoring is planned to take place during 'termly planning ... monthly curriculum reviews' (Phase 1-3) and these sessions are described as opportunities for the '*teachers also to have bonding [sic]*' (Phase 1-6) and viewed as formal mentoring events that the principal manages (Phase 1-8). The mentors mentioned in these interviews were identified as senior teachers; the principals themselves would at times be the mentor for the new or beginning teacher.

While the Skills Framework has identified the key personnel responsible for the mentoring that occurs in the EC sector, only one interviewee had developed a structure/framework for mentoring that was specifically meaningful or relevant in their setting. In this setting, a multi-level approach to mentoring had been developed with the senior centre leader mentoring the leadership team, who, in turn, mentored the senior teachers for each level, who then were mentors to the junior teachers. This structure was created '*so that there is more than one person the mentee can refer to*' (Phase 1-1). At this centre, mentors were therefore formally assigned by the centre leader and mentees were informed that they '*have every right to go to them because they are their assigned mentors ... so the teacher doesn't feel, 'oh, I'm disturbing her. I'm imposing'* (Phase 1-1). While the other interviewees in this study stated that there was a lack of a formalized structure to their approach in developing mentoring relationships in their centres, it was possible for them to also assign mentors to new teachers within their organizations. Three interviewees called this pairing a *'curriculum level buddy'* (Phases 1-4, 1-5, 1-7), while others (Phases 1-1, 1-2, 1-3, 1-6, 1-8) distinguished between mentors and buddies in their centres.

Analysis of the interviews also suggests that in general EC educators in Singapore did not volunteer to mentor and were usually selected or tasked to do so by the employer, a senior employee or the government. For some larger organizations, mentors were assigned from a centralized department of the organization rather than teachers from within the setting. Other than the particular setting with the formalized mentoring structure, mentoring was for new teachers and existing teachers were typically identified as mentors. However, there were no formal mentoring programmes available for experienced teachers who remained with the same employer for many years. Gardiner and Weisling (2015) describe such actions as mentoring 'outside' of teaching practice; actions that occur outside of working directly with children. 'Inside' mentoring is that which impacts directly on teaching practice (2015: 2), and Gardiner and Weisling argue that both types of mentoring can be complementary and enhance teaching practice.

Discussion

The Skills Framework employment tracks can be seen as a nascent conceptualization for considering different areas of mentoring relevant to EC educators in Singapore. With the distinction between the leadership and teacher tracks, the mentoring that takes place within each track can, in fact, include mentoring for centre leadership ('outside' mentoring) and mentoring for curriculum leadership ('inside' mentoring). Except for the setting with a formalized structure for mentoring, all other mentoring practices that were described focused on the mentoring of 'inexperienced' EC educators with little or no mention of mentoring that occurs in the sector for senior and experienced EC educators other than them being mentors to others. The potential impact of such a focus of mentoring in the sector, which may benefit in reducing the attrition rate for beginning EC educators, could contribute to stagnation and a misconception of mentoring that mentors do not need to be mentored. As one of the interviewees expressed their thoughts about this: '*in terms of mentoring there should be a structure ... I hope that everyone can be mentored ... I think ECDA (Early Childhood Development Authority) actually needs to look into that if we want to retain senior people*' (Phase 1-4). Another interviewee described this to be '*for people like us who are in between [sic] ... people who are mentoring mentors, how do we do that, how do we balance that kind of handholding with them ... people like us we need to know how to support better*' (Phase 1-7).

In April 2016, a national EC leadership programme Principal Matters was launched to extend the capacity of centre leaders in the country. Participants from the programme were paired with eight selected experts in the sector who served as mentor and friend to these centre leaders as part of the six-month-long programme. Using a Behavioural Competency Model (Lien Foundation, 2016), the programme aimed to develop future-ready pre-school principals who lead the team, lead themselves and lead in the community (Korn Ferry Hay Group, 2016: 5). The programme provides opportunities solely for a select group of senior EC educators in the sector, primarily principals who are to be mentored, and does not extend to those experienced EC educators who are senior teachers in the sector. No formal evaluation of this programme is available to enable us to understand its impact on the EC sector and the growth in capacity of the individuals involved. To date, no national frameworks or programmes have been introduced to develop senior EC educators who do not assume a centre leadership role.

Conclusion

As a small nation state, Singapore continues to use a national approach in its attempt to promote the development of the EC sector. Mentoring in the sector currently caters to two ends of the professional career pathways: at induction for beginning EC educators (which we argue is more like coaching) and at the senior level for those EC educators who are leading EC centres. No national framework for mentoring has been developed to capture the continued development of EC educators through the different occupational pathways and there is a need for differentiating leadership from curriculum mentoring that is relevant to the EC sector in Singapore.

> **Reflective Questions**
>
> 1 Is there a national mentoring and coaching framework in place within your country? Do you see this as important?
> 2 If there is no framework in place, how would you design this and what key elements should it contain?

References

Athanases, S. Z., Abrams, J., Jack, G., Johnson, V., Kwock, S., McCurdy, J., and Totaro, S. (2008) Curriculum for mentor development: problems and promise in the work of new teacher induction leaders. *Journal of Curriculum Studies*, 40 (6): 743–770. DOI: 10.1080/00220270701784319.

Australian Children's Education and Care Quality Authority (2018, February). *National quality standard*. Available online: https://www.acecqa.gov.au/nqf/national-quality-standard (Accessed 4 July 2018).

Bryant, L. and Gibbs, L. (2013) *A director's handbook: managing an early education and care service in NSW*. Marrickville, NSW, Community Child Care Co-operative.

Elek, C. and Page, J. (2018) Critical features of effective coaching for early childhood educators: a review of empirical research literature. *Professional Development in Education*, 1 (19): 567–585. DOI: 10.1080/19415257.2018.1452781.

Gardiner, W. and Weisling, N. (2015) Mentoring 'inside' the action of teaching: induction coaches' perspectives and practices. *Professional Development in Education*, 1–16. DOI: 10.1080/19415257.2015.1084645.

Ingersoll, R. M. and Strong, M. (2011) The impact of induction and mentoring programs for beginning teachers: a critical review of the research. *Review of Educational Research*, 81 (2): 201–233. DOI: 10.3102/0034654311403323.

Izadinia, M. (2016) Student teachers' and mentor teachers' perceptions and expectations of a mentoring relationship: do they match or clash? *Professional Development in Education*, 42 (3): 387–402. DOI: 10.1080/19415257.2014.994136.

Korn Ferry Hay Group (2016) *Behaviours that matter: a behavioural competency model for early chidlhood centre leadership*. Singapore, Lien Foundation.

Lien Foundation (2016) Principals matter – new leadership programme to gear up 150 preschool principals for the future. Press release. Available online: http://www.lienfoundation.org/sites/default/files/Presser%20Principal%20Matters%20FINAL.pdf (Accessed 13 February 2017).

Ministry of Education Singapore (2010) *SPARK: Singapore pre-school accreditation framework*. Singapore, Ministry of Education.

Ministry of Social and Family Development Singapore (2012) *Achieving excellence through continuing professional development: a CPD framework for early childhood educators*. Singapore, MSF. Available online: http://www.childcarelink.gov.sg/ccls/uploads/CPD_Guide_5_FA.pdf (Accessed 7 May 2014).

Nolan, A. (2017) Effective mentoring for the next generation of early childhood teachers in Victoria, Australia. *Mentoring and Tutoring: Partnership in Learning*, 25 (3): 272–290. DOI: 10.1080/13611267.2017.1364800.

Rodd, J. (2013) 4th edn. *Leadership in early childhood: the pathway to professionalism*. Crows Nest, NSW, Allen and Unwin.

Schatz-Oppenheimer, O. (2017) Being a mentor: novice teachers' mentors' conceptions of mentoring prior to training. *Professional Development in Education*, 43 (2): 274–292. DOI: 10.1080/19415257.2016.1152591.

SkillsFuture Singapore (2016a) *Introduction to the ECCE skills map*. Singapore, SkillsFuture. Available online: http://www.skillsfuture.sg/docs/SkillsFramework/ECCE/SF_ECCE_Skills_Map.pdf (Accessed 5 May 2017).

SkillsFuture Singapore (2016b) *Skills framework for early childhood care and education: a guide on occupations and skills*. Singapore, SkillsFuture. Available online: http://www.skillsfuture.sg/docs/SkillsFramework/ECCE/SF_ECCE_Guide_2016.pdf (Accessed 16 May 2017).

Waniganayake, M., Cheeseman, S., Fenech, M., Hadley, F., and Shepherd, W. (2012) *Leadership: contexts and complexities in early childhood education*. Docklands, VIC, Oxford University Press.

Wong, D. and Waniganayake, M. (2013) Mentoring as a leadership development strategy in early childhood education. In Hujala, E., Waniganayake, M., and Rodd, J. (eds) *Researching leadership in early childhood education*. Tampere, Tampere University Press. pp. 163–180.

10

Individualized *yet* Standardized Approaches to Coaching in Early Childhood Education

Karrie Snider and Maggie Holley

Chapter Summary

National attention to improving Early Childhood Education (ECE) in the United States has stimulated discussion and research about which features of pre-school experiences contribute the most to improved ECE programme quality (Barnett and Frede, 2017; Pianta, Downer and Hamre, 2016). In 2017, the National Institute for Early Education Research at Rutgers University added benchmarks to the Early Learning and Development Standards for measuring programme quality and it identified coaching as a strengthening agent in ECE professional development systems (Barnett et al., 2017). Since US pre-school children currently receive only moderate levels of quality teaching to effect social, emotional and behavioural outcomes and very little support in developing cognitive and language capacities (Hamre, 2014; Office of Head Start, 2016), coaching is a promising practice to increase learning for both children and teachers.

Current research has sought: 1. professional development approaches that consider the divergent knowledge, skills and circumstances of ECE teachers; and 2. features of coaching that improve teaching (Phillips *et al.*, 2016). In this chapter we present solutions to the dual requirements for coaching diverse Early Childhood professionals. We describe an integration of adult learning theory (Kolb, 2014), teacher development (Glickman, 2002; Glickman, Gordon and Ross-Gordon, 2018) and evidence-based coaching (Rush and Shelden, 2011), all of which individualize yet standardize coach-teacher interactions. Finally, we highlight the coach-teacher interactions from our research.

In this chapter we cite the coach-mentor, who is a non-evaluative instructional leader whose goal is to empower teachers' cognitive autonomy. The coach-mentor is a mediator between professional development knowledge and improved ECE programme outcomes. The coach-mentor possesses expertise and effectively communicates the linkage between teachers' advanced development and children's enriched learning.

Introduction

Head Start, the largest federally funded ECE programme in the US, serves the nation's most economically vulnerable families and children. In September 2016, the Office of Head Start bolstered programme standards related to coaching, as evidence strongly suggests that coaching increases Head Start outcomes (Diamond and Powell, 2011; Morris *et al.*, 2014; Son *et al.*, 2013). For example, coaching increased effective teacher-child interactions (Hindman and Wasik, 2012; Vartuli *et al.*, 2014). Coaching predicted high quality environments and parent involvement in a nationally representative sample of 2,457 Head Start pre-schoolers (Son *et al.*, 2013). In short, coaching builds teachers' capacities (Rush and Shelden, 2011).

Understanding Teacher Development

US ECE professionals vary in characteristics that are related to career preparation, credentials, expertise and working conditions (Phillips *et al.*, 2016). Early Childhood teachers also vary in their beliefs about effective teaching practices (i.e. Guo *et al.*, 2011; Vartuli, 1999). Such differential patterns in teaching quality characteristics require coach-mentors to understand the unique development of individual adult learners (Glickman *et al.*, 2018). Targeted coaching increases both teachers' instructional efficacy and positive outcomes for children (Shidler, 2009).

How Teachers Learn

David Kolb's (2014) Experiential Learning Theory informs coach-mentors about the nature of teacher learning. Kolb's interactionist epistemology conceptualizes learning as an individualistic cycle where 'knowledge is created through the transformation of experience' (Kolb and Kolb, 2013: 49). Like Dewey, Piaget, Vygotsky, Freire and others, Kolb believes that learning occurs as internal conflict (cognitive dissonance) and arises to refashion knowledge through experience (2014). Adult learners engage 'in a spiral of learning that embeds [the learner] in a co-evolution of mutually transforming transactions between [themselves] and the world' (Kolb, 2014: 13), thereby producing unique patterns of thought and possibility (2014). Thus, teachers engage in observing, reflecting, adapting and acting within daily, unique improvisational experiences. They constantly evaluate these events, integrating observations into theories, positing actions and enacting teaching practices retrieved during this highly integrative process.

Teachers' individual experiences and beliefs and how they function as thinkers affects their engagement, learning and success in professional development processes. A coach-mentor's goal is to increase teachers' capacities toward autonomous thinking and action, advancing teachers along a continuum of intellectual development, despite individual differences in teaching characteristics. Glickman's (2002) and Glickman *et al.*'s (2018) conceptual model of teacher development explains the dispositional and cognitive differences in teacher characteristics and specifically, teacher commitment and teacher abstract thinking.

How Teachers Develop

Teacher commitment to professional development varies from low to high (e.g. little to high concern for improving child outcomes and little to high prioritization for personal growth) (Glickman, 2002). Teachers' abstract thinking exists along a continuum from simple to complex. Highly abstract teacher-thinkers are autonomous, self-actualizing and creative in generating a comprehensive self-improvement plan. Low-abstract teacher-thinkers may approach coach-mentors by saying, 'tell me what to do', as they lack discernment regarding what or how to improve.

Content with daily routines, low-commitment/low-abstract thinking teachers exhibit limited commitment to improving, cannot conceptualize ways to improve and consider others as sources for difficulties (administration, families, children, etc.) (Glickman, 2002). High-commitment/low-abstract thinking teachers are highly committed but unfocused and thus unable to think comprehensively through problems and take realistic actions towards improvements (2002). 'Analytical observers', i.e. low-commitment/high-abstract thinking teachers, approach improvement issues with understanding but take limited steps towards carrying out action plans (2002). The 'professional' demonstrates high-commitment/high-abstract thinking displayed through continual self-improvement, a positive influence on children and colleagues and are 'thinkers and doers' (2002: 89).

Once coach-mentors analyse teacher characteristics they select an interpersonal approach for guiding coach-teacher interactions, ranging from the most teacher-autonomous approach to the most coach-controlled: non-directive (independent teacher develops own plan); collaborative (coach and teacher create a mutual plan); directive-informational (teacher requires expert-given information/coach-suggested plan); and directive-control (teacher requires step-by-step coach-assigned plan) (Glickman *et al.*, 2018). Coach-mentors enhance coaching practices with appropriate interpersonal behaviours, such as listening, clarifying, encouraging, reflecting, problem-solving, negotiating, directing and reinforcing (2018). Since the goal of coaching is to strengthen teacher development, coach-mentors shift approaches (non-directive, collaborative, directive-informational and directive-control) over time as they continually reassess patterns of teacher development.

Finally, evidence-based coaching practices comprise the coaching cycle: joint planning (agreed-upon actions to take place in between coach-teacher interactions); observation (examination of practices); action/practice (actual events where skills are practised and refined); reflection (analysis of progress); and feedback (specific, objective reaction and affirmation) (Rush and Shelden, 2011). Evidence of coaching practices may include: systematic documentation (teachers' journals, child assessment data); scores on classroom quality measures (i.e. Classroom Assessment Scoring System

(Pianta *et al.*, 2008); Early Childhood Project Approach Fidelity (Vartuli *et al.*, 2014); and teachers' perceptions of coaching.

Application of Theory and Practice: Our Work to Improve Teaching and Learning Quality

In our year-long professional development study, coach-teacher interactions aspired to improve classroom quality across five Midwestern US Head Start programmes. Coaching goals targeted the **curriculum** (the Project Approach;[1] Helm and Katz, 2014), **instruction** (teacher-child interactions measured by the Individualized Classroom Assessment Scoring System (CLASS); Pianta *et al.*, 2008) and **assessment** practices (Desired Results Developmental Profile; California Department of Education, 2015) of twenty-one Head Start teachers. Over 350 children represented economically, culturally, linguistically and racially diverse familial backgrounds. For example, programmes served Hispanic and African American families and children and children with special needs.

A coaching team of nine coach-mentors partnered with individual teachers. Coaches held advanced degrees in ECE (i.e. master's or doctoral levels) and were members of the study team (not programme employees). Research coordinators met twice a month with the coaching team to facilitate and support coach-mentors' engagement with their respective teachers. Open communication, site visits and individual meetings supported the ongoing coach-teacher interactions. In addition, the team worked collaboratively with programme administrators as needed.

Coaching occurred weekly (for two hours in total) per teachers' availabilities. Weekly logs documented coach-teacher action steps, inquiry and reflections, which supported coach-mentors' ongoing evidence-based decision-making. Initially, coach-mentors established rapport, identified teacher strengths and clarified needs. Throughout the year, coach-teacher interactions were responsive to individual coachee needs. As teachers' patterns of learning changed, so did the coach-mentors' approaches within specific coaching practices, namely joint planning, action/practice, feedback and reflection.

---

[1] See our study website: https://www.projectapproachkc.org/coaching-took-kit/coaching-in-project-abc2 for further information.

Coach-mentors' descriptions of teacher behaviours reflected the four patterns of teacher development. Initially, some teachers showed reluctance or resistance. This small set of teachers represented Glickman's (2002) conception of low teacher commitment and low teacher abstracting thinking. This was apparent in the statements made to their coach; for example, they did not understand why they were required to participate in this professional development. In fact, early on, one teacher removed herself from the project and eventually left her teaching position. During this time, directive-informational and directive-control approaches governed coach-teacher interactions. For example, the coach was constantly brainstorming how to direct teacher actions yet offer choices; frequently applying listening, clarifying and negotiating within the coaching practices of joint planning and action/practice.

Many teachers represented Glickman's (2002) high-commitment/low-abstract-thinker characteristic, as they were unsure of what to do or where to begin. We expected this, with so many teachers implementing the curriculum (i.e. the Project Approach) for the first time. At first, these teachers concentrated on general teaching processes, managing children's behaviours or learning how the Project Approach fitted within their daily routines. This was evident when reviewing the coaching logs. Teachers' comments were more generic: *'Learning is engaging when it is hands-on'*; *'It takes a lot of planning ahead of time'* and *'[I am learning] to listen to what children are interested in.'* Coaches spent time in joint planning, providing information, step-by-step instruction and resources to help teachers develop fundamental skills. This group of teachers tried new things out, were excited about the coaching process, but were saying, *'Tell me what to do next.'* During coach-teacher interactions, coaching practices reflected a directive-informational approach, as coaches were the source of information. Based on mid-year survey data, teachers viewed and respected coaches-as-experts, which created productive coaching. Coach-mentors were sure to direct instructional improvements by individualizing yet standardizing the action steps, clarifying the teacher's point of view and reinforcing new knowledge in order to propel the teacher towards independence.

Few teachers in our study represented Glickman's (2002) third type of teacher, the 'analytical observer', apart from one teacher. She was very creative and often philosophical in her approach to thinking about project work with children. At times, it was very difficult to rein her in and encourage her to stick to agreed-upon plans or even just select an appropriate project topic. New ideas would misdirect her actions and progress. Once the teacher had a firm understanding of how to go about implementing the Project Approach, the coach observed a more self-regulated teacher and thus a shift in teacher development. While it was obvious to the coach that the teacher appreciated a more collaborative interpersonal approach, this did not sufficiently help here early on in guiding the teacher. The coach adopted a directive-informational approach. Coach-teacher interactions then helped the teacher 'stick to it' and actually see progress in the classroom project.

Finally, several teachers demonstrated high-commitment and high-abstract thinking. These teachers were self-starters. As such, coaches used non-directive approaches. Some teachers actually shifted to this developmental level over the course of the project year. This was particularly evident in the increasing sophistication of teacher reflections recorded each week:

We [teachers] *don't have to be so in control. We can be the guide. Things that interest them* [children] *lead to more engagement.*

[on children's learning] *They are very curious; wasn't as apparent before starting project work. Surprised by how high level their questions are.*

How important the environment is in figuring their [children's] *interest. The change in centers I made really made a difference in children's excitement and interest.*

Discussion: Evidenced-Based Coaching Resulted in Improved Teaching and Learning Outcomes

After a full year of systematic coaching, qualitative evidence revealed the learning processes for teachers and children. Over 220 coaching cycles targeted teachers' implementation of the Project Approach. As a result, teachers' scores improved on all thirty-six items of the Early Childhood Project Approach Fidelity measure. Interestingly, teachers increased the most on items that were related to implementing project activities: using children's questions to guide curricula, connecting children's prior knowledge and culture to activities and accommodating children's individual differences. From fall to spring, teachers increased their use of responsive, child-centred instructional strategies as measured by CLASS, which contributed to creating positive learning environments. Teachers managed children's behaviour and organized the learning environment with increased efficiency. Most importantly, teachers increased their use of effective questioning, language modelling and feedback during conversations and learning activities. Children's engagement with peers, teachers and tasks and their use of communication increased across the coaching year, thereby exceeding established norms on a child observation measure.

Conclusion

Coaching is complex, necessary work for helping to advance teaching quality and improve the learning outcomes for children, particularly children who are at risk of failing in their future formal school experiences. Coaching, when *individualized yet standardized*, places teachers' unique needs at the heart of coach-teacher interactions. Coaches can hone their coaching towards specific goals, which increases teachers' efficacy and produces quality pre-school learning environments. Developmental understandings (Kolb, 2014; Glickman, 2002) and evidence-based approaches (Glickman *et al.*, 2018; Rush and Shelden, 2011) strengthen coach-teacher interactions. Interpersonal approaches and behaviours (Glickman *et al.*, 2018) enhance the coaching practices and optimize the professional development growth of ECE teachers.

Reflective Questions

1 Using Glickman's model, what types of teachers do you or the teachers you are coaching represent? Why?
2 How can you apply individual *yet* standardized practices to your coaching?
3 What interpersonal behaviours are you using to reflect teachers' perceptions and guide them towards improved practices?

Recommended Reading

Glickman, C. D. (2002) *Leadership for learning: how to help teachers succeed*. Alexandria, VA, Association of Supervision and Curriculum Development.

Helm, J. H. and Katz, L. (2014) 3rd edn. *Young investigators: the project approach in the early years*. New York, NY, Teachers College Press.

Project Approach, The (2017) Available online: https://www.projectapproachkc.org/coaching-took-kit/coaching-in-project-abc2 (Accessed 17 July 2019).

Rush, D. D. and Shelden, M. L. L. (2011) *The early childhood coaching handbook*. Baltimore, MD, Paul H. Brookes.

References

Barnett, W. S. and Frede, E. C. (2017) Long-term effects of a system of high-quality universal preschool education in the United States. In Blossfeld, H.-P., Kulic, N., Skopek, J., and Triventi, M. (eds) *Childcare, early education and social inequality: an international perspective*. Cheltenham, UK, Elgar Publishing. pp. 152–173.

Barnett, W. S., Friedman-Krauss, A. H., Weisenfeld, G. G., Horowitz, M., Kasmin, R., and Squires, J. H. (2017) *The state of preschool 2016*. New Brunswick, NJ, National Institute of Early Education Research. Available online: http://nieer.org/state-preschool-yearbooks/yearbook2016 (Accessed 10 January 2018).

California Department of Education (2015) *Desired Results Developmental Profile (2015) A developmental continuum from early infancy to kindergarten entry: preschool comprehensive view*. Sacramento, CA, California Department of Education, Early Education and Support Division. Available online: http://www.cde.ca.gov/sp/cd/ci/drdpforms.asp (Accessed 15 December 2017).

Diamond, K. E. and Powell, D. R. (2011) An iterative approach to the development of a professional development intervention for Head Start teachers. *Journal of Early Intervention*, 33 (1): 75–93.

Downer, J. T., Booren, L. M., Lima, O. K., Luckner, A. E., and Pianta, R. C. (2010) The Individualized Classroom Assessment Scoring System (inCLASS): preliminary reliability and validity of a system for preschoolers' competence in classroom interactions. *Early Childhood Research Quarterly*, 25 (1): 1–16.

Glickman, C. D. (2002) *Leadership for learning: how to help teachers succeed.* Alexandria, VA, Association of Supervision and Curriculum Development.

Glickman, C. D., Gordon, S. P., and Ross-Gordon, J. M. (2018) 10th edn. *SuperVision and instructional leadership: a developmental approach.* New York, NY, Pearson.

Guo, Y., Justice, L. M., Sawyer, B., and Tompkins, V. (2011) Exploring factors related to reschool teachers' self-efficacy. *Teaching and Teacher Education,* 27 (5): 961–968.

Hamre, B. (2014) Teachers' daily interactions with children: an essential ingredient in effective early childhood programs. *Child Development Perspectives,* 8 (4): 223–230.

Helm, J. H. and Katz, L. (2014) 3rd edn. *Young investigators: the project approach in the early years.* New York, NY, Teachers College Press.

Hindman, A. H. and Wasik, B. A. (2012) Unpacking an effective language and literacy coaching intervention in Head Start: following teachers' learning over two years of training. *The Elementary School Journal,* 113 (1): 131–154.

Kolb, D. (2014) 2nd edn. *Experiential learning: experience as the source of learning and development.* Upper Saddle River, NJ, Pearson.

Kolb, D. and Kolb, A. (2013) *The Kolb learning style inventory 4.0: a comprehensive guide to the theory, psychometrics, research on validity and educational applications.* Boston, MA, Hay Resources Direct.

Morris, P., Mattera, S., Castells, N., Bangser, M., Bierman, K., and Raver, C. (2014) *Impact findings from the Head Start CARES demonstration: national evaluation of three approaches to improving preschoolers' social and emotional competence.* OPRE Report 2014-44. Washington DC, WA: Office of Planning, Research and Evaluation, Administration for Children and Families, U.S. Department of Health and Human Services. Available online: https://www.mdrc.org/sites/default/files/HSCares_2014%20Impact%20Report.pdf (Accessed 5 January 2018).

Office of Head Start (2016) *A national overview of grantee CLASS scores in 2016.* Washington DC, WA, Office of Head Start. Available online: https://eclkc.ohs.acf.hhs.gov/publication/national-overview-grantee-classr-scores-2016 (Accessed 15 December 2017).

Phillips, D., Austin, L. J. E., and Whitebook, M. (2016) The early care and education workforce. *The Future of Children,* 26 (2): 139–158.

Pianta, R., Downer, J., and Hamre, B. (2016) Quality in early education classrooms: definitions, gaps and systems. *The Future of Children,* 26 (2): 119–137.

Pianta, R., LaParo, K., and Hamre, B. (2008) *Classroom assessment scoring system.* Baltimore, MD, Paul H. Brookes.

Project Approach, The (2017) Available online: https://www.projectapproachkc.org/coaching-took-kit/coaching-in-project-abc2 (Accessed 17 July 2019).

Rush, D. D. and Shelden, M. L. L. (2011) *The early childhood coaching handbook*. Baltimore, MD, Paul H. Brookes.

Shidler, L. (2009) The impact of time spent coaching for teacher efficacy on student achievement. *Early Childhood Education Journal*, 36 (5): 453–460.

Shonkoff, J. P. and Phillips, D. A. (2000) *From neurons to neighborhoods: the science of early childhood development*. Washington DC, WA, National Academies Press.

Son, S. H. C., Kwon, K. A., Jeon, H. J., and Hong, S. Y. (2013) Head Start classrooms and children's school readiness benefit from teachers' qualifications and ongoing training. *Child and Youth Care Forum*, 42 (6): 525–553.

Vartuli, S. (1999) How early childhood teacher beliefs vary across grade level. *Early Childhood Research Quarterly*, 14 (4): 489–514.

Vartuli, S., Bolz, C., and Wilson, C. (2014) A learning combination: coaching with CLASS and the Project Approach. *Early Childhood Research and Practice*, 16 (1–2). Available online: http://ecrp.uiuc.edu/v16n1/vartuli.html (Accessed 5 December 2017).

Part II

Appreciative Inquiry: Examples from Practice

Introduction

The examples in Part II offer the reader the opportunity to reflect on the international practice of mentoring, coaching and supervision in England, Ireland, Belgium, Australia, New Zealand, Singapore, South Africa, USA and Canada. Using practical examples, the case studies broaden understanding of theory and practice and provide a starting point for reflecting on issues common to all working in the Early Years field. Their scope and range take the reader on a journey through an exploration of models of supervision, coaching and mentoring that are suitable for Early Years' professionals. They allow the reader to engage with ideas and to think about the complexities of professional support and intervention at many levels. An Appreciative Inquiry approach is used in order to reflect on what worked and why and to build on the successes. The case studies highlight the particular practice undertaken and give the reader insight into how to manage mentoring, coaching and supervision. It is hoped that practitioners will find these useful in helping to develop new skills or extend existing ones within the field of coaching and mentoring.

They examine the following common themes: mentoring and coaching to enhance teacher confidence; inclusive practice that takes account of adult and child starting points and 'voice'; and deepening reflective capacity. Whether the structures are creative or more formal, there is an emphasis on the way in which partnerships can be created through reflective practice and an experiential approach to personal professional development. Reflective questions are posed at the end of each case study to prompt reflection and suggest application to your own practice.

Taken together, the chapters unearth a rich tapestry of the practice of coaching and mentoring and provide opportunities to explore the underpinning theory and research and how these might work in practice. They offer a range of examples designed to showcase international practice models and explore current issues. Examples highlight the benefits of working together in developing a shared philosophy and culture and celebrating success. Again, the important role that the leader plays is explored, as well as the need for a safe space from which to foster professional identity and reflection on practice.

The concept of 'diversattitude' is introduced within the case studies from Belgium; here, a positive attitude to diversity and how we can be empowered to learn through each other is developed. As the landscapes of practice are changing, new ways of communicating and developing coaching and mentoring are needed. For example, many people now work from home, or work in isolation, and others hot-desk at their place of work where the busy daily schedule may mean that supportive conversations no longer take place by the photocopier or the coffee machine. Within nursery settings, busy schedules and part-time working may have implications for team meetings. With this in mind, new ways of working, such as peer mentoring, emails, phone conversations, are needed to create the safe space that practitioners need in order to engage in professional conversations and to explore issues that they encounter. An example of such a model of working can be seen in the Canadian case study, and practical examples of managing such professional conversations within the UK are discussed.

These are followed up by two detailed case examples from the USA that explore how coach-teacher interactions facilitate teacher-child interactions within Head Start classrooms. An evidence-based approach illuminates the coaching practices that support teachers' capacities to strengthen their classroom outcomes. The examples from Belgium demonstrate the critical importance of relationships and the value of creativity modelled by the way the Early Childhood pedagogue training programme is structured and delivered. The second example from England shares the approach taken by a mentor and coach, and the final example from South Africa highlights how students can overcome challenges and become mentors to practising Early Years teachers in supporting them as they promote more inclusive practice.

All the case studies highlight the importance of a philosophy of staff ownership of their professional learning and the need for continuous collaboration and engagement with one another within emotionally safe spaces. While reading the case studies it is useful to reflect on the changes that may be necessary to envisage a future where Early Years is recognized and new, innovative approaches to professional development and learning are instigated and valued within supportive and nurturing communities of practice.

11

Appreciative Inquiry Mentoring to Implement the Early Childhood Bicultural Curriculum

Chris Jenkin

Case Study Summary

Aotearoa New Zealand has many types of Early Childhood education (indigenous centres, state kindergartens, private- and community-run sessional and full-day care and education, home-based care and parent-led play centres). The Ministry of Education mandates that all centres implement the national Early Childhood curriculum *Te Whāriki* [The Woven Mat] (Ministry of Education, 1996; 2017), which was the 'first bicultural curriculum statement developed in New Zealand. It contains curriculum specifically for Māori immersion services [and] the bicultural nature of curriculum for all Early Childhood services' (Ministry of Education, 1996: 7). Given that Early Childhood teachers of Māori descent make up 9 per cent (Ministry of Education, 2014) of teachers, it is not surprising that many struggle to implement Māori language, customs and knowledge. This case study shows how teaching staff at Aro Arataki Children's Centre enhanced their bicultural practices. It includes ideas and strategies that may be relevant and useful in other contexts where colleagues work with children from diverse cultural and language backgrounds.

Introduction

Aro Arataki Children's Centre is a new purpose-built mainstream multi-room centre attached to a large Auckland District Health Board service. Area One, where the case study took place, has fifteen full-time children aged 2 years and under. In order to attend the centre at least one parent or grandparent has to be associated with the hospital service.

The educators were at different stages of being qualified, with four of the five staff involved in a course of study: Chris was studying for an Early Childhood postgraduate qualification; Nilmini was in the final year of a bachelor's degree; Shani was in her last semester of her Diploma of Teaching; Margaret had just started the first year of her course; and Peggy had completed her degree eight years previously. Having shared their stories of best practice using the Appreciative Inquiry approach (Whitney and Trosten-Bloom, 2003), the team met twice to develop further strategies for success.

Strategies for Success

Two sessions of coaching and mentoring from an Appreciative Inquiry approach enabled the teachers to build on their past experience. They reflected on their practice as they individually and collectively focused on appreciating best practice. As the teachers continued to implement the bicultural curriculum, they developed strategies for success, which included finding suitable resources, fostering team cohesion, developing leadership skills and implementing the practice of ownership.

The teachers at the Aro Arataki Centre identified that one of their strategies for success involved learning from staff who attended tertiary courses in Early Childhood education: *'We didn't know ... commonly used words like milk bottle, lie down, but we asked Shani who asked her lecturer when she is in her class what is the Māori word for milk bottle, lie down'* (Tr: N). Such Teacher education providers were a source of specific answers about the bicultural curriculum. Having somewhere to go to augment their knowledge and have questions answered enabled the teachers to expand their understanding.

An integral part of Māori culture is singing waiata [songs]. Chris shared how this strategy enabled her to learn and practise te reo Māori [Māori language]: *'I memorized Māori lyrics and sang action songs in Māori language to children. I followed colleagues to sing songs in Māori. Children began to understand te reo Māori'* (Jl: C). Not only was Chris able to learn more te reo Māori by singing waiata, but she was supported by her team in developing these skills, which, in turn, enabled children to extend their knowledge. Resources such as games, books and puzzles were available to support te reo Māori. Some of these were made by the staff, as Shani noted: *'I made some Māori resources ... followed by the song. It's on the wall. Pungāwerewere* [spider] – *it's about spiders ... the different colours of spiders and we counted the spiders and we made the colours, the shapes.'*

As staff supported each other, it was evident that they derived confidence and pleasure from their achievements. This is an important aspect of Appreciative Inquiry. Peggy expressed this sense of achievement: *'We sang many action songs, such as "Piko,* [bend] *Toru* [three]*!" The children were happy and they did a lot of "Paki paki"* [clap]*. I was quite thrilled to take part in waiata and putting my effort* [in] *to say the words.'* Margaret, too, enjoyed the fulfilment that came with children's responses to her effort: *'I felt great satisfaction when the children responded with some of the books I read to them.'*

Success became possible as teachers drew strength from the mentoring and coaching approach of Appreciative Inquiry. The team approach means that teachers support each other's efforts, but it would be unrealistic to expect this to be consistently effective. All working relationships have their rocky moments, and Early Childhood teaching teams are no exception. What does work is to use people's strengths to resolve those difficulties (McNamee, 2003). However, colleagues can resent being called upon to provide support, as Shani expressed: *'I was not happy when the other staff called me to participate and sing. I was thinking, "why can't she sing without me?" It is true that I am learning Māori as a module for my studies. Everybody should take ownership and practice.'* As Shani reflected on being called upon to support other teachers, she noted: *'I like team work, but as Early Childhood teachers we need to take ownership and work confidently. Next time I will ask the other teachers to sing without me. I will tell them I will listen and tell them if there is anything wrong. I will make sure that they practice confidently.'*

Shani had worked through what happened and was able to consider a strategy that would support both herself and the other teachers. In other words, she was working from an Appreciative Inquiry model for dealing with the inevitable difficulties that can arise. Although the teachers encountered difficulties, these were resolved through the consideration of positive strategies.

Reflection

While the case study of Aro Arataki shows Appreciative Inquiry in action with the bicultural curriculum in Aotearoa New Zealand, teachers reading this will want to be able to develop strategies for success within their own practice, centres and programmes. This reflective section, while building on the case study, provides theory and ideas that all teachers can use for their own development.

Appreciative Inquiry Approach

Sharing best practice enabled all the teachers in the team to make a connection with each other by hearing the narratives of their most effective bicultural practice. It also enabled them to be clear about each other's level of skills and confidence. The main learning from the Appreciative Inquiry coaching and mentoring was that each person had a narrative from which they could build their knowledge, skills and confidence. Another key realization was that, although individually teachers at the centre had made previous attempts to implement the bicultural curriculum, they had not worked together as a team in this area. Mentoring and coaching through the process of Appreciative Inquiry enabled the teachers to work together, to see each other's strengths and to develop a shared philosophy with strategies for success.

Resources

Coaching and mentoring from an appreciatively oriented evaluation begins by taking stock of resources, 'to mine the resources and strengths that are part of the program in order to improve or in some way alter the parts that are not working' (McNamee, 2003: 37). Resourcing the Early Childhood curriculum is an important aspect of programme delivery, regardless of the approach taken, for teachers to be successful and this was no different in Aro Arataki. To effectively implement the bicultural or any curriculum there must be, according to Cubey (1992), sufficient resources. Indeed, within New Zealand the curriculum document *Te Whāriki* 'supports the cultural identity of all children ... each early childhood education service should ensure that programmes and resources are sensitive and responsive to the different cultures and heritages' (Ministry of Education, 1996: 18).

With regard to honouring and including indigenous perspectives in Early Childhood programmes, genuine indigenous knowledge is crucial, including the use of indigenous resources and crafts (Moore and Hennessy, 2006; Ritchie and Rau; 2006). Language and culture are entwined and difficult to separate (Corson, 1990). Incorporating language other than the one which is dominant has been shown to advantage children (Gonzalez-Mena, 2006). Second language learning can be challenging, especially for monolingual adults. Using music and singing (as Chris did) to learn a foreign language is a practical strategy, because as well as creating a good atmosphere in the classroom, it is useful for teaching the rhythm of language (Shtakser, 2001).

Theories of Team

In the group, teachers identified the value of the team, as summed up by Margaret: '*You need team support to keep the fires going.*' Teamwork is a central part of Early Childhood education practice. It is the way in which teachers work towards collectively planning and supporting each other. In this way, as well as learning from each other they develop the ability to determine the skills of their colleagues and achieve greater confidence in what they are doing. Part of being in a team involved developing an understanding of and sharing ideas about bicultural pedagogy, as well as fostering the opportunity to learn from each other. In their research Ritchie and Rau (2006) reported that 'co-researchers felt the implementation of Tiriti-based [bicultural] programmes was more effective when the teaching team held a shared philosophy and commitment' (2006: 20).

Team cohesiveness was developed through activities such as sharing food. This enabled them to talk about the challenges they encountered, to show themselves as vulnerable and to expose self-doubt, all of which contributed to building trust.

Because teachers were exchanging ideas, listening to each other and moving beyond individual and even isolated implementation, they were able to gain confidence as a team. This is consistent with observations made by Reid and Stover (2006), who noted that 'groups can show resilience, efficacy and an ability to achieve in the face of great odds' (2006: 23), but for this to happen two conditions have to be present. Firstly, a whole-team approach that emphasises working from a platform of success. Second, the importance of a strong leader – this cannot be over-emphasised.

Leadership

Shani was not the designated leader responsible for managing day-to-day processes (Cardno and Reynolds, 2009), but more importantly she became the leader who took on responsibility and ownership for implementing the bicultural curriculum. Hayden and Gibson (2000) state that: 'leadership refers to vision and influence. By vision we mean the foresight, imagination and commitment to devise new and better ways; and by influence we refer to the capacity to motivate others to participate in the realization of the vision' (2000: ii).

Research on self-review in an Early Childhood Centre (Grey, 2004) revealed that an effective leader was important in facilitating group processes in order for change to occur. Strong, responsible leadership, which Shani provided, enabled the team to own their actions with the bicultural curriculum. She had the ability to influence the other team members (Hayden and Gibson, 2000) and in doing so 'created the impetus for change' (Duhn, 2010: 55).

Ownership

However, for someone to be a leader, there needs to be those who are followers. As Sergiovanni (1992: 71) states, 'followers are people committed to purposes, a cause, a vision of what the school is and can become, beliefs about teaching and learning, values and standards to which they adhere, and convictions'. While the team looked to Shani for guidance, they all shared the same vision, philosophy and action for implementing the bicultural curriculum. However, members of the team need to take ownership and be prepared to take action. As can be seen from Shani's reflections, she saw the importance of each team member taking ownership of the curriculum rather than relying on the leaders or 'expert'. Bishop (2008) describes ownership as ensuring that the 'original objectives of the reform are protected and sustained' (2008: 55). Ownership occurs when learning is central to classroom exchanges and relationships, thus replacing deficit thinking by teachers, which Bishop claims results in negative relationships between students and teachers.

In Early Childhood education, believing that the bicultural curriculum is difficult to implement becomes a self-fulfilling prophecy. By practitioners being positive and supportive of each other and by building on what they already know, successful implementation will become inevitable and this is the advantage of coaching and mentoring from the Appreciative Inquiry perspective. As Duhn and Craw (2010: 68) state, 'teachers are in the privileged position of making a difference in children's understandings of themselves and others'.

In Aro Arataki Centre teachers needed to move to beyond being committed to the bicultural curriculum to assuming, instead, a sense of personal responsibility. In other words, the sense of ownership was so strong, they would implement the curriculum even without the support from their teams. This also meant that they would transfer their sense of ownership into their future endeavours if ever they moved to other centres.

Conclusion

Utilizing Appreciative Inquiry in Early Childhood within a coaching and mentoring framework has implications for putting theory in practice, rather than espoused theory in use (Argyris and Schön, 1974). Theory in practice emphasizes Appreciative Inquiry for each centre in order for practitioners to effectively plan together so that collaborative development occurs. Argyris and Schön (1974) discuss the difference between 'theories of action which exist as espoused theories and so theories-in-use, which govern actual behaviour' (1974: 29). At Aro Arataki, where Appreciative Inquiry was utilized and the focus was on what worked, teachers were proud of and thrilled by their achievements. Strong, responsible leadership enabled the team to own their actions in Tiriti-based curriculum. They were keen to share their knowledge beyond their own team. Their positive focus produced positive results.

> **Reflective Questions**
>
> Team members discussed the effective ways in which they implemented the bicultural curriculum, one of which was working together as a team.
>
> 1. Reflect on a time when working as part of a team either enhanced or could have enhanced your mentoring/coaching. What can you identify as the key strategies inherent in your reflection of team work?
> 2. Strategies were identified, such as memorizing content to be delivered; supporting team members as they developed skills; using relevant resources; encouraging participant responsiveness; and acknowledging/celebrating success. Which of these strategies would be effective in your work? Build a mind map of effective strategies for your work.
> 3. What are the skills that need to be developed further, or new skills to be acquired?
> 4. What would be suitable ways of celebrating success in your cultural and professional context?

References

Argyris, C. and Schön, D. (1974) *Theory in practice: increasing professional practice.* San Francisco, CA, Jossey-Bass Publishers.

Bishop, R. (2008) GPILSEO: a model for sustainable educational reform. *New Zealand Journal of Educational Studies,* 43 (2): 47–62.

Cardno, C. and Reynolds, B. (2009) Resolving leadership dilemmas in New Zealand kindergartens: an action research study. *Journal of Educational Administration,* 47 (2): 206–226.

Corson, D. (1990) Bilingualism and second language teaching (SLT) across the curriculum. In Corson, D. (ed.) *Language policy across the curriculum.* Clevedon, Multilingual Matters. pp. 159–206.

Cubey, P. (1992) Responses to the Treaty of Waitangi in early childhood education. Master's thesis, Wellington, New Zealand, Victoria University of Wellington.

Duhn, I. (2010) The centre is my business: neo-liberal politics, privatisation and discourses of professionalism in New Zealand. *Contemporary Issues in Early Childhood*, 11 (1): 49–60.

Duhn, I. and Craw, J. (2010) Embracing the complexity of a socio-cultural pedagogy: interpersonal relationships as a vehicle for learning. In Clark, B. and Grey, A. (eds) *Āta kitea te pae Scanning the horizon. Perspectives on early childhood education*. Auckland, New Zealand, Pearson.

Gonzalez-Mena, J. (2006) 5th edn. *Diversity in early care and education: honoring differences*. New York, NY, McGraw-Hill.

Grey, A. (2004) The quality journey: is there a leader at the helm? *New Zealand Research in Early Childhood Education*, 7: 91–102.

Hayden, J. and Gibson, H. (2000) Management and leadership: editorial. *Australian Journal of Early Childhood*, 25 (1): 1–2.

McNamee, S. (2003) Appreciative evaluation within a conflicted educational. *New Directions for Evaluation*, 100 (Winter): 23–40.

Ministry of Education (1996) *Te whāriki. He whāriki mātauranga mō ngā mokopuna o Aotearoa: early childhood curriculum*. Wellington, New Zealand, Learning Media.

Ministry of Education (2014) *Education counts: annual ECE census report 2014*. Wellington, New Zealand, Ministry of Education. Available online: https://www.educationcounts.govt.nz/publications/series/annual-early-childhood-education-census/annual-early-childhood-census-2014 (Accessed 26 January 2016).

Ministry of Education (2017) 2nd edn. *Te whāriki. He whāriki mātauranga mō ngā mokopuna o Aotearoa: early childhood curriculum*. Wellington, New Zealand: Ministry of Education. Available online: https://www.education.govt.nz/assets/Documents/Early-Childhood/Te-Whariki-Early-Childhood-Curriculum-ENG-Web.pdf (Accessed 14 July 2018).

Moore, P. and Hennessy, K. (2006) New technologies and contested ideologies: the Tagish first voices project. *The American Indian Quarterly*, 30 (1 and 2): 119–137.

Reid, R. and Stover, S. (2006) Can we do what we set out to do? A reflective model of group agency. *The First Years: Nga Tau Tuatahi. New Zealand Journal of Infant and Toddler Education*, 8 (1): 23–27.

Ritchie, J. and Rau, C. (2006) *Whakawhanaungatanga: partnerships in bicultural development in early childhood care and education*. Wellington, New Zealand, Teaching and Learning Research Initiatives. Available online: http://www.tlri.org.nz/tlri-research/research-completed/ece-sector/whakawhanaungatanga%E2%80%94-partnerships-bicultural-development (Accessed 17 July 2018).

Sergiovanni, T. J. (1992) *Moral leadership: getting to the heart of school improvement.* San Francisco, CA, Jossey-Bass.

Shtakser, I. (2001) *Using music and songs in the foreign language classroom.* Available online: https://dokumen.tips/documents/using-music-and-songs-in-the-foreign-language-classroom.html (Accessed 12 December 2018).

Whitney, D. and Trosten-Bloom, A. (2003) *The power of appreciative inquiry: a practical guide to positive change.* San Francisco, CA, Barrett-Koehler Publishing Inc.

12

Finding Community Through an Induction Support Pilot Project

Laura K. Doan

Case Study Summary

The case study considers the impact of a pilot project carried out in British Columbia, Canada, designed to support professional educators in developing their identity through mentoring and peer support.

Introduction

This project involved twenty-two Early Childhood educators in British Columbia, Canada. The participants, who were working in eight different early learning programmes, ranged from those who were newly qualified with a few weeks' experience to those who had been in the profession for thirty-five years. The aim of the project was to support the ongoing professional identity development of both new and experienced Early Childhood educators and to address the lack of formal support to new educators and the difficulty in accessing professional development for all Early Childhood educators.

The project involved peer mentoring, professional development, online support and visits to early learning programmes. This pilot project was based on previous research with beginning Early Childhood educators, where the induction support received was haphazard and unreliable (Doan, 2014). For example, when asked about the mentoring they had received in their first year of work, 51 per cent of participants indicated that they had received none or little and commented that they wanted induction support in the form of mentoring or peer support, observations, feedback and professional development. Furthermore, as many as 50 per cent of beginning Early Childhood educators in British Columbia leave the field within the first five years of starting work (Early Childhood Educators of British Columbia (ECEBC), 2012).

Scenario

Participants in the induction support project were involved in introductory meetings in which Early Childhood educators shared their interests. Figure 12.1 shows how the meetings are conducted, with participants considering topics for discussion during peer mentoring. Participants found their own peer mentor and together they connected over email, telephone and/or face-to-face meetings, as shown in Figure 12.2, which supported confidence, as shown in Figure 12.3.

There was a range of experiences for the participants. One peer mentor who was acting as a coach was asked to collaborate with a peer by focusing on a specific case within her studies, and she found she learned alongside the newer educator. She reported, '*I learned probably just as much or maybe even more than she learned in that conversation too. So I think that's the value of peer mentoring or peer support. If you can learn alongside one another, it's not necessarily teacher and student, it's coming together.*'

Some participants spoke about the importance of knowing that there were people they could call on for support. Educators shared specific challenges within the workplace that hindered their ability to obtain the support they needed. These included lack of time within the day to talk with colleagues, reluctance to open up about problems and the desire to appear competent. For some participants, it came as quite a relief to know that some of their co-workers (who were part of the project) were interested in peer mentoring and this opened up opportunities for dialogue as the participant felt much more confident in asking for support. One participant described it as follows:

Finding Community: A Support Pilot Project 127

Figure 12.1 Induction

Figure 12.2 Peer mentoring

A lot of people [in the project] were people I kind of knew or were colleagues already, but maybe wouldn't have reached out to them before because I didn't know that they were interested in providing support or needed support. Our jobs are very busy and so I often don't want to bother people 'cause usually those extra things have to be on our own time ... knowing that they were all interested in both mentoring and being mentored helped me feel more confident to reach out.

Gaining confidence is an important aspect of peer mentoring and is an issue discussed regularly at project meetings. It is not always visible but nevertheless is an essential component to the success of the project. One participant, who had been an Early Childhood educator for over thirty years, became aware of the importance of mentoring: 'Now that I'm a little bit older and more experienced, I'm realizing that, you know, I can be a mentor, and I can also be mentored. I like that, that we can learn from one another, and I think that is something to be really intentional about.' This participant went on to make some changes directly in her programme. This included reassuring her staff that open communication was welcome and that they would not be judged: 'I'm giving you the permission to ask me when you don't know something. Don't be afraid to, you know, clarify something if you're uncertain. Don't be afraid to make mistakes because we can learn together. We can try something and if it doesn't work, we can talk about it and then try something else.'

Figure 12.3 Gaining confidence

Perspectives/Issues

At times, Early Childhood educators find themselves working in an environment where they feel isolated, despite the fact they have co-workers. One reason for this was that due to staff shortages Early Childhood educators move quickly into positions of leadership and many do not have adequate training or experience. Bloom (2007) argues that new directors may be experiencing their own form of survival, where they are just trying to get through the day and are unable to support new Early Childhood educators and/or focus on communication structures between staff. This simple diagram (Figure 12.4) illustrates the fact that, while there are educators working within the same job site, the structures for communication are not automatically present.

In contrast to the above model, new Early Childhood educators want to be valued, included on the team, given feedback and offered opportunities for professional development, and they want mentors who show an interest in them (see Figure 12.5).

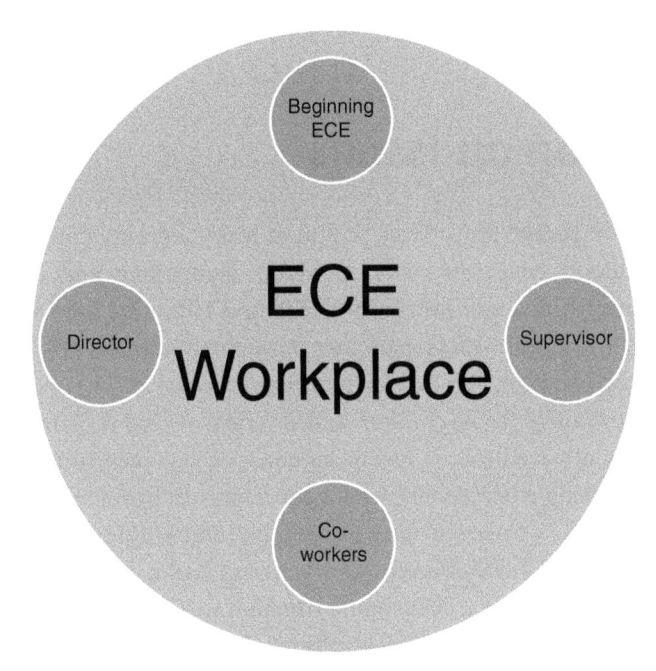

Figure 12.4 ECE workplace

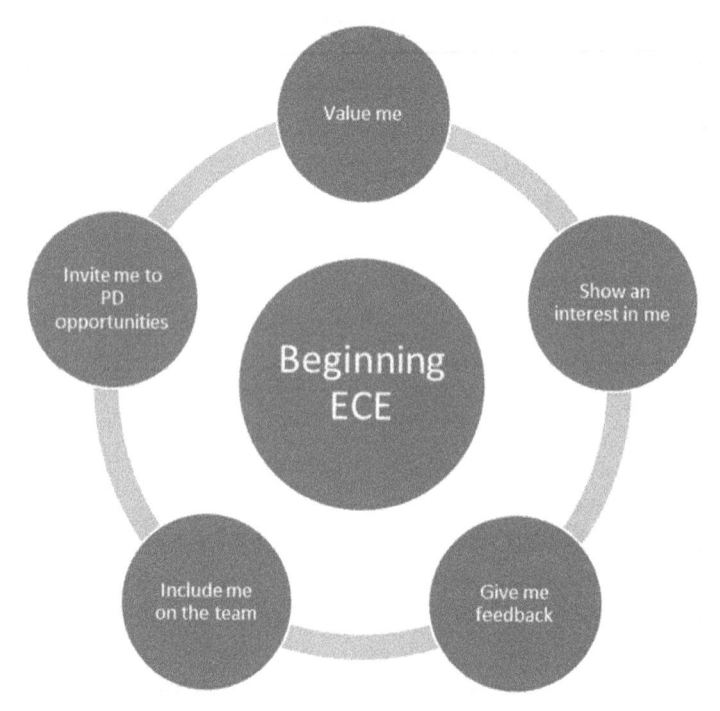

Figure 12.5 Beginning ECE

Circles around "Beginning ECE": Value me; Show an interest in me; Give me feedback; Include me on the team; Invite me to PD opportunities

Reflection on Issues

This induction project took place within an early learning context where Early Childhood educators work in highly demanding and fast-paced environments. In this context, Early Childhood educators have very little time, if any, to connect with one another throughout the day as there is very little time for planning or discussing professional issues. The work day is spent 'on the floor' with the children and, as one participant shared, getting support from other educators has to be done 'on our own time'. This can result in a working environment where educators are working in isolation, without the benefit of hearing other perspectives and working as a team. For example, an Early Childhood educator who has had a difficult encounter with a family member or a challenging situation with a child would benefit from having time to connect with a colleague, to receive both support and practical help. Despite the challenges within an early learning programme, mentoring can occur within and outside of the workplace and the benefits for all parties make it worthwhile to try it out.

As previously mentioned, in the context of where this study took place, 50 per cent of Early Childhood educators leave the early learning field within the first five years of starting work (ECEBC, 2012). This is a startling statistic and, while not all educators may be leaving the field due to a lack of mentoring, I believe it is part of the equation. Katz (1972) has described an Early Childhood educator's first year as being one of 'survival', where he or she is simply trying to make it through the day. It is during this time period especially that Early Childhood educators need mentoring support as they take on additional responsibilities and experience work outside of the post-secondary system. Teacher efficacy (Tschannen-Moran, Woolfolk Hoy and Hoy, 1998) comes out of Bandura's concept of self-efficacy (1997) and relates to the educator's beliefs about their own abilities as an educator and their abilities to make changes within an early learning programme. Early childhood educators who receive quality mentoring have the opportunity to grow their teacher efficacy. Moreover, having a mentor who can share their challenges openly to others can help to normalize the 'survival' mode that the new Early Childhood educator may be experiencing and this can create space for honest dialogue about issues.

Mutual Learning

As the mentors in this study have shared, there are benefits for new and experienced Early Childhood educators when they come together to support each other through peer mentoring. Whether it is through an email, phone call or face-to-face meetings, peer-mentors who engage with issues of practice and take a break from the day-to-day work opt instead to reflect upon and problem-solve the potential issues. I would argue that teacher efficacy can improve for both new and experienced Early Childhood educators when they engage in peer mentoring, and this can contribute to a higher job satisfaction (Skaalvik and Skaalvik, 2009). Furthermore, successful peer mentoring can support the development of collective efficacy, a term that refers to people's 'shared belief in their collective power to produce desired results', and this is an important factor in collective agency (Bandura, 2001: 14). The early learning field is one where, depending on the context one is working in, there are often questions about the value and worth of the work that Early Childhood educators do, and I would argue that taking part in a mentoring relationship can help to sustain educators when they need it the most. Being able to share with a mentor and hear their reflections can help Early Childhood educators to recognize the value of the work they are doing.

Opening Up

Peer-mentors in this study spoke about the importance of opening up, being willing to share a concern, question and/or a desire for mentoring. Depending on the work site, this can be a very challenging thing to do. In many situations, new Early Childhood educators are given the same workload as experienced Early Childhood educators, and in essence are expected to do the same job, despite the fact that they are new. Mentors who step in to support new Early Childhood educators recognize that professional identity does not happen overnight and takes time to develop (Katz, 1972; Vander Ven, 1988). Furthermore, mentors who can be intentional in supporting educators around them can do much to assist new educators at a time when they may need it the most, and this can result in new educators successfully entering the profession. What does being intentional look like? This can include taking the time to reflect and think about the educators around you. How long have they been in the field? How are they doing currently? Have you had time to check in with them, letting them know you care? Being aware, being present and being willing to step outside of your comfort zone to let a new Early Childhood educator know you are there can make a huge difference to someone who may otherwise feel quite isolated and alone.

One issue for mentors to consider is their comfort level with knowledge with which they may be unfamiliar. Given that in this study the experience of the Early Childhood educators ranged from several weeks to thirty-five years in the early learning field, there is going to be a variety of educational experiences and mentors should expect to hear about new ideas related to programming, child guidance and pedagogical documentation. For example, in the British Columbia context, the British Columbia Early Learning Framework was introduced in 2009 and put great emphasis on the use of pedagogical narrations or learning stories as a way for educators to document the children's learning. While new Early Childhood educators will have great familiarity with pedagogical narrations, experienced Early Childhood educators may not, and this is okay. Mentors do not need to be experts on all things related to early learning, nor is this expected. In fact, I would argue that mentors who position themselves as being open to learning from the person they are mentoring help to build a relationship that is mutually beneficial. Moreover, this kind of attitude and practice recognizes that the work done by Early Childhood educators is, in fact, not simple but deeply complex and professional, requiring ongoing learning (Pacini-Ketchabaw *et al.*, 2015).

Reflection

As a mentor, how comfortable am I with uncertainty? Being a mentor does not mean you are an expert in all things related to early learning. Quite the contrary. Being a mentor includes being open to learning new things, being available and being willing to hear the experiences of others. Given the complexity of the work involved in early learning, one person cannot possibly know everything and while new Early Childhood educators will need support, they may also be the one you are learning from, given that they have just recently completed their training. You may be in a situation where you are being asked questions about something with which you are unfamiliar. See this as an opportunity to learn together.

Reflective Questions

1. As a mentor, how intentional am I being in my role as a mentor? What am I actually doing to let others know that I am ready and available as a mentor? How do I actively support the educators around me?
2. Given how busy the early learning environment is, and the lack of time for reflection and joint planning, what can you do as a mentor to connect with another educator? Is there a way to creatively plan the daily schedule to make use of common break times? If you mentor an educator who works in a different programme, how can you make use of online technology as a tool to support your communication?
3. If you find yourself in an early years setting where mentoring is not practised, how might you open up dialogue with the educators to see if they are open to this?
4. What are your thoughts on the practice of mentoring as a way of supporting the professional work that early years professionals are involved in?

References

Bandura, A. (1997) *Self-efficacy: the exercise of control.* New York, NY, W. H. Freeman and Company.

Bandura, A. (2001) Social cognitive theory: an agentic perspective. *Annual Review of Psychology*, 52 (1): 1–26.

Bloom, P. J. (2007) *From the inside out: the power of reflection and self-awareness.* Rosemont, IL, New Horizons.

Costigliola, B. and Peek, S. (2009). *A bulletin of the child care.* Human Resource Sector Council.

Doan, L. (2014) The early years: an exploration of the experiences and needs of novice early childhood educators in British Columbia. Dissertation, Calgary, AB, University of Calgary.

Early Childhood Educators of British Columbia (2012). *May 2012 is child care month: early childhood educators matter to BC's economy.* Press release. Available online: http://www.ecebc.ca/news/ECEBC_ChildCareMonth_2012.pdf (Accessed 27 December 2018).

Katz, L. (1972) *Developmental stages of preschool teachers.* Urbana, IL, Educational Resources Information Centre Clearinghouse on Early Childhood Education.

Nicholson, S. and Reifel, S. (2011) Sink or swim: child care teachers' perceptions of entry training experiences. *Journal of Childhood Teacher Education*, 32 (1): 5–25.

Pacini-Ketchabaw, V., Nxumalo, F., Kocher, L., Elliot, E., and Sanchez, A. (2015) *Journeys: reconceptualizing early childhood practices through pedagogical narration.* Toronto, ON, University of Toronto Press.

Skaalvik, E. M. and Skaalvik, S. (2009). Does school context matter? Relations with teacher burnout and job satisfaction. *Teaching and Teacher Education*, 25: 518–524.

Tschannen-Moran, M., Woolfolk Hoy, A., and Hoy, W. K. (1998) Teacher efficacy: its meaning and measure. *Review of Educational Research*, 68: 202–248.

Vander Ven, K. (1988) Pathways to professional effectiveness for early childhood educators. In Spodek, B., Saracho, O., and Peters, D. (eds) *Professionalism and the early childhood practitioner.* New York, NY, Teachers College Press.

13

Coaching Teams of Early Years Professionals throughout a County in England

Becky Poulter Jewson

Case Study Summary

This case study considers the need for and development of a coaching strategy for Early Years practitioners based in a pre-school setting in the south of England.

Introduction

The pre-school is set in an affluent suburban (Department for Communities and Local Government, 2015) area of England (with approximately 10,000 residents of all ages) and is attached to a small community school. The school does not oversee the pre-school, although it rents the premises to them and to afterschool clubs. Many of the children attend the school when they are old enough; this promotes good transitions as the children know the environment well. The pre-school is open for thirty-eight weeks of the year and follows the school term dates as many families have siblings at the school and pre-school.

The pre-school has the resources for twenty-one children between the ages of 2 and 4 years. The number of children attending at any one time is usually sixteen. The setting has a strong ethos, based around quality interactions and teaching through child-led interests and provocations, enabling children to feel listened to and valued and encouraging them to grow in confidence and independence, not only for their time at pre-school but for their future life. Figure 13.1 shows the nursery garden. The activities that take place here give the children the opportunity to learn independently.

In England there is a statutory requirement set out in the Early Years Foundation Stage (Department for Education, 2017) for all staff to have regular supervision or professional conversations; this comes from the need for all people working with young children to be listened to and for their concerns to be understood (Tickell, 2011). The term 'professional conversations' encompasses the process of mentoring and coaching where future outcomes and personal goals are focused upon and support is offered so that personal and professional growth are nurtured. Regular meetings foster reflective

Figure 13.1 Nursery garden fostering independent learning

discussions, help alleviate pressures, support staff as they understand and act upon safeguarding concerns and encompass a containment and reciprocal approach (Solihull, 2018). After discussions with colleagues and following shared good practice meetings, it was concluded that mentoring sessions should be held regularly approximately every six weeks (Skinner, 2017). The meetings are one-to-one and usually last for about an hour; however, they do sometimes last longer as mentees do not like to feel rushed and this is their time away from a very busy childcare environment to actually be really listened to and reflect professionally without interruption. The importance of setting a regular date that is not going to change and where both parties have the time to prepare is paramount. Professional conversations should follow the same pattern of questions and the discussions cover the previous actions.

Within the setting a professional coaching and mentoring template focuses the discussion on current and future goals and outcomes – see Figure 13.2.

Mentoring and Coaching Template — *thriving Language*

Example of professional conversation lines of discussion Coaching and Mentoring	Reflective discussion
Starting point: where are you now?	Assessing how much capacity mentee has to move forward Think not overwhelmed or under-stimulated Positive aspects Challenging aspects Barriers
Manageable understanding of discussion processes	Structuring ideas and thoughts Creating an achievable and realistic plan of how mentee can proceed (mentee needs to take ownership in order to move forward)
Understanding what motivates and drives mentee	Viewing self professionally Viewing self personally Maintaining momentum Future goals

Figure 13.2 Mentoring and coaching template

Mentoring and coaching at the setting are present in action and at evaluation. Peer observations are used for this, with direct feedback being given to the team and then reflected upon within dedicated daily evaluation times. Professional conversations are recorded and acted upon in the daily short-term planning and also referred to for more in-depth mentoring and coaching with the team (see Figure 13.2). Mentoring at the setting has a planned time and is held on the day when no children are present. Interruptions are minimal and outcomes can be actioned immediately where possible. This uses the non-contact time allocated to the team and is highly valued as reflection and team discussion time. Staff at the setting are not taken out of ratio as there are no funds to bring in cover staff and the children's continuity of care may become disrupted. Therefore, a team decision was made to carry out recorded professional conversations away from the setting if dates are compromised. This has been necessary so that they can still take place regularly as a time lapse may make a supervision meaningless (Twigg *et al.*, 2013: 75). Even when carefully planned, meetings do sometimes have to change, for example, due to staff illness, safeguarding meetings, transition records and assessment deadline.

As the setting lead, I mentor and document the professional conversation of the team individuals; however, this is not open to me as a manager. I have regular meetings with a supportive committee lead, although these do not follow the same format, as the committee lead is a volunteer parent. I have paid for professional supervision and mentoring when I have recognized I need more support and guidance. There is a paradox of knowing how important it is to professionally discuss outcomes and concerns, yet many settings (including mine) do not have an area manager to act as the facilitator of these.

I have been trained in mentoring and supervision in a previous post; therefore, I have an understanding of what is expected and why professional conversations should be highly valued. After discussions in meetings with other Early Years providers, there does not seem to be clarity on how mentoring, coaching and supervision should be carried out or what the content and length should be. Appraisals are often mistaken for professional conversations, or a group team meeting may take place which is not individualized. Professional reflective conversations seem to be misunderstood and then perhaps misrepresented 'as something else to do'. Coaching, mentoring and supervision training for settings are not free or easily accessible. Yet there is a statutory requirement for supervision, developed to protect children and give a voice to Early Years workers.

At local Early Years providers meetings, we have discussed creating a group of managers who could, with guidance and trust, mentor each other. I have shared formats with the group so that we have a starting point.

Facilitating Peer Reflection through Coaching and Mentoring

Managers may feel they have no one to mentor or coach them and as such are continuously 'holding' their teams' personal and professional concerns. Does this imply that all managers may be faultless or have endless empathy and the broadest of shoulders to carry everyone's thoughts and not discuss their own? Discussions at local Early Years providers meetings appear to confirm this; the most senior managers do not have supervision, coaching or mentoring as there is no one to carry out this role. This may add to the pressure of their role of a proactive and reflective leader and diminish their ability to facilitate others' practice. How does a manager with no facility for supervision safeguard their well-being? Safeguarding of children may be compromised if there is no confidential arena to discuss individual concerns and actions. This is an area discussed in more depth in Chapter 5.

Further reflections showed that many managers have a misunderstanding of the purpose of professional conversations and how to implement critical reflections in practice without a structure and time to do so (Twigg *et al.*, 2013: 75). Comments from manager's network meetings are revealing: *'When will we fit that in'*; *'No room to do it in'*; *'We do carry out appraisals, another thing to do.'* There appears to be a training need to develop a network of meaningful mentoring and professional discussions, thereby enabling positive and sustained long-term outcomes for managers who engage (Sheridan *et al.*, 2009).

This has been discussed and realized at Early Years providers network meetings. Training for mentoring and professional conversation has developed and is available locally for all employees in the Early Years workforce. Figure 13.3 depicts the possible impact of professional conversation (Thriving Language, 2018). The insightful comment by a manager attending the training conveys their feeling: *'If you don't know how or what's expected but you know you have to carry out professional conversations, it becomes a bit scary to admit that you don't know how to.'*

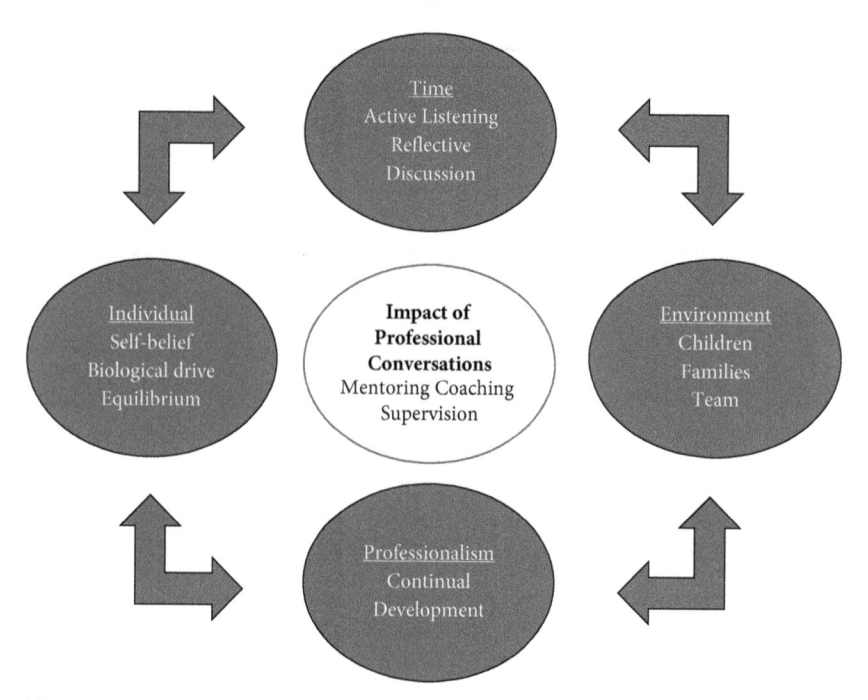

```
              Time
         Active Listening
           Reflective
           Discussion


  Individual                          Environment
  Self-belief        Impact of         Children
  Biological drive  Professional       Families
  Equilibrium       Conversations      Team
                   Mentoring Coaching
                    Supervision


         Professionalism
            Continual
           Development
```

Figure 13.3 Interconnecting processes *Impact of Professional Conversations*

My Reflections

In a previous Early Years role I worked within the safeguarding arena and was fortunate to have excellent professional mentoring training. From this, I recognized that to empower others to make a difference I need to be able to discuss my worries and concerns and explore my reflective thoughts. Most importantly, I understood when I was holding too many concerns and when I needed to talk confidentially to another professional. When professional conversations were timetabled, this allowed me to feel that I was supported in my role.

Currently, I do not have this facility within the pre-school, so professionally I have sought mentoring for which I pay when needed. I also work alongside a professional NHS colleague and she coaches me reflectively, which enables me to build my understanding of myself personally and professionally. There is a risk in Early Years to be selfless with our own health and always put others first; this serves very little positive purpose and may lead to psychological and physiological 'burn out' (Hozo *et al.*, 2015). To take time for 'you' could enable you to have clarity of thought and actions, both personally and professionally. Personal aspects of life may have an effect on work and professionalism, so to discuss these confidentially with a non-judgemental fellow professional may ensure a better understanding of their impact (Tickell, 2011).

Professional Discussions: The Impact and Outcomes of Mentoring Sessions

My colleague and I held professional discussions about her mentoring sessions. She has had mentoring sessions for two years and has developed a good understanding of their benefits and why they are necessary. We discussed the need for these sessions to be private and where possible uninterrupted, giving further authenticity. If there are personal or professional concerns, the mentee will need to have the space and time to honestly discuss these without fear of anyone hearing or misinterpreting their thoughts and words. There must be a trust that the mentor will not share the session notes. However, there is an understanding that actions may need addressing and safeguarding concerns or unprofessional acts will definitely be acted upon. Actions need to be agreed jointly, but do not have to be implemented by the mentor. The mentor should not try and 'fix' everything and there should be a shared responsibility for moving forward and deciding the necessary actions to enable this. Mentees should not feel 'done to'; they will need to be an integral part of the processes.

My colleague feels supported and can talk to me or another team member at an appropriate time. She knows she has a set date to discuss professional issues. She feels valued and her opinion is listened to and, therefore, if a matter needs addressing sooner, she initiates a conversation prior to her next session. This approach may be the key to an integrated team and successful mentoring; it is not a time to store up all of the angst or misunderstandings. It can be a time to look forward to a firm belief in enabling deeper reflective practice and a better environment for all.

Other team members also have a role and, with permission from the mentee, a good course of action could be to share ideas and include other team members, with the intention that authentic fruition of ideas becomes a reality. Cohesive, holistic practice with an embedded ethos is developed and grows over time, with deep levels of understanding for all individuals in the team. This includes encouraging their motivations, ideas and growth within their current role and progression. Most importantly, in our setting mentoring provides an understanding of how individuals can be a key influence on the child's and family's life daily, weekly, monthly and for life.

Reflecting on Good Practice through Group Mentoring and Coaching and the Impact Upon the Setting

The setting is small and busy and, while it can accommodate twenty-one children, we decided to cap the number of children attending to sixteen. This decision was made through professional conversations in the format of group coaching. Staff reflected that having more children at the setting would compromise on the quality of care at the pre-school and that we would also need to employ another member of the team. The group coaching enabled a whole team approach to evaluate the environment and for all the team's ideas to be discussed and professionally challenged.

Reflection

Robust professional conversations may encourage staff retention as staff feel more valued, listened to and they may have a sense of belonging (Twigg et al., 2013). Through creating wider communities of practice for coaching and mentoring networks Early Years teams may gain clarity and develop understanding of the wider influence they hold on children's immediate emotional and educational well-being and the impact they have on future outcomes.

A term developed and used at network meetings – 'discussion before issue' (Thriving Language, 2017) – may be credited as enabling productive talks in practice amongst Early Years professionals. We discuss and offer constructive, reflective support, working through differing thoughts and ideas before they become an issue. We recognize that there will be conflict at times (Rodd, 2006). However, this does not stop us engaging in difficult conversations.

Professional conversations that are reflective:

1 **allow** flexibility of environment;
2 **consider** cost implications (time in lieu may be offered to mentor and mentee);
3 **enhance** practice;
4 **enable** better team work;
5 **increase** welfare of staff and children;
6 **support** individuals to feel valued and understood.

Conclusion

Despite the constraints of time and budgets, it is possible to set up a robust system of coaching and mentoring for all practitioners within Early Years settings where there is the will to do so.

Reflective Questions

1 Consider any potential risks in one senior member of staff being responsible for all mentoring/coaching/supervisions.
2 To what extent should practitioners receive standardized training for mentoring/coaching/supervision? How could this be developed/monitored?
3 What is the level of understanding of mentoring/coaching/supervision in the Early Years environment?
4 Consider the potential impact of mentoring/coaching/supervision on the professional status of the Early Years sector and the individual.

References

Department for Communities and Local Government (2015) *English indices of deprivation*. Available online: https://www.gov.uk/government/statistics/english-indices-of-deprivation-2015 (Accessed 15 December 2017).

Department for Education. (2017) *Statutory Framework for the Early Years Foundation Stage: setting the standards for learning, development and care for children from birth to five.* Available online: https://www.gov.uk/government/publications/early-years-foundation-stage-framework-2 (Accessed 13 January 2017).

Department for Education (2016) *Disqualification under the Childcare Act (2006) statutory guidance for local authorities, maintained schools, academies and free schools.* Available online: https://www.gov.uk/government/publications/disqualification-under-the-childcare-act-2006t (Accessed 15 December 2017).

Hozo, E., Sucic, G., and Zaja, I. (2015) Burnout syndrome among educators in preschool institutions. *Journal of the Academy of Medical Sciences of Bosnia and Herzegovina,* 27 (6): 399–403.

Rodd, J. (2006) 3rd edn. *Leadership in early years.* Maidenhead, Berkshire, Open University Press.

Sheridan, S. C., Marvin, C., Knoche, L. (2009) Professional development in early childhood programs: process issues and research needs. *Early Education and Development,* 20 (3): 377–401.

Skinner, R. (2017) 'Item 3: understanding supervision', *Minutes of early years providers meeting 3 October 2017,* Gloucestershire, Early Years Network.

Solihull Approach (2018) '1st session training: containment and Reciprocity', *Notes of Solihull training meeting 7 September 2018,* Birmingham, UK, Solihull Approach.

Thriving Language (2017) *Supervision.* Available online: http://rebeccajskinner.wixsite.com/thrivinglanguage/training (Accessed 27 December 2018).

Thriving Language (2018) *Interconnecting processes impact of professional conversation.* Available online: www.thrivinglanguage.co.uk (Accessed 27 December 2018).

Tickell, C. (2011) *The Early Years Foundation Stage (EYFS) review.* Available online: http://www.gov.uk/government/uploads/system/uploads/attachment_data/file/516537/The_early_years_foundation_stage_review_report_on_the_evidence.pdf (Accessed 14 November 2017).

Twigg, D., Pendergast, D., Fluckiger, B., Garvis, S., Johnson, G., and Robertson, J. (2013) Coaching for early childhood educators: an insight into the effectiveness of an initiative. *International Research in Early Childhood Education,* 4 (1): 75.

14

Using Collaborative Coaching When Teachers are Experts

Karrie Snider and Maggie Holley

Case Study Summary

The goal of coaching in Early Childhood education is to empower teachers. When teachers improve dispositions, knowledge and skills, children's development and learning strengthens. The way in which coach-teacher interactions are shaped depends upon the unique patterns of adult learning (Kolb, 2014) and teacher development (Glickman, 2002; Glickman, Gordon and Ross-Gordon, 2018) (see Chapter 11). Given the differential nature of Early Childhood teachers' development, supervisors may wonder, 'Do *all* teachers *need* coaching?'

In this case scenario, we describe the experiences of Susan, a teacher-expert, and her coach-mentor who utilized collaborative coaching practices during a year-long study of professional development.

Introduction

Susan was a teacher participant in a community-university partnership developed to enhance the teaching and learning outcomes of five pre-school programmes in a Midwestern metropolitan region of the United States. A research team of coach-mentors provided individualized

(Kolb, 2014; Glickman, 2002; Glickman, Gordon and Ross-Gordon, 2018) yet standardized (Rush and Shelden, 2011) coaching to forty-five Head Start lead and assistant teachers. The goal of the study was to increase teachers' capacities for implementing the curriculum (the Project Approach, Katz and Chard, 2014; Helm and Katz, 2014) instruction (teacher-child interactions measured by the Classroom Assessment Scoring System (CLASS); Pianta, Hamre and LaParo, 2008) and assessment practices (Desired Results Developmental Profile; California Department of Education, 2015). Participants gave informed consent with regard to the use of programme, classroom and child data.

Susan taught in a full-day pre-school programme. Her classroom comprised approximately twelve to fifteen pre-school children, ranging in ages from 3 to 5 years. She had one consistent assistant teacher. Most of the children's families represented diverse cultural and linguistic backgrounds. For example, Spanish was the home language of many children in the classroom. Susan was fluent in both English and Spanish. She held a two-year college degree and an entry-level professional certificate (Child Development Associate). At the time of the study, Susan had been in the Early Childhood field for over fifteen years.

Case Scenario

Walking into Susan's classroom at the beginning of the study, her coach-mentor immediately sensed a positive, organized classroom. Susan designed the physical environment to support children's creative activities, such as painting, building with blocks or investigating living things. Susan and her assistant teacher frequently facilitated rich conversations with small groups of children. Susan's pre-schoolers were well behaved. When Susan redirected children's behaviours, she used positive statements such as, 'There are too many friends in this centre now. Let me help you find other things you can play.'

Susan provided a stable and stimulating learning environment throughout the entire study. Observers conducted fall and spring research observations using CLASS (Pianta, LaParo and Hambre, 2008). Observation ratings revealed Susan's consistent implementation of high quality teacher-child interactions. She was supportive of children's autonomy. She frequently provided activities that interested her students and allowed extended time for play in her daily schedule.

In the first months of the study, observers using the Early Childhood Project Approach Fidelity Form (ECPAF) (Vartuli, Bolz and Wilson, 2014) observed more evidence of project work in Susan's classroom than in most all other classrooms in the study, even though her ECPAF scores revealed she had room to grow. As evidenced in coaching logs, many teachers during this time worked on the 'basics' (i.e. setting up classroom rules and routines, managing small groups appropriately, implementing successful transitions, etc.). Susan had previously implemented the Project Approach so her 'readiness' was no surprise. For these reasons, Susan's coach-mentor initially wondered, 'What would I bring to Susan's learning and development?'

Based on Susan's demonstrated expertise, the coach-mentor employed collaborative supervision (Glickman *et al.*, 2018) to create a partnership. For instance, the coach-mentor prioritized interpersonal behaviours such as clarifying, listening, reflecting and presenting (see Chapter 11). The coach-mentor used clarifying statements to determine the focus of the coaching. The coach-mentor listened to Susan's needs and perspectives, selectively offering her own suggestions for what Susan might try next. For example, the initial coaching log showed Susan's plan for getting started with a project. The partners determined activities to spark children's thinking. Susan also discussed creating a Teacher Anticipatory Web (Helm and Katz, 2014). The supervisory strategies facilitated Susan's autonomy as she was the one who directed the coach-teacher interactions and determined action steps, rather than the coach-mentor.

When the partners determined areas for Susan's growth, she effortlessly took risks to try new teaching strategies. Susan sometimes planned 'crafts' in addition to other academic-focused activities. Her coach-mentor provided Project Approach resources and together they explored the importance of creating authentic learning activities. The shared readings prompted discussions of how to avoid more popularized, yet 'empty' activities like crafts when conducting project work (i.e. avoiding rote, single-concept activities – colours, shapes or alphabet letters versus relevant, real and integrated concept activities).

Surprisingly to the coach-mentor, Susan did not regularly participate in children's project investigations even though she organized the classroom by implementing child-centred activities. Through reflection and feedback (Rush and Shelden, 2011), questions surfaced about instructional strategies that would help Susan increase her active facilitation of children's project time. Over time, Susan's comments in the coaching logs reflected her pride and excitement for conducting project work alongside the children. *'I just* need to be brave ... learning is work to do with children.' Later coaching logs continued the development of this theme, '[I] *am learning with children and from children during project work.'*

Susan's coach-mentor and administrators viewed her as confident in working and communicating with her families, yet she had struggled with this aspect of teaching from the start. Susan's self-report on a measure of self-confidence in culturally responsive teaching (CRT) practices (Siwatu, 2007) provided a different perspective. While she reported strong CRT efficacy overall, she was least confident in working with diverse families or planning learning experiences based on the children's cultural backgrounds. Coaching logs revealed this same pattern (*'It is hard to* [work] *with families'*; '[I am] *not learning much* [about families] *yet'*). She made progress in this area, but it took six months before she communicated personal growth (*'Parents can get motivated watching their children learn'*). The coach-mentor listened to Susan's concerns and gave Susan suggestions week after week for improving family engagement (i.e. how to communicate project work; how to create a newsletter; how to invite parents into the classroom; how to explain the ways in which project work develops children's reading, writing and maths skills).

Together, Susan and her coach-mentor negotiated weekly action steps. They utilized the Project Approach Planning Journal (Helm and Katz, 2014) extensively so that Susan would have a written record of her progress and strategies after the coaching period was over. Susan and her coach-mentor developed a very collegial relationship, in which they could both speak frankly and openly about teaching. Susan's knowledge of the Project Approach appeared strong in the beginning but was truly strong by the end of the study year.

Perspectives

From the Coach-mentor's Perspective

According to her coach-mentor, Susan was 'all in, all the time' and highly motivated to be a good teacher. She demonstrated high commitment to her students and to the Early Childhood profession. She displayed strong knowledge and confidence for teaching with the Project Approach. The coach-mentor valued her coaching role and looked forward to the weekly coach-teacher interactions.

Susan's strengths challenged the coach-mentor. While some supervisors might view Susan as easy to coach or not needing coaching at all, the coach-mentor took her task seriously. She considered coaching approaches that would be most effective for challenging Susan's intellectual growth and passion for teaching. With the help of the study team, the coach-mentor viewed this as an opportunity to make the coaching practices explicit so that Susan might transfer coaching skills to her work with assistant teachers and peers. Over the course of the year, evidence of Susan's personal growth energized the coach-mentor, creating a sense of fulfilment. The coach-mentor believed Susan would work at a high level even after the coaching process was finished.

From the Teacher's Perspective

Susan liked teaching with the Project Approach. Through prior successes, she understood the benefits of the Project Approach for teachers and children. Susan was excited to learn alongside the children. Even though others saw her as a teacher-expert, Susan wanted to learn more. She was concerned about her ability to work effectively with all families. She collaborated with her coach and tried new teaching techniques. Because of her self-improvement, she expressed pride for helping the children (and herself) learn so much.

Susan valued her coach. On a measure of coaching practices (Rush and Shelden, 2006) she rated her coach as 'high' on all items. She maximized her coaching time by taking ownership from the start. She was always prepared and followed through on agreed-upon plans. She kept her own journal with detailed notes in order to be able to replicate the new processes she learned through coaching.

From the Administration's Perspective

Susan's administration considered her a 'star worker'. They gave her more latitude to carry out her own ideas in the classroom than they did the other teachers. Susan's administrators were very happy to have such a dedicated teacher whom they knew could work independently. They were pleased that such exciting learning opportunities were happening in her classroom. Frequently, her administrators brought visitors to her classroom because they viewed Susan to be a model teacher. Yet, like her coach-mentor, Susan's administrators viewed her as more skilled in some areas than Susan viewed herself.

Reflection

As we saw in Susan's scenario, 'professional' teachers or teacher-experts possess high commitment and high abstract thinking (Glickman, 2002). These qualities are visible in teacher-experts' on-the-spot thinking, solutions-driven actions, continual self-improvement and positive influence on children and colleagues (2002). Teacher-experts have similar or more expertise than their supervisors (Glickman *et al.*, 2018), which requires sophisticated and skilful approaches for shaping coach-teacher interactions. Research suggests coach-mentors should carefully select non-directive or collaborative supervisory behaviours for coaching teacher-experts and that given a choice, most teacher-experts prefer a collaborative approach (2018).

During initial research team meetings, the coach-mentor showed delight in being able to focus on the Project Approach right from the start. The coach-mentor carefully reflected on how to incorporate collaborative supervision (Glickman *et al.*, 2018) and as a result quickly earned Susan's trust through the formation of a collegial coach-teacher relationship. Trust is critical in creating successful coaching (Glickman *et al.*, 2018). Susan's coach-mentor used collaborative behaviours consistently, which fostered mutually determined goals.

Teacher-experts may have undiscovered areas for improvement. Many believed Susan to possess effective skills for working with diverse families, yet she was uncertain about her capabilities in this area. Teachers may be reluctant to share such thoughts with supervisors-as-evaluators. We can surmise from this that, instead of making assumptions about teachers' skills or judgements regarding who is or is not a good candidate for coaching, coach-mentors should concentrate on providing effective collaborative coaching to get to the heart of teachers' needs.

Like Susan's coach-mentor, supervisors may question whether teacher-experts need coaching or ongoing supervision. In some Early Childhood programmes, teacher-experts may experience little involvement or monitoring from administrators, which includes reduced cycles of formal teacher performance observations. Supervisors may use non-directive behaviours, taking a hands-off approach, as Susan's administrators demonstrated. Such behaviours include acting as a sounding board for teacher-experts and refraining from giving teacher-experts suggestions. Susan's coach-mentor frequently listened to Susan, selectively provided guidance or reinforced Susan's self-directed initiatives.

Once Susan's needs began to surface, coaching conferences centralized on joint planning. Susan requested help to plan project-related activities or to help her problem-solve (i.e. how to find a guest speaker on the project topic). Susan tested out ideas and made improvements quickly in some areas, such as increasing her direct involvement in children's activities. When necessary, the coach-mentor modelled Project Approach teaching competencies and allowed time for Susan's mental rehearsal of such methods during reflective conversations. Together, the partners explored the possible benefits of Project Approach teaching experiences and expanded Susan's pre-existing skills.

These experiences were very different from most other coach-teacher interactions in our study. For example, a preponderance of coach-teacher interactions in the first three to four months for other teachers focused on improving general teaching practices, such as establishing rules, setting up procedures and most of all managing instances of negative child behaviour. For teachers who demonstrated the need to grasp entry-level knowledge of Early Childhood principles, let alone knowledge of the Project Approach, coach-mentors used a more directive approach (Glickman et al., 2018). While all teachers in the study made progress, with Susan, her coach-mentor spent less time on foundational learning and could focus more quickly on specialized learning.

It is certainly noticeable that Susan demonstrated effective teaching prior to participating in coaching. Susan consistently provided high quality teacher-child interactions by creating a responsive, stimulating and project-rich learning environment for her pre-school students. Researchers captured her high quality teaching practices using the CLASS (Pianta et al., 2008) and ECPAF (Vartuli et al., 2014) measures as a pre/post measure during the study. Yet, Susan improved her specialized teaching skills, such as working with families, because of her efforts and the collaborative partnership with a coach-mentor.

Large national studies of early education in the United States have challenged assumptions regarding the relationship between teacher credentials (i.e. training and preparation, year of experience) and programme quality (i.e. ratings on CLASS scores) (Pianta et al., 2005). Unlike the majority of lead teachers in the study, Susan possessed a two-year college degree and an entry-level certificate in Early Childhood education. She was a valued employee and frequently participated in professional development initiatives. These factors, coupled with Susan's many years of experience teaching pre-school children aged 3, 4 and 5 years, probably contributed to her exhibited teaching qualities, along with skills she had developed through ongoing professional learning opportunities.

Conclusion

Success for coaching the teacher-expert depends upon how coach-teacher interactions are designed to meet the strengths and needs of teachers – even teacher-experts. Individualized (Kolb, 2014; Glickman *et al.*, 2018) yet standardized (Rush and Shelden, 2011) coaching practices foster growth for teachers with varied backgrounds, experiences and expertise (i.e. Hindman and Wasik, 2012). Based on this case scenario, we can surmise that despite the initial training or skills with which teachers enter the coaching relationship, coaching benefits all teachers.

Reflective Questions

1. What do you think are the main reasons this teacher was so successful?
2. What do you think contributed to the successful coach-teacher interactions?
3. How can a coach challenge a teacher like Susan, when as a teacher-expert she excelled so much on her own and is so self-motivated?
4. What supervisory behaviours have you used to build trust and create a collaborative partnership with peers or coachees?
5. How does Susan's story remind you of a young learner?

References

California Department of Education (2015) *Desired Results Developmental Profile (2015) A developmental continuum from early infancy to kindergarten entry: Preschool comprehensive view.* Sacramento, CA, California Department of Education, Early Education and Support Division. Available online: http://www.cde.ca.gov/sp/cd/ci/drdpforms.asp (Accessed 27 December 2018).

Glickman, C. D. (2002) *Leadership for learning: how to help teachers succeed.* Alexandria, VA, ASCD.

Glickman, C. D., Gordon, S. P., and Ross-Gordon, J. M. (2018) 10th edn. *SuperVision and instructional leadership: a developmental approach.* New York, NY, Pearson.

Helm, J. H. and Katz, L. (2014) 3rd edn. *Young investigators: the project approach in the early years.* New York, NY, Teachers College Press.

Hindman, A. H. and Waskik, B. A. (2012) Unpacking an effective language and literacy coaching intervention in Head Start: following teachers' learning over two years of training. *The Elementary School Journal*, 113 (1): 131–154.

Katz, L. and Chard, S. (2014) 3rd edn. *Engaging children's minds: the Project Approach.* Santa Barbara, CA, ABC-CLIO, LLC.

Kolb, D. (2014) 2nd edn. *Experiential learning: experience as the source of learning and development.* Upper Saddle River, NJ, Pearson.

Pianta, R., Howes, C., Burchinal, M., Bryant, D., Clifford, R., Early, D., and Barbarin, O. (2005) Features of pre-kindergarten programs, classrooms, and teachers: do they predict observed classroom quality and child-teacher interactions? *Applied Developmental Science*, 9 (3): 144–159.

Pianta, R., LaParo, K., and Hamre, B. (2008) *Classroom assessment scoring system.* Baltimore, MD, Paul H. Brookes.

Rush, D. D. and Shelden, M. L. (2006) Coaching practices rating scale for assessing adherence to evidence-based early childhood intervention practices. *CASEtools*, 2 (2): 1–7.

Rush, D. D. and Shelden, M. L. L. (2011) *The early childhood coaching handbook.* Baltimore, MD, Brookes Publishing Company.

Siwatu, K. O. (2007) Preservice teachers' culturally responsive teaching self-efficacy and outcome expectancy beliefs. *Teaching and Teacher Education*, 23 (7): 1086–1101.

Vartuli, S., Bolz, C., and Wilson, C. (2014) A learning combination: coaching with CLASS and the Project Approach. *Early Childhood Research and Practice*, 16 (1–2), Available online: http://ecrp.uiuc.edu/v16n1/vartuli.html (Accessed 27 December 2017).

15

Coaching When Teacher Commitment, Confidence and Knowledge are Developing

Karrie Snider and Maggie Holley

Case Study Summary

This case concerns a community-university partnership to enhance the teaching and learning outcomes of five pre-school programmes developed in a Midwestern metropolitan region of the United States. Community concern about the preparedness of urban pre-school children for formal schooling led to this year-long study of professional development. A research team of coach-mentors provided individualized yet standardized coaching to forty-five lead and assistant teachers with the goal of increasing teachers' capacities in implementing curriculum, instruction (teacher-child interactions measured by the CLASS) and assessment practices.[1]

Participants in this study were the teachers, families and children of the participating sites, and as such provided informed consent with regard to the use of programme, classroom and child data.

---

[1] See Kolb, 2014; Glickman, 2002; Glickman, Gordon and Ross-Gordon, 2018 (for individualized coaching); Rush and Shelden, 2011 (for standardized coaching); the Project Approach, Katz and Chard, 2014; Helm and Katz, 2014 (for curriculum implementation), Pianta, Hamre and LaParo, 2008 (for teacher-child interactions measured by the CLASS); and the Desired Results Developmental Profile and California Department of Education, 2015 (for assessment practices).

Introduction

The Head Start teacher (Michelle) described in this case was teaching in a full-day pre-school programme. Her classroom comprised approximately sixteen to eighteen pre-school children, ranging in ages from 3 to 5 years. The teacher described in this case was teaching in a full-day pre-school programme. Her classroom comprised approximately sixteen to eighteen pre-school children, ranging in ages 3 to 5 years. Most of the children's families represented ethnicities and linguistic backgrounds different from Michelle's. Michelle held a Bachelor of Science in Early Childhood Education and certification in Early Childhood/Elementary Education.

Case Scenario

Michelle's previous teaching experiences had been in elementary settings. She believed preschool teaching was not as important as elementary school teaching. Her administrators tried to guide her, but she felt she didn't need their help. While she agreed to carry out requests, she did not always follow through completely, thus demonstrating her hesitancy to take the risks necessary to improve her practice.

Michelle saw herself as a manager rather than a teacher because the children were 'too young' to learn deep concepts. This attitude was evident in the research data collected from fall classroom observations. For example, observers noted that Michelle's teacher-child interactions (i.e. the Classroom Assessment Scoring System (CLASS), Pianta *et al.*, 2008) rarely facilitated children's thinking by asking higher-level questions or by supporting them to connect with their prior knowledge, or by integrating learning experiences from activity to activity. Michelle provided time in her daily schedule for extended periods for play and Project Approach activities, but there was little evidence of project work in the environment, activities or interactions as observed in the fall using the Early Childhood Project Approach Fidelity Form (ECPAF) (Vartuli, Bolz and Wilson, 2014).

Michelle did not speak each family's home language, as the assistant did; consequently, her relationships with both children and families were superficial and less personal than the relationships between the assistant and the children and families. Michelle indicated strong beliefs in effective culturally responsive teaching strategies, yet, like other teachers in the study, self-reported ratings on a confidence measure (Siwatu, 2007) reflected she was not efficacious in using these instructional strategies. She rated herself least confident on items that described communicating with families and children who spoke a language other than English. She spent considerable time throughout the year looking at other employment positions.

While strong in content related to elementary teaching, Michelle's knowledge of Early Childhood education was limited. For example, early on the coach-mentor spent considerable time discussing with Michelle general teaching practices, such as facilitating smooth transitions, rather than the goals of the professional development study. Her ability to manage children's behaviour improved over time, but it was difficult for her to navigate the complexities of the Early Childhood classroom and 'put it altogether', leading to a disorganized schedule-less day.

During the first twelve weeks of the study, coach-teacher interactions consisted heavily of observation, feedback and reflection (i.e. Rush and Shelden, 2011), often with the coach-mentor presenting resources and teaching the coachee possible classroom management strategies. Reflection (Rush and Shelden, 2011), however, focused more procedural practice rather than Michelle's deeper analysis of teaching. At Michelle's request, the coach-mentor modelled various basic teacher practices, such as storytelling, child guidance strategies and asking open-ended questions. These early coach-teacher interactions built foundational process skills in both the children and the teacher. Around sixteen weeks into the school year, Michelle was more efficacious with classroom management. Her coach-mentor observed that she was then open to focusing on the Project Approach, the original intent of the coaching.

By the end of the study (nine months after the professional development began), Michelle's implementation of effective teaching practices and use of the Project Approach had increased significantly. On the CLASS measure, her assigned ratings shifted from below (in the fall) to above (in the spring) national norms. Most notable were her improvements in consistently scaffolding children's higher order thinking, providing high quality feedback and increasing classroom conversations to facilitate children's language development. In addition, Michelle implemented the Project Approach with increased fidelity, particularly by creating a project-rich environment and consistently facilitating project-related activities. She also significantly increased on self-reported ratings that measured her teaching efficacy, even on items capturing her beliefs for working and communicating with families whose home language was different from hers.

Perspectives

From the Coach-Mentor's Perspective

Early in the professional development process, the coach-mentor was frustrated at not being able to coach on the Project Approach topic as planned. She worried about the time it was taking Michelle to make progress and if Michelle would ever be able to carry out a project like other teachers in the study. The coach-mentor shared feelings of disappointment with the research team when the teacher agreed to try new strategies, but then actually was unable to take the risk to try them out with the children. The coach-mentor was also concerned about coaching on basic teaching practices because she did not want to interfere with the role of the on-site supervisor who was providing classroom support on those aspects of teaching, while the study coach-mentor provided content coaching on the Project Approach.

Although the coach-mentor had years of experience working in the field of Early Childhood education, she was challenged at how to shape the coach-teacher interactions week after week. This was primarily true in the first three months, when the coach-mentor viewed progress towards the study goals as slow. The research coaching team brainstormed through issues and supported the coach-mentor to feel productive in her coaching. Furthermore, the research coordinator reminded the team that foundational processes of teaching and learning (such as organized small groups and learning centres, using open-ended questions to elicit children's ideas and managing challenging child behaviours) were critical to the successful implementation of the targeted curriculum, instructional and assessment practices.

From the Teacher's Perspective

Michelle was frustrated because she felt like everyone was telling her what to do, even though she had been a teacher for over five years. She was also frustrated because her confidence in general teaching practices was limited. Early in the study, Michelle's classroom was characterized by low levels of effective supports to manage children's behaviours positively and to engage children in learning activities. At times, she was observed to be providing limited to no instructional teacher-child interactions that promote children's learning by way of analysis, reasoning, creating, planning, producing and evaluating. Instead of recognizing this, Michelle tried to manage children's behaviours and organized the learning environment with reactive rather than proactive strategies (such as using ineffective redirection, lacking routines and procedures that children understood, or providing clear learning targets). This was very frustrating for her. Although she believed in effective teaching practices, she had little confidence or self-efficacy that she could implement those same practices in her classroom independently.

Michelle was also lacking confidence in working with families whose linguistic backgrounds were different from hers. For the first three to four months of the study, Michelle's comments in coaching logs indicated that she was continually wondering how to involve families in her classroom, but more specifically how to communicate with families. The incongruence between Michelle's native language and the home language of families contributed to her feelings of self-doubt. At times it appeared that she was just 'going through the motions' of taking care of children rather than seeing her role in early education as facilitating meaningful inquiry learning experiences through collaboration with children and families.

From Administration's Perspective

Michelle's administrators were frustrated by her lack of confidence in managing children's behaviours because they thought she was more experienced when they hired her. They were frustrated because she did not follow through on directions. They were also concerned about her lack of progress towards the initial goals of the study. Frequently, her administrators asked the coach-mentor for reports on Michelle's progress.

Reflection

According to David Kolb's (2014) Experiential Learning Theory, the adult's knowledge develops through two types of learning experiences: grasping experience – taking in information and transforming experience – interpreting and acting on information. We can learn from Michelle's scenario that sometimes the teacher's capacity (as the adult learner) for being able to grasp out of or discern from an experience what is to be learned is suppressed. Michelle, possessing a four-year college degree in the Early Childhood field, certainly had demonstrated teaching competencies at the earliest stage of her career; yet her experiences in elementary settings had an impact on her view of teaching early learners, as well as her view of teacher-as-caregiver rather than teacher-as-thinker.

Week after week, Michelle's coaching logs revealed the same discussion over basic teaching functions in Early Childhood classrooms. She demonstrated knowledge in more elementary school teaching functions, such as the integration of technology. Independently, she was not able to make sense of the experiences within her own pre-school classroom, create a plan of action and test out possible solutions. Michelle's lack of self-efficacy may have been the contributing factor that left her uncertain about how to function as a teacher of pre-school children in this setting, thus, stifling her ability to grow as an adult learner.

When certain situations suppress the adult's ability to think and act, the adult is unable to transform experiences into new knowledge. When Michelle doubted her capabilities, she shied away from tasks or she remained stagnant week after week, month after month. This pattern of behaviour reflected Michelle's lack of motivation and her inability to persist in the face of challenges and expend effort towards solving problems (i.e. Theory of Self-Efficacy, Bandura, 1997). Such doubts about one's capacities often leads to 'low aspirations and weak commitment to ... goals' (Bandura, 1997: 39). Because self-efficacy is so fragile to a specific experience or task (Bandura, 1997), given Michelle's success in elementary teaching, she may have not ever encountered such issues as she was in this early learning environment.

Problem-solving, recreating understandings and taking risks to test out new ideas, as discussed in Kolb's (1984) theory, are also believed to be the characteristics of teachers who demonstrate high commitment to their profession and high levels of abstract thinking (Glickman, 2002; Glickman, Gordon and Ross-Gordon, 2018). Michelle's initial behaviours, however, were indicative of low teacher commitment and low teacher abstract thinking on Glickman's (2002) continuum of teacher development (see Chapter 11). Teacher commitment includes the concepts of self-assurance, willingness, motivation and interest (2002). She demonstrated low self-assurance and limited motivation. She was constantly seeking verbal feedback from her coach-mentor by asking, *'Am I doing this alright?'* Bandura (1997) reminds us that when individuals perceive such low efficacy about themselves in their given work position, they are slow to make progress in the face of obstacles, they lose hope in themselves easily and may become disinterested. While Michelle verbally said that she was committed to take on tasks when meeting with her coach-mentor, but for nearly half of the coaching study period she often did not follow through.

Left alone, Michelle may have remained stagnant in her attempts to teach pre-school children. Michelle's coach-mentor initially utilized supervisory behaviours indicative of the directive control supervision (Glickman *et al.*, 2018). This supervisory approach is applied 'in limited circumstances when teachers possess little expertise, involvement, or interest with respect to an instructional problem and time is short' (2018: 155). Michelle's coach-mentor definitely felt pressed for time. Four months into the study, however, Michelle reported favourable feelings towards the support she was receiving from her coach-mentor via a confidential survey to obtain teacher feedback about coaching practices (i.e. Coaching Practices Scale, Rush and Shelden, 2006). This evidence of coaching practices assured the coaching team that responsive coach-teacher interactions were making a difference for Michelle's teaching and the learning of the children in her care. In fact, by the end of the study Michelle's teacher development had moved away from low teacher commitment and low abstract thinking. Consequently, the coach-mentor's supervisory approach had shifted to a more directive informational approach. Because Michelle was new to learning the Project Approach, this supervision approach was appropriate, as the coach-mentor was the source of information and facilitated the weekly action steps. Michelle's teacher-child interactions towards the end of the study fostered a much more intellectually challenging learning environment for the children. She expressed deepened understandings of how young children learn, how she had improved in her own teaching and how she could foster future relationships with families and children when a language barrier is perceived.

Reflective Questions

1. In addition to starting with the basics and assuring the coach-mentor that their questioning was not too advanced, what else would you suggest for this coach in supporting this teacher's low confidence, low commitment and low knowledge of Early Childhood teaching?

2 What would you suggest the Programme Administrators do to help encourage and retain this teacher?
3 Why do you think teachers go through struggles like Michelle's?
4 What do you think would have happened if the coach-mentor had given up?
5 How do you, as a coach, refrain from doing too much for this teacher, but instead help her feel safe enough to take reasonable risks and reach out for assistance in the classroom?
6 How does the coach-mentor help the lead teacher collaborate with the assistant teacher to address her low self-efficacy related to communicating with families?

References

Bandura, A. (1997) *Self-efficacy: the exercise of control*. New York, NY, W. H. Freeman and Company.

California Department of Education (2015) *Desired results developmental profile (2015) A developmental continuum from early infancy to kindergarten entry: preschool comprehensive view*. Sacramento, CA, California Department of Education, Early Education and Support Division. Available online: http://www.cde.ca.gov/sp/cd/ci/drdpforms.asp (Accessed 27 December 2018).

Glickman, C. D. (2002) *Leadership for learning: how to help teachers succeed*. Alexandria, VA, ASCD.

Glickman, C. D., Gordon, S. P., and Ross-Gordon, J. M. (2018) 10th edn. *SuperVision and instructional leadership: a developmental approach*. New York, NY: Pearson.

Helm, J. H. and Katz, L. (2014). 3rd edn. *Young investigators: the project approach in the early years*. New York, NY: Teachers College Press.

Katz, L. and Chard, S. (2014) 3rd edn. *Engaging children's minds: the project approach*. Santa Barbara, CA, ABC-CLIO, LLC.

Kolb, D. A. (1984) *Experiential learning: experiences as the source of learning and development*. Englewood Cliffs, NJ, Prentice-Hall.

Kolb, D. (2014) 2nd edn. *Experiential learning: experience as the source of learning and development*. Upper Saddle River, NJ, Pearson.

Pianta, R., LaParo, K., and Hamre, B. (2008) *Classroom assessment scoring system*. Baltimore, MD, Paul H. Brookes.

Rush, D. D. and Shelden, M. L. (2006) Coaching practices rating scale for assessing adherence to evidence-based early childhood intervention practices. *CASEtools*, 2 (2): 1–7.

Rush, D. D. and Shelden, M. L. L. (2011) *The early childhood coaching handbook*. Baltimore, MD, Brookes Publishing Company.

Siwatu, K. O. (2007) Preservice teachers' culturally responsive teaching self-efficacy and outcome expectancy beliefs. *Teaching and Teacher Education*, 23 (7): 1086–1101.

Vartuli, S., Bolz, C., and Wilson, C. (2014) A learning combination: coaching with CLASS and the Project Approach. *Early Childhood Research and Practice*, 16 (1–2). Available online: http://ecrp.uiuc.edu/v16n1/vartuli.html (Accessed 27 December 2018).

16

Cultural Awareness, Narratives and Identity: The Pedagogical Coach as a Facilitator for Quality in ECEC in Belgium

Kaat Verhaeghe and Joke Den Haese

Case Study Summary

The following two cases focus on the development of a positive attitude to diversity (diversattude) through the creation of a culturally aware professional identity. This approach uses the coachee's own story as a starting point towards professional growth.

Introduction

In 2004, a participatory approach to quality assessment was introduced in the Netherlands. It defined quality as a negotiable construct that is jointly determined by parents, childcare workers, children and the management board of childcare centres (Peeters, 2014). Since 2014 there has been a pedagogical framework in Flanders, with a concise vision for quality childcare. It clarifies what childcare means to children, families and society. The framework offers direction and a firm basis from which to work (MeMoQ, 2014).

Belgium was one of the only European countries where no undergraduate degree in Early Childhood education existed (Bauters and Vandenbroeck, 2017). A study on professionalism in Flemish childcare and some international reports were making the case for a bachelor's degree to break the cycle of de-professionalization. In September 2011 the initial training course Pedagogy of the Young Child was established. This pedagogical course focuses on continuous professional coaching of the Early Years (EY) (Peeters, 2014; Urban et al., 2012).

Eurofound (2015) showed that coaching in practice provides the best chance of supporting professionalization. It must be focused on the invoking of intrinsic motivation (Eurofound, 2015). Educational professionals, steered by their perspective on reality (Golombek, 2017), have a significant impact on the behaviour of children in contexts of diversity (Vandenbroeck, 2001). A clear understanding of meaning and values helps to clarify the goals that govern these actions (Stelter and Law, 2010). Having a diversattude (Verhaeghe and Den Haese, 2018) and deepening the cultural awareness of the coach and coachee creates a conscious professional identity is the focus of the following case studies.

Narrative Coaching: The Narrative as the Starting Point for Professional Growth

Context: Being in Times of Becoming

'All we have is who we "are", and this in turn shapes what we do. Being is sometimes thought of as something intangible, abstract, or even ineffable, but it is actually quite real ... Being is the context from which all of our thinking and actions spring' (Hargrove, 2003: 45).

Nowadays, the discourse of developmental psychology guides our perspective in ECEC. It pushes us into the future. Lifelong learning is the conviction as we feel obliged to constantly develop (Stelter, 2009). There is no time for the here-and-now. But is this present moment not valuable?

In these crazy times of 'becoming', this case study focuses on 'the being' of people: their identity.

Personal identity is at the core of professional identity. We believe it is hard to professionalize without paying attention to norms and values and the recognition that everyone is determined by his/her unique view on the world (Verhaeghe, Den Haese and De Raedemaeker, 2016a and 2016b). How can we coach starting from 'the being' of people? The practice-based research that was conducted in two childcare centres in Brussels and Rotterdam resulted in the creation of a narrative coaching method consisting of two phases: 'the telling of the story' and 'bringing the story in the here-and-now'. Every phase has two conversations. In describing the method, we will explore the role of the narrative coach and the creation of the narrative space.

This method is a framework that gives structure. It is important that this structure remains in the background as a source for potential questions, rather than in the foreground as expectations to which the coachee and his/her stories must conform (Drake, 2007: 289). The most important compass during the coaching process is the coachee with his/her story, values, words and dreams.

Under the Surface of Action

Many coaching methods are goal- or problem-oriented (Stelter, 2009). There is a focus on behaviour. Why we act in a certain way remains in the subconscious is and pre-reflective. The personal interpretative framework steers the actions of the Early Childhood Professional (ECP). Ideas about education, the professional role and the child image influence behaviour and intentions (Golombek, 2017; Vanassche and Kelchtermans, 2014). These ideas are formed by our upbringing and the experiences we have throughout our lives. They are co-created through the interaction of past, present and future. Especially prevalent in educational professions, these influences are unmistakable. To understand actions and convictions, the identity of the ECP is considered: their narrative is the starting point in creating pedagogical quality from within.

Narrative coaching is part of what Stelter and Law (2010) call third-generation coaching. This is coaching from a reflective perspective. The focus is on the exploration of values and meaning-making. 'Things become meaningful, when we understand our own way of sensing, thinking and acting, by telling certain stories about ourselves and the world in which we live' (Stelter, 2009: 212). Coaching is seen as a conversational process through which the coachee gets deeper insight. 'It wants to unravel the current view on reality' (Stelter, 2007: 191). It is a conversation where one transfers the tacit knowledge into language, thereby making actions reflective and present (Stelter, 2007). 'The stories people tell in coaching are windows into their identities' (Drake, 2007: 284). Values are the implicit foundation of action, connecting actions and conviction. Much of the time the coachee is not conscious of his/her values. 'They will usually lie dormant under the surface of action' (Stelter, 2017: 338). To explore these values, we need time. 'Coaching, as a way of lingering, a process of slowing down to think and reflect' (Stelter, 2018: 11). Narrative coaching creates a cultural awareness which can be a point of departure for the creation of alternative narratives. Through co- and re-construction of our stories we can grow. Narrative coaching tries to obtain a conscious professional identity.

Reflection

This section provides an illustration of a coaching process that can inspire coaches. The narrative perspective on the role of the coach and the creation of the narrative space hopes to offer an alternative way of looking at professionalization. It hopes to do what narrative coaching wants to do: slowing down and creating time to think and reflect. What are we doing in our coaching practice today? How does this resonate with our own norms and values as a coach? From which perspective on humanity do we work in our coaching? Do we coach for tomorrow or yesterday? And what about the here-and-now?

Phase 1: The Telling of the Story

This first phase focuses on creating trust. It is about identifying the 'way of being'. We start from the first-person perspective to grasp the subjective reality. The coachee gains insight into him/herself and the world. We verbalize what mostly stays in the subconscious. The question, 'who are you?' is the point of departure. We strive for identity awareness. The narrative model believes that human beings express themselves through stories. Identity moves in a chaotic world that needs stories to make it accessible (Bleyen, 2008).

We need to create a safe narrative space in which the coachee dares to speak. 'A narrative coach creates a holding container in which people can courageously and creatively bring their narrative material into the world' (Drake, 2014: 125). Coaching outside of the workspace makes it possible to speak, free from power structures. It facilitates the telling of the story, creating an openness that transforms the content of the coaching session and the relationship with the coach.

In our first case study, the first narrative space was a nearby park where the participants took a walk; this can be regarded as nature coaching. The openness and quietness of nature engendered a comfortable atmosphere. Walking side-by-side fostered the building of trust. There was no confrontation. The coachee guided the walk; she decided which way to go. The non-verbal body language became more open throughout the conversation. Sometimes you could see the coachee's reflective processes through the way she walked – slow or fast; coming to a halt; looking back or staring into the distance; hesistating to go left or right; sometimes wandering off the road in search of something.

The second conversation was conducted on a bench in the same park. The coach and coachee wanted to stop walking and sit down. They slowed down their paces, stood still and took time to reflect. It was an interpretation of 'the art of lingering'. The coach had to let go and be amazed. She followed the footsteps of the coachee. This enabled the coach to be open to receive the story, without judgement. It was a kind of phenomenological observation, without interpretation, purely as information. It called out for acceptance. The coach listened with 'a third ear'. Empty and full. Empty because it is unprejudiced. Full because of the attention. The coach asked open questions, summarized and paraphrased. She was really present. It showed the art of listening and the power of silence. It was a form of generous listening and sometimes naive wondering. The listening is active yet non-directive, engaged yet non-attached, deeply present yet keenly observant (Drake, 2014). The coach must be aware of her own bias and how this can steer the conversation. A meta-level that is always present. 'We need to understand more fully the degree to which coaches steer clients' storytelling into their own preferred frames and language' (Drake, 2007: 290). The coach acted with continuous attention on the narrative basic attitude (Figure 16.1).

Throughout the process it becomes more important to ask sensitive questions. These help the coachee to encounter the implicit and

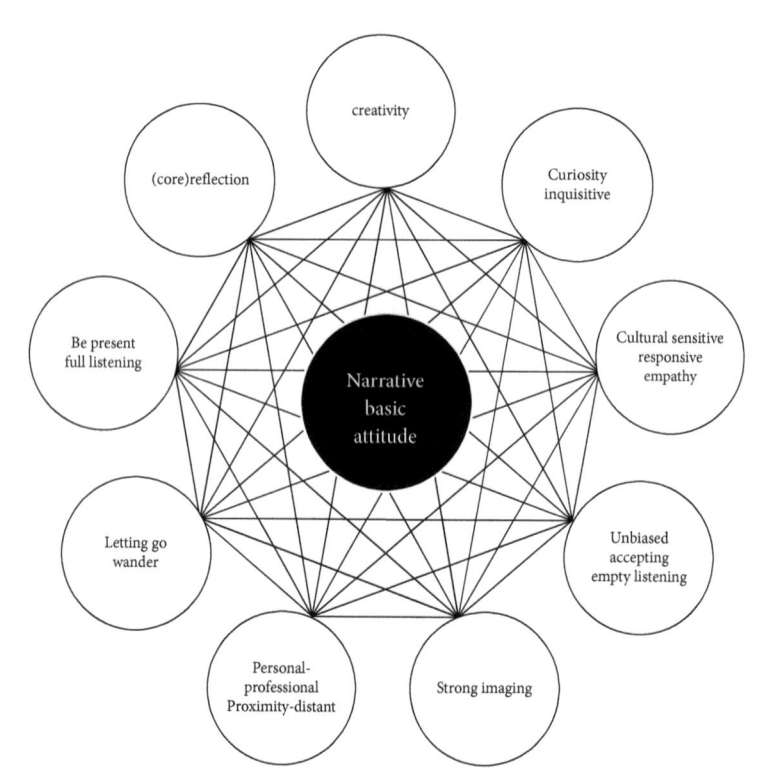

168   Mentoring and Coaching in Early Childhood Education

Figure 16.1 Narrative basic attitude (Verhaeghe et al., 2017)

Figure 16.2 Phase 2: Bringing the story into the here-and-now

pre-reflective dimensions of his/her being. (S)he searches for meaning. 'The coach should support the process of verbalizing experiences and knowledge by, for example, inviting the coachee to employ metaphors and analogies in his/her use of language' (Stelter, 2007: 194). Such conversations in coaching often reveal that certain values and convictions have a very long history, connecting with persons, situations and cultural contexts that the coachee is part of and that carry great importance for them (Stelter, 2017). They show the connection between past and present, for example:

> *I have missed this during my own childhood. I don't want them to miss out. It is so important that we cuddle them and comfort them. When I was 12 years old, my father told me I was not allowed to cry anymore. I feel it, but most of the times I don't show it. I feel it inside, sometimes they tell me I'm too distant, but that's not true.* (Conversation 2, Coachee 1)

Phase 2: Bringing the Story into the Here-and-Now

In the second phase the identity awareness is broadened and contextualized. Identity is socially constructed (Bruner, 2002). It is a co-construction between teller and listener. Every narrative expression must be understood in the context of its assumed audience (Stelter and Law, 2010). When we become aware of the storylines that determine us, we can find alternative stories to compose our identity (Freeman, 1993). Figure 16.2 demonstrates the importance of building narratives together to weave stories that develop identity.

From a constructivist perspective, everything that has meaning in life has its origin within a set of social relationships; values are not absolute but the result of a process of negotiation. The coach co-reflects as a collaborative partner in the process. (S)he invites people to see their stories through other perspectives. It is a conversation in which we are open to being transformed by what we encounter. The narrative space, tea-time coaching in a nearby pub; a table between two chairs. There is something between us. A place where we lay our thoughts on the table and meet each other.

Through thematical analysis of the first two conversations key themes emerge. The coachee is asked if s(he) recognizes himself/herself. This allows reflection about which values form a vital aspect in their life. It is a process that involves the respondents and provides insight in which values steer action. These are reported hierarchically.

Vital themes are disclosed. These themes have the potential to deepen, renew and strengthen the story. The themes are explored through imaginative techniques like metaphors, images, art, poetry and literature. It offers a third-person perspective that creates a distance from 'the self'; a meta-level that enables us to look differently at the things that are closest to us. 'This approach is about a shift from thinking about a story as a fixed commodity transmitted from one person to another to thinking about a story as co-created within a narrative space that lies between, yet beyond, the participants' (Drake, 2007: 289). The identity experiences a temporal coherence. It is present and verbalized. The aim is to create cultural awareness: awareness of the influence of the other. Alternative perspectives are explored, unobvious connections are being made and the coach confronts the coachee and challenges his/her perspective.

Example 1: Cats and Dogs ... Babies and Toddlers

A coachee was wrestling with the fact that she would be transferred to the toddler group. She could not explain why she would rather stay with the babies. It was a feeling. Throughout her story 'dogs' were a vital theme. By using the dog as a metaphor she gained insight into her 'way of being'.

Coach: *'Why aren't you a cat person?'*

Coachee: *'I don't like the independence of the cat. I'd rather have a dog, who comes to you, who needs you. Now that I think about it, it's like the difference between babies and toddlers. I find it important that the children need you. And then when you come in they start calling your name ....'* (Conversation 2, Coachee 2)

After the deepening of the vital themes, a safe environment to experiment in the here-and-now is created. 'A here-and-now focus has many advantages. It provides a safe laboratory in which to experiment with new behaviours and to experience new voices before trying them in the world' (Drake, 2007: 289). The narrative was contested and placed in the context of the childcare centre.

The coach mirrors and confronts. New storylines are co-created in the dialogue. The coach suggests a counterplot to explore different possibilities. This makes alternative storylines and unique outcomes possible.

> *Stories move in circles. They don't move in straight lines. So it helps if you listen in circles. There are stories inside stories and stories between stories, and finding your way through them is as easy and as hard as finding your way home. And part of the finding is getting lost. And when you're lost, you start to look around and listen.* (Metzger, 1992)

Reflective Questions

1 How do you use the narratives of your coachee in your practice?
2 How can the role of the narrative coach inspire you?
3 From which perspective on humanity do you coach?
4 What is the place of identity, of being, of norms and values in your own coaching practice?

Growing Through Art

Context

In the bachelor's degree in ECEC, art is a substantial part in the curriculum. Taking initiatives, making choices and inventing different roles are important competences. Mentors in this programme relate to art to foster this part of their education. In a time where children's growth and education often seem to be approached in a reductionist, fragmented way, we believe in this alternative perspective.

Art influences the future ECPs during their learning programme. We have chosen to give them the experience of art, rather than observing art. Therefore, the concept of 100 languages is integrated (Edwards *et al.*, 2012). We use art in everyday interactions to inspire a culture of inquiry. We believe that creativity originates from a need to communicate and form dialogue. We assume that the benefits of introducing the arts into learning environments showcases a balanced intellectual, emotional and psychological development of individuals and societies. Being sensitive to art facilitates the interaction with children and empowers participants to engage in reflective thinking (Nussbaum, 2016).

We believe changes must be made to prepare ECPs to experience the reality of a diverse world. Educators working in Early Childhood settings need to acquire a 'diversattude', a positive attitude towards diversity (Verhaeghe and Den Haese, 2018).

Growing Through Art

It is often liberating to observe children who re-invent the world with their fantasy, without fear and full of self-awareness. Failure is not an issue. Children seize the moment to use their imagination. This includes playing and participating in activities without apparent purpose, consequence or result. If we want children to be powerful, failure is the place where learning begins, because every error generates a new opportunity.

Allison Gopnik (2010) indicates that 'trying things out' in different ways and with many attempts seems to be an effective way to advance in the world. Our experiences as children influences the way we shape our lives. For children, inventing and creating is a way of existing (Gopnik, 2010).

For the ECP to connect with others, observing children provides a powerful reflection tool to rebuild their own imagination as communication strategy. The child turns out to be the mentor. This is why, in the courses of the 100 languages, the future ECPs are invited to explore the child within. In each of us, a child is still present and it is a challenging adventure to make this child visible again.

Their own narrative is the focus in this project, 'Discover the child within'. The future ECPs recall and write about their own childhood memories and they create a new story together. The diversity of the group is a meaningful advantage. The students connect, learning about themselves in relation to the others and through the language of art. A multi-disciplinary team of artists guide them through this process. Visual art, movement, drama and music are integrated and inspire participants to recall the stories. Mentoring through different perspectives is crucial to the approach.

The environment can be a mentor who speaks, inviting co-creation. Nature is one of the languages chosen participants to meet in an intercultural way. When students go outside, nature creates a specific space in which they can learn. Stories can be told and shared through nature, as a way to express and connect. Future ECPs interact with children using materials such as clay and

Figure 16.3 Letting the story emerge

creations with branches and leaves, rather than spoken language. Through play and invention, they create the space needed to let the story of the other emerge, to listen and hear the different point of view and to conclude that we are different and similar at the same time. Figure 16.2 illustrates this.

Letting the Story Emerge

What does the world look like through another's eyes? What does an experience feel like to someone else? To make this reflection possible, we ask these future ECPs to develop their own cultural map, asking the following questions: 'Who am I?', 'Which cultural experiences were the keys to my becoming?' and 'Who was guiding me through my story?' The participants think about metaphors, pictures and paintings to bring the cultural map alive. They read each other's map and search for what is not obvious, dialogue about it, share meaning and values. It is a beautiful moment of connection (Figure 16.3). They become aware of their framework in relation to the other and start to realize they have a lot in common. They become each other's mentors.

Reflection

'Culture' can refer to a community which shares common experiences that shape the way its members understand the world. As Martha Nussbaum (2016) explains, we empathize with those who are similar to us, but when we are aware of our own identity, what we believe in, what we stand for and what made us to who we really are, it will create an openness to a diversity of other identities.

Narrative imagination, the ability to be an intelligent reader of another person's story, makes it possible to think what it might be like to be in someone else's shoes (Nussbaum, 2016). An important concept in this is play. When we play, we make space for joy; we feel free to invent, reconsider and fantasize. We change identity, experiment and open up towards the other. As adults, we need these playful moments to become flexible in our thoughts and to think critically, to feed our imagination and empathize in order to understand the role and stories of others.

Narrative imagination demonstrates artistic rather than scientific skills in education. In our utilitarian society, unfortunately, there is little space for critical reflection. An artistic approach can, through imagination, motivate individuals to argue and debate with nuance and understanding. This capacity is essential for a successful democracy (Nussbaum, 2016). ECPs should encourage children in critical thinking that is necessary for independent and intelligent resistance to the power of blind tradition and authority (O'Brien in Nussbaum, 2016). In order to be a genuine tool for democracy, narrative imagination is based on an understanding of humans as basically pluralistic. If we assume that the 'role of the other' is critical to our development, the more choice we have in languages to assimilate, the more opportunity we have to understand and empathize. It is important to clarify the answer to the question, 'what are those languages we grow through?'

Growing through art is about mobilizing the power of art, as a language, where art is used in a specific way to reach out to people, not to make artists out of them, but to help them come to terms with the emotions and circumstances that they might otherwise find hard to express. Instead of teaching how to look at art, we talk about how to look at life through art. The arts are unique in the fact that information and values can be communicated through media other than verbal/language. Josh Lacey (2009) adds: 'Through artful activities, we are playing and stimulated to rid the adult minds of inhibitions and return to the joys of being a child.

Theatre, dance, storytelling, exhibitions ... even a walk in the wood ... are strong ways to rekindle the imaginative confusion of our childhood and force us to experience the world anew.'

When we invite the Future ECP to grow through art, often it is a revelation to them as they learn about themselves, the children and the people they meet.

Future ECP Reflection 1

'The 100L brought back the child in me and experiencing the sessions and workshops, I could express myself and go back to that child that was not seen when I was little. It touched me, I felt liberated ... free in a certain way.' (Future ECP)

According to Van Heusden (2010), art is a mirror of life. Art is important because it helps us to understand ourselves and others. It contributes to our consciousness, to our self-image and our identity. It shows where dialogue with the other can start and become meaningful (Van Heusden, 2010). Therefore, diversity can be considered as a meaningful mentor. Diversity is used to empower each other and enable us to learn to understand each other's filter. Clearly, attention should be paid to developing the imagination of young people, especially if we assume that intercultural exchange is needed. Our complex and changing society can only benefit by giving meaning to intuition and inventiveness in dialogue between different groups (Colpaert, 2007).

Reality cannot be perceived simply by using the language of reason, the 'logos'. We had better not lose sight of the myth and the muse. Every culture has demonstrated that the true meaning of life can only be understood by using other languages, or the 'mythos' (Colpaert, 2007). Intercultural exchange will not succeed unless the importance of imaginative element is fully appreciated (Colpaert, 2007). As people come together, they encounter moments when they just do not understand each other's thinking. These are moments of tension and conflict, when ideas collide. These moments can fracture or deepen relationships. The frustration of not understanding nor being understood dissolves when we see each other's thinking, when thinking and reflection become visible through artful activities. We embrace a positive attitude towards diversity, a 'diversattude' (Verhaeghe and Den Haese, 2018).

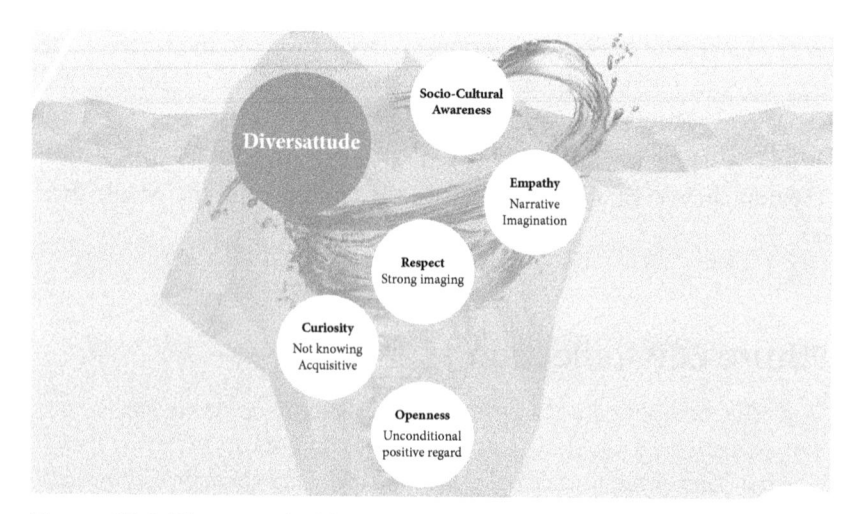

Figure 16.4 Diversattude (Verhaeghe and Den Haese, 2018)

Circles in figure: Diversattude; Socio-Cultural Awareness; Empathy — Narrative Imagination; Respect — Strong imaging; Curiosity — Not knowing, Acquisitive; Openness — Unconditional positive regard.

This 'diversattude', illustrated in Figure 16.4 above, is shown in the way in which the ECP is socio-culturally aware and understands that, by questioning his own identity, which is the sum of his experiences and through discussion and reflection, there is a place for the other, which allows his/her frame of reference to extend. Starting from our narrative we meet the other empathetically and accept 'the other' unconditionally in their diversity as an inspiring and powerful mentor (Verhaeghe, Den Haese and De Raedemaeker, 2016a and 2016b).

Future ECP Reflection 2

'The content of the arts and cultural education course was an inspiring adventure. I had always been attracted to the life stories of people who were different from me. If I want to get to know someone, I don't want to talk about the weather. I want to talk about what he/she finds breathtaking works of art and why. I want to know about their fears and what their reaction is face to face with it. What is the very first experience from childhood they remember? How is their family and where do they come from? ... Everything is culture. Culture in the broad sense of the word tells us who we are and who the other is. And I think one cannot exist without the other. Everything that I find important in life is culture. I never knew that the meaning of the word culture was so all-encompassing. For me the pieces finally felt into place.' (Future ECP)

Conclusion

We should strive toward becoming self-critical practitioners who see the world through different perspectives and who are being inspired by a multitude of languages. We refer to the idea of multi-perspective, most commonly used as a concept of narration or storytelling where more than one perspective is represented and often discrepant viewpoints are employed. Here, multi-perspectivity is considered as the force of the sum of the parts. The big picture offers a fuller and truer image of the truth. We will feel enriched if we dare to look at the surrounding reality this way. Through art, we discuss, we dialogue ... we bridge. We connect.

Reflective Questions

1. How can art inspire you as a professional?
2. How do you use multi-perspectivity in your work?
3. How can the idea of 100 languages inspire you?
4. What can imagination mean for your practice?

References

Bauters, V. and Vandenbroeck, M. (2017) The professionalisation of family day care in Flanders, France and Germany. *European Early Childhood Education Research Journal*, 25 (3): 386–397.

Bleyen, J. (2008) Praten over seks? Theoretische kwesties in verband met oral history. In Dupont, W. and de Smaele, H. (eds) *Belgische tijdschrift voor nieuwste geschiedenis, themanummer hedendaagse geschiedenis van de seksualiteit in België*, 38 (3–4): 323–347.

Bruner, J. (2002) *Making stories*. New York, NY, Farrar, Straus and Giroux.

Colpaert, M. (2007) *Where two seas meet*. Leuven, Lannoo Campus.

Drake, D. B. (2007) The art of thinking narratively: implications for coaching psychology and practice. *Australian Psychologist*, 42 (4): 283–294.

Drake, D. B. (2014) Narrative coaching. In Cax, E., Bachkirova, T., and Clutterbuck, D. A. (eds) *The complete handbook of coaching*. London, Sage. pp. 117–130.

Edwards, C. P., Gandini, L., and Forman, G. E. (2012) *The hundred languages of children: The Reggio Emilia experience in transformation*. Santa Barbara, CA, Praeger.

Eurofound (2015) *Early childhood care: working conditions, training and quality of services – A systematic review*. Luxembourg, Publication Office of the European Union.

Freeman, M. (1993) *Rewriting the self. History, memory, narrative*. London, Routledge.

Golombek, M. (2017) Opvoedingsidealen in de praktijk. In Bekker, J., De Deckere, H., De Jong, W., Meer, M., Van der Poel, V., Schonewelle, I., and Viëtor, H. (eds) *De pedagoog in de spotlights: Opvoedingsidealen vanuit verschillende contexten*. Amsterdam, SWP. pp. 61–71.

Gopnik, A. (2010) *The philosophical baby*. London, Picador.

Hargrove, R. (2003) Revised edn. *Masterful coaching*. San Francisco, CA, Jossey-Bass Pfeiffer.

Lacey, J. (2009, 8 August) Geraadpleegd van. Available online: https://www.theguardian.com/books/2009/aug/08/philosophical-baby-alison-gopnik-review (Accessed 3 April 2019).

MeMoQ (2014) A pedagogical framework for childcare for babies and toddlers. Available online: https://www.kindengezin.be/img/pedagogische-raamwerk-engelseversie.pdf (Accessed 3 April 2017).

Metzger, D. (1992) *Writing for your life*. San Francisco, CA, HarperCollins Publishers.

Nussbaum, M. (2016) *Not for profit. Why democracy needs the humanities*. New Jersey, NJ, Princeton University Press.

Peeters, J. (2014) Country position paper on ECEC of the Flemish Community of Belgium. In Aarsen, J. and Studulski, F. (eds) *VVersterk in international perspective: early childhood and care in six countries*. Utrecht, The Netherlands, Sardes. pp. 17–28.

Stelter, R. (2007) Coaching: a process of personal and social meaning making. *International Coaching Psychology Review*, 2 (2): 191–201.

Stelter, R. (2009) Coaching as a reflective space in a society of growing diversity – towards a narrative postmodern paradigm. *International Coaching Psychology Review*, 4 (2): 207–217.

Stelter, R. (2017) Working with values in coaching. In Bachkirova, T., Spence, G., and Drake, D. (eds) *The Sage handbook of coaching*. London, SAGE Publications. pp. 331–345.

Stelter, R. (2018) *The art of dialogue in coaching. Towards transformative exchange*. London, Taylor & Francis.

Stelter, R. and Law, H. (2010) Coaching – narrative-collaborative practice. *International Coaching Psychology Review*, 5 (2): 152–164.

Urban, M., Vandenbroeck, M., Van Laere, K., Lazzari, A., and Peeters, J. (2012) Towards competent systems in early childhood education and care. Implications for policy and practice. *European Journal of Education*, 47 (4): 508–526.

Vanassche, E. and Kelchtermans, G. (2014) Teacher educators' professionalism in practice: positioning theory and personal interpretative framework. *Teaching and Teacher Education*, 44: 117–127.

Vandenbroeck, M., (2001) *The view of the Yeti: bringing up children in the spirit of self-awareness and kindredship*. The Hague, Bernard van Leer Foundation.

Van Heusden, B. (2010) *Cultuur in de spiegel*. Groningen, Rijksuniversiteit Groningen.

Verhaeghe, K. and Den Haese, J. (2018, 18–31 August, Budapest, Hungary) Being in times of becoming. Conference paper, Dublin, Ireland, European Early Childhood Education Research Association.

Verhaeghe, K., Den Haese, J., and De Raedemaeker, G. (2016a, 31 August–3 September, Dublin, Ireland) Narrative coaching in early childhood education and care. Conference paper, Dublin, Ireland, European Early Childhood Education Research Association.

Verhaeghe, K., Den Haese, J., and De Raedemaeker, G. (2016b, 31 August–3 September, Dublin, Ireland) The narrative of the early childhood professional. Conference paper, Dublin, Ireland, European Early Childhood Education Research Association.

Verhaeghe, K., Den Haese, J., De Raedemaeker, G., and Govers, D. (2017, 29 August–1 September, Bologna, Italy) Narrative coaching as a way to enhance pedagogical practice from within. Conference paper, Dublin, Ireland, European Early Childhood Education Research Association.

17

Three Key Stages in Mentoring and Coaching

Michael Gasper

Introduction

This particular Appreciative Inquiry is a personal reflection on the nature and processes of mentoring and coaching and the characteristics that help them to work well. Any examples given are a mosaic of extracts from different stages in my professional life. They are anonymous constructs used as illustrations. The reflection focuses on the different stages within the overall process of mentoring and coaching, as the title indicates: Stage 1 – beginnings – includes preparation and planning before the first face-to-face meeting; Stage 2 – middles – the stage following the establishing of trust and a working relationship; and Stage 3 – endings – deal with closure.

Prologue

My informal introduction to mentoring and coaching began to emerge in my childhood in my interactions with older neighbours, family or school friends who acted as guardians and guides. I learned to watch what they did and listen to what they said. I understood that vicarious experience could save time and trouble; avoid adult censure; or earn adult praise. As my life has progressed, I have been actively or passively mentored and coached by colleagues who were more experienced and by peers who supported each other. In Wenger *et al.*'s (2002) terms we were cultivating our own

'Community of Practice'. In hindsight, these formative years were invaluable in learning the basic skills in which mentoring and coaching are grounded, most importantly: listening and asking rather than telling, learning to suspend judgement, reading body language and allowing silence. This has served me well and helped me to understand that we all learn as much from our mistakes as from our successes, if we can step back and get beyond the raw personal emotion or others' censure. As I moved into leadership, the Community of Practice comprised headteacher colleagues at local and national levels; began to extend to include staff within the educational psychology, social services and health sectors; and eventually encompassed those working in community mental health. I learned that the world could be seen through different lenses and education was not the centre of the universe, but part of a solar system of mutually beneficial agencies.

What I learned from the partnerships with colleagues from health and education was the value of inter-agency cooperation. Working together to support families of pre-school and Early Years children introduced me to yet more perspectives. At the end of the 1990s, I left education to join the Early Years research team led by Chris Pascal and Tony Bertram, which further developed the skills that underpin mentoring and coaching. My role was to coordinate the research into the Early Excellence Centres programme, collate the data and check the reports. These pre-school settings received government funding to establish professional training and to disseminate best practice in pre-school and Early Years education. For the first time I witnessed national decision-making first hand. I also visited settings across the country as the programme expanded from nine to eleven settings in the first year and continued to expand over a three-year period.

Settings were linked with a university local to them and had academic support and a dedicated research team member. In this role I became a mentor as well as a researcher. I learned more about listening and mentoring. The initial loss of some of the original leaders prompted Sheila Thorpe OBE and me to conduct research into the leadership of settings in the programme. We discovered that all of those who had been there from the start and who remained had some form of mentor or coach, formal or informal. Sheila continued the research, and when the programme merged with Sure Start and neighbourhood nurseries to become Children's Centres she was part of the Pen Green team who designed the National Professional Qualification in Integrated Centre Leadership (NPQICL). Karen John was the team member responsible for developing the mentoring element of the programme and for designing and leading training for mentors.

This training and the associated programme became a life-changing experience for me, as well as for the participants. The experiential (Kolb, 1984) ethos of the training programme, the mentor support for participants and the nature of the centre-based assessment brought all my previous experiences together.

What then, have I learned that is worth sharing?

Reflections 1: Stage 1 – Beginnings

Meeting a new mentee for the first time presents opportunities and challenges. I try to find out what I can about their position and role in their setting or organization before contacting them. On award-bearing courses I have known the course in which they are involved as a tutor and mentor and I have knowledge and experience of pre-school and Early Years working. I know that the first move is mine and that I need to lead, but without dominating. My first contact is by email. I introduce myself and explain my role in relation to the course and sketch an outline of the shape of the mentoring components: the number of times we will meet over the year at a location away from their workplace that is convenient to both of us and where it is comfortable for listening. The mentee will indicate the most appropriate dates and times. I also ask them to reflect upon what they want me to include and to send these to me in advance. It is important to remember that it can be challenging for some Early Years practitioners to allow themselves the time and space away from their place of work for their own benefit.

First meetings set the tone for the relationship. For mentoring or coaching the relationship is critical (Cox *et al.*, 2014). Establishing the tone, style and purpose of the relationship is essential from the start. I visualize the relationship as a 'dance' where the lead changes, but within an overall context and with a clear purpose and where the mentor or coach retains control of the timing, while the mentee influences the direction and pace. From the start, my aim is to put the mentee at their ease. The location can help if chosen well. It needs to be somewhere accessible and reasonably public but comfortable. Coffee shops, hotel lobbies, rail station cafés can all work well provided they are not too busy, and a public park or open space works well if the weather allows. The session will last for up to three hours, so refreshments on hand will also help.

I aim to arrive early, so that I can introduce myself to the serving staff, at the venue, especially if I am likely to use the place again. I try to choose a position where the mentee and I can face each other, each with a clear view of the other, but with a comfortable space between us. I like to refresh what I already know about the mentee before they arrive. Recognizing someone you have never met can be a challenge and photographs do not always help, so it is as well to give the mentee some idea of how to recognize you. When they arrive, greeting them with a smile, making eye contact and being friendly without being too familiar should help. It is important to look out for the signals they give you; they may be nervous or uncertain.

I begin by re-capping on the reasons for meeting and the purpose parameters of the sessions. Establishing clear boundaries is essential: I make it clear what is meant by confidentiality, particularly in terms of disclosures that cross legal boundaries or those which are beyond the remit of our shared brief, or which require more specific expert help. Creating this 'contract' is important because it is agreed jointly: the mentee has part ownership, setting the tone for an equal partnership. How things progress after this, particularly in the initial meeting, depends on the mentee. They may want to know more about me and my background or they may wish to share more of their own, but at some point it is useful to outline again the context and purpose of the meeting and the areas they wish to cover. It is sometimes helpful to explore their expectations, hopes or fears by asking what they want from the sessions. Initially I will be mostly listening, perhaps asking questions for clarification. I try to maintain eye contact and be aware of any subtle changes in their tone or body language.

I try not to make written notes while the mentee is speaking, other than a word or two that I can go back to if necessary. 'Active listening' (Parsloe and Leedham, 2009: 141–145) is a key skill for mentoring and coaching. It means really concentrating on what is being said and its meaning, actual and hidden. Where there is a natural pause, I summarize what I have heard and make notes once the mentee has agreed that what I have described accurately reflects their perspective. This can sometimes open new pathways or areas: a mentee might come back to a point or name without realizing they have done so. Drawing this to their attention can help to open hidden areas or unlock closed areas.

As the session progresses emerging threads can usually be identified and time allowed for reflection. The mentee's response to these new understandings will provide insights into their feelings which may be positive or negative. As a mentor I need to maintain a positive approach and help the mentee to appreciate their own strengths wherever possible. Humour can help if opportunities arise.

There are occasions when a mentee may be reluctant to engage: they may keep the conversation at a superficial level, avoid eye contact, give short answers that discourage further comment or even produce a verbal torrent which limits real interaction, although this may also indicate that they need to get rid of so much it can only be released as a 'waterfall'. In these cases a mentor or coach must find a way past the initial 'block'. I have found it necessary on some occasions to share how their opening words appear to me as a listener and I ask them if that is right and, if so, why it is necessary. On other occasions it has been better to allow the stream to diminish before saying anything, perhaps asking how they feel after the release of so much emotion.

Reflections 2: Stage 2 – Middles

The middle period may not be a timed central point. It may occur earlier or later, but it is the period following the initial 'ice breaking' and establishing of a connection. Towards the end of the initial period it is useful to review what has been discussed and summarize any key points. It is important to make sure the areas that the mentee wanted to cover are being discussed or to ask them if they wish to adjust priorities. By this time both mentor and mentee should be more at ease with each other and this part of the session is likely to be even more productive. Trust is critical and cannot be rushed, but should be developing by this stage.

This time can often be the most productive as it is when the mentee is prepared to share more deeply felt or deeply hidden issues, or to reflect more deeply on those raised initially. Schön (2013) refers to 'reflection on action', and this stage can help the mentee develop or extend their reflective capacity by pausing and deconstructing their initial statements and begin to explore what lies behind them. It can also be a point at which I need to be aware of the boundaries and to keep the mentee within them. Mentoring and coaching are not counselling. Any suspicion that the mentee's needs may be better met by other professionals with specific qualifications must be shared with them, and they should be encouraged to seek more appropriate help, even if that means accompanying them to seek it. This is an extreme scenario, but it can happen. It can be useful to call a 'comfort break' and take refreshments: it does provide a break from the intensity and allows mentor or coach and mentee space to reflect. I have often used this to think how to move forward, particularly when a mentee has been reluctant or simply very hard to get to know.

In most cases this 'middle' stage provides the safe place for the mentee to identify issues behind the initial concerns shared and their own emotional responses to these and to begin to acknowledge how this has affected them in the past. It is a space to reflect on possible scenarios to take forward and on strategies to achieve them. This is perhaps where the approach of a coach may differ from that of a mentor, depending on the agreed remit they have. A mentor might ask how the mentee could respond and assist them by talking through a strategy or scenario. A coach might provide possible alternatives and describe what these would involve. In either case the aim is to assist the mentee to move forward more confidently and with a better understanding of themselves as well as the context and others involved. A well-informed mentor or coach may well use specific metaphors, such as 'Iceberg theory',[1] or techniques, such as the 'GROW' model (Grow, Reality, Opportunity, Will)[2] or 'Socratic questioning'[3] to assist the mentee in moving forward more confidently. These and similar tools or techniques need to be part of the resources a mentor or coach has at their disposal and, incidentally, they reinforce the need for training for mentors and coaches wherever they are used.

Once again, at the end of this period reviewing what has been covered and how far the mentee has progressed is usually a positive experience.

---

[1] Iceberg Theory is the notion that what we see or are aware of is only part of a larger set of issues, circumstances or understandings. It is useful to encourage mentees to begin to think more deeply beyond the immediate issue or need – see https://www.londonleadershipacademy.nhs.uk/sites/default/files/uploaded/Introduction%20to%20the%20Iceberg%20model_FINAL_25%2003%202015.pdf (Accessed 16 July 2019).
[2] Grow, Reality, Opportunity, Will or GROW is an acronym to remember four aspects when reflecting on progression or development as an individual, team or organization – see Parsloe and Leedham (2009) and https://www.performanceconsultants.com/grow-model (Accessed 27 December 2018).
[3] Socratic questioning is a technique of answering a response with a more probing question to encourage deeper reflection, for example, Mentor – 'Why is this such an issue for you?'; Mentee – 'I don't know'; Mentor – 'Why is that?' See Cox, Backirova and Clutterbuck (2014) and https://www.intel.com/content/dam/www/program/education/us/en/documents/project-design/strategies/dep-question-socratic.pdf (Accessed 27 December 2018).

Reflections 3: Stage 3 – Endings

It is the mentor or coach's responsibility to maintain the health and well-being of the mentee during the session and especially at the end. Judging when to begin drawing a session to a close and allowing space to achieve a positive end is as important as the beginning. This part of the process provides time for an overview of the whole session from the perspective of the mentee and the mentor or coach. Stepping back and sharing the emotional journey, as well as the specific points covered, should enable the mentee to recognize their strengths, think about how these can be used in the future and to discern strategies and aims going forward. I try to use this time and space to agree on what we have covered, making notes as we discuss each aspect. The notes will also contain agreed aims and strategies for the practitioner to achieve. These notes will then be shared with the mentee who will have opportunity to edit them, in which case we both agree the final version. This also provides a starting point for the next session where one is planned.

In addition, I complete my own reflections in my personal professional journal, recording my own thoughts and feelings and what I feel went well or how my approach could be improved next time. This has sometimes shown more clearly the areas that have not been discussed or it has enabled me to see where a mentee has been focused solely on actions and processes and has avoided any personal reflection or reference to emotional responses.

It can sometimes happen that, right at the point of departure, a mentee will choose to reveal or share an important issue, event or feeling. As a mentor I have experienced this more than once and each time I have felt that I had been left with another person's burden, not knowing quite what to do with it. In each case I have left it to the mentee to raise it again. Perhaps it is an indication of trust that they could share it at all. The timing suggests ambivalence in terms of the mentee wanting to address it. It was included in my notes, which were then shared and agreed, and it did provide a focus for the next session. In some ways this is an echo of 'moments of disconnect' (Megginson and Clutterbuck, 2009), where the mentor or coach 'begin to doubt their own ability'. Such apparently negative moments, as Clutterbuck and Megginson suggest, can be turned into positives. I have had occasion to ask a mentee to 'help me out here …' and together we have deconstructed and re-constructed the issue, how it has emerged, what it might mean and how we both might deal with it positively. It can also be the case that a mentee achieves success by recognizing and 'owning' the issue.

Conclusion

Early Years practitioners have often little formal training or in-service development. Their focus is on the children in their care and they can be reluctant to recognize or set aside time for their own needs. Mentoring and coaching can provide a space in which to acknowledge their strengths and consider how to be even better at what they do. It has been my privilege to see individuals progress over time and become more confident about themselves and their ability to meet the demands of the children and their organization when they are given time and space and someone to actively listen to them.

> **Reflective Questions**
>
> 1 How far does the 'three stage process' match your experience?
> 2 How often is time and space made to foster effective mentoring or coaching support?

References

Cox, E., Bachkirova, T., and Clutterbuck, D. (2014) 2nd edn. *The complete handbook of coaching.* London, Sage.

Early Excellence Centre, Pilot Programme Second Evaluation Report 19 2000–2001. Available online: https://dera.ioe.ac.uk/4667/1/RR361.pdf (Accessed 26 December 2018).

Kolb, D. A. (1984) *Experiential learning.* Englewood Cliffs, NJ, Prentice Hall.

Megginson, D. and Clutterbuck, D. (2009) *Further techniques for coaching and mentoring.* Oxford, Butterworth.

Parsloe, E. and Leedham, M. (2009) 2nd edn. *Coaching and mentoring: practical conversations to improve learning.* London, Kogan Page.

Schön, D. (2013) *The reflective practitioner: how professionals think in action.* London, Ashgate.

Wenger E., McDermott, R., and Snyder, W. M. (2002) *Cultivating communities of practice.* Boston, MA, Harvard Business Press.

18

Using Pre-service Teachers as Mentors to In-service Early Years Teachers to Promote Meaningful Child Participation

Naseema Shaik

Introduction

In a South African higher education context based in the Western Cape, final year Foundation Phase pre-service teachers are required to spend six weeks in a Grade R (reception year) class. The first three weeks occur at the beginning of the second term and the second session occurs at the beginning of the third term of the year. The pre-service teachers have limited time in this class as they only spend the first year practicum and their final year practicum (practical study) in Grade R. In their second and third years of study the pre-service teachers spend their practicum in Grade one, Grade two and Grade three classes.

During their academic year pre-service teachers receive extensive cognitive coaching on child participation. During the first practicum they are required to observe the type of pedagogy that is undertaken in a Grade R context and then provide feedback at a dialogic session. At the feedback session the coach facilitates conversations and questioning strategies using dialogue as the main means of obtaining feedback and supporting the pre-service teachers.

Reflective Narrative

During the dialogic session the pre-service teachers were highly perturbed by the ways in which the in-service teachers adopted pedagogy. The following excerpts show the attitudes of the in-service teachers, with whom the pre-service teachers are working, towards child participation:

> 'What the teacher says goes, so children don't have a chance to say anything and that is exactly what we're doing; we're killing our children because we're not giving them the opportunities to say anything. It's all about what the teacher says and what she is giving you and that's right – which is wrong because children are born with child participation in themselves and if we do not give them a chance to be heard we are not allowing them to be critical thinkers.'
>
> 'Children are shouting and the teacher is listening … but doesn't really motivate and encourage that child.'
>
> 'She does not ask, 'what do you mean' and how and actually get their ideas in the classroom. It doesn't happen.'
>
> 'You know during teaching practice, I said to myself that I'm going to give my children the opportunity to speak but they don't speak. When they [are] supposed to be doing work now they want to chat you know. Because the teacher doesn't do it so you kinda like what must I do?'
>
> 'The teacher wants the children to work in their workbooks so there is no time to talk to the children and to genuinely listen to them. The Grade R has now become a mini Grade one.'
>
> 'The teacher believes that children must not be heard but [that] they need to listen to her. It makes it difficult for us to invite child participation because the teacher is in charge of her class and we cannot do anything but follow what she wants us to do.'
>
> 'She has no understanding about what child participation is … '

The above excerpts show that there is a dissonance between pre-service teachers' and in-service teachers' understanding of child participation. The dissonance limits the potential for child participation to take place. This means that the pre-school teachers do not have the chance to learn how to develop this aspect of their practice and enhance their understanding. Due to the in-service teachers' limited understanding of what child participation means and its potential for valuing children's opinions and to give children a voice, the in-service teachers cannot further extend the concept of child participation beyond the coaching that the pre-service teachers receive during their training.

As a group, we decided that for the second session of the practicum we would find ways to implement child participation and to work collaboratively with the in-service teachers so that they would better understand the concept of child participation by using Shier's (2001) Model of Participation (see Figure 18.1). This model is built on five levels of participation:

1. Children share power and responsibility for decision-making.
2. Children are involved in the decision-making process.
3. Children's views are taken into account.
4. Children are supported in expressing their views.
5. Children are listened to.

At each level of participation, the Grade R in-service teachers may have different degrees of commitment, which are known as 'openings', 'opportunities' and 'obligations'. An opening occurs when a Grade R teacher is ready to accept that children need to participate and gives a personal pledge to facilitate this. An opening might not be implemented, however. Opportunities occur when an opening is put into practice; for example, staff might be given training in how to invoke child participation. An obligation is honoured when opportunities are incorporated into the policies of the setting. There is, therefore, an obligation on the staff to ensure that participation is integrated into the system (Shier, 2001).

During the second practicum, pre-service students introduce Shier's model of participation to the pre-service teachers and pose questions relating to the five levels of participation to obtain feedback from the in-service teachers as to how they invite participation. These questions stimulate the in-service teachers to think about, reflect upon, plan and evaluate opportunities they might take advantage of to encourage and implement child participation. The key idea here is collaboration (Kellett, 2010) and so there is co-construction between the pre-service teachers and the in-service teachers. Shier alerts us to the fact that using the model in the form of questions should not be restricted to a tick-box exercise. For example, if the Grade R in-service teachers' response to any of the questions was no, the pre-service teachers should then probe the Grade R teachers further by asking questions such as, 'What do we need to do so that we can …?'; 'Are we in a position to face the challenges considering the diversity of children in the Grade R context?' This helps them explore the possibilities open to them. Shier (2001) proposes that the model should be used as a first step in developing an action plan to enhance child participation.

Pre-service Teachers Mentoring Teachers 191

Levels of *Participation*

⇩

5. Children share power and responsibilities for decision making.

4. Children are involved in decision-making processes?

3. Children's views are taken into account.

2. Children are supported in expressing their views.

1. Children are listened to.

START HERE

Openings>Opportunities>Obligations

| Are you ready to share some of your adult power with children? | Is there a procedure that enables children and adults to share power and responibility for decisions? | Is it a policy requirement that children and adults share power and responsibility for decisions? |

| Are you ready to let children join in your decision-making processes? | Is there a procedure that enables children to join in decision-making processes? | Is it a policy requirement that children must be involved in decision-making processes? |

This point is the minimum you must achieve if you endorse the UN Convention on the Rights of the Child

| Are you ready to take children's views into account? | Does your decision making process enable you to take children's views into account? | Is it a policy requirement that children's views must be given due weight in decision-making? |

| Are you ready to support children in expressing their views? | Do you have a range of ideas and activities to help children express their views? | Is it a policy requirement that children must be supported in expressing their views? |

| Are you ready to listen to children? | Do you work in a way that enables you to listen to children? | Is it a policy requirement that children must be listened to? |

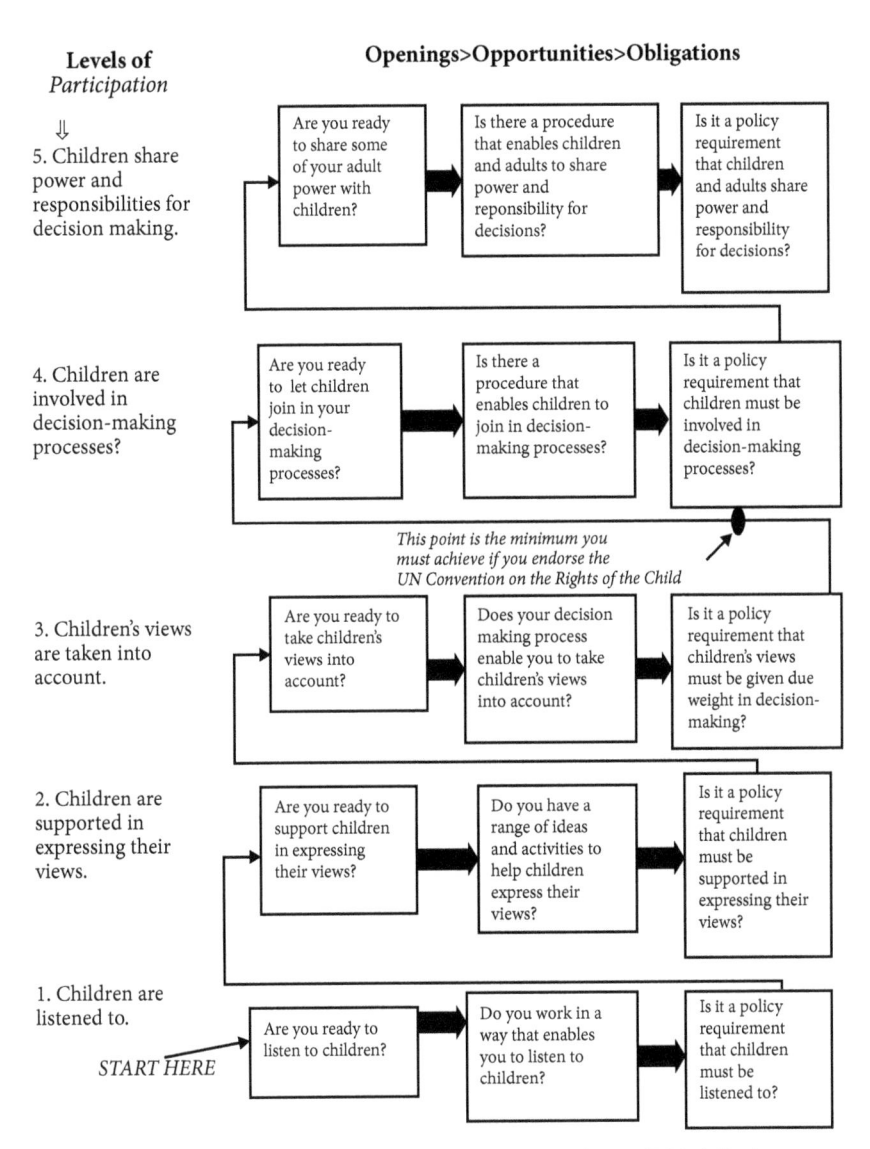

Figure 18.1 Shier's model of participation, from Shier (2001) Pathways to participation: openings, opportunities and obligations. *Children and Society*, 15: 107–117, at p. 111

After the second practicum there is another dialogic session. The feedback received looks at how the pre-service teachers used Shier's model of participation and how the in-service teachers responded to it. Here are some of the responses from the pre-service teachers: '*The mentor teachers* were not aware of Shier's model of participation'; 'They did not understand child participation as placing so much of an emphasis on children's voice, opinion and decision-making.'

Although there is much more work to be undertaken in order for genuine child participation to be implemented, the in-service teachers are now aware of using Shier's model as a guideline when inviting child participation throughout the daily programme in an integrated way that respects the voice of the child.

The above case study shows how the pre-service teachers were encouraged to change their role as pre-service teachers to becoming mentors to in-service teachers in order for child participation to be realized. While cognitive coaching is being offered to pre-service teachers for child participation to become a reality in the South African context, there also needs to be more research into how coaching can stimulate in-service teachers' understanding and implementation of child participation.

Reflective Questions

1 How do these examples resonate with your own experience?
2 'The Grade R has now become a mini Grade one.' Is this statement true in your context? If not, how have you avoided it? How might mentoring and coaching help to change this?
3 If we do not give children a chance to be heard we are not allowing them to be critical thinkers. How are children's voices heard in your situation? What helps or hinders critical thinking in young children?
4 How might greater convergence of theory and practice be achieved between those being trained to teach in Early Years and practising teachers?
5 In this study 'novice' Early Childhood educators have valuable ideas to share with experienced teachers. How does this match traditional forms of mentoring and coaching?
6 How might mentoring and coaching help serving teachers to be open to change?

References

Kellett, M. (2010) Small shoes, big steps! Empowering children as active researchers. *American Journal of Community Psychology*, 46 (1–2): 195–203.

Shier, H. (2001) Pathways to participation: openings, opportunities and obligations. *Children and Society*, 15: 107–117.

19

Critical Reflections on Emerging Themes

Michael Gasper and Rosie Walker

As coaching and mentoring policy and practice develops within the workplace, our definitions of what these are change. Within the chapters of this book, the definitions that have been given reflect their themes and these may differ. However, the broad themes are evident and perhaps more useful to consider than precise definitions. As can be seen from the chapters and case studies, coaching and mentoring is most effective when used positively to empower practitioners to achieve the best outcomes for children and families and to provide quality services. The book provides many examples.

However, there are contributions, taken from the different countries, that expose a number of tensions in respect to coaching and mentoring. Not least is the contradiction between the regulatory and policy expectations and what can actually be offered at a grassroots level. For example, there is a recognition by policy-makers, as discussed in Chapter 2, that coaching and mentoring has a key part to play in the global agenda for integrated working and adopting a life-course approach to caring for citizens within differing societies. But, as the case studies show, there are often not the skill sets, funding, time or emotional or physical space for this to be adequately resourced. For example, the UK Early Years Foundation Stage (EYFS) identifies coaching as an essential part of supervision, which is a requirement for all staff. Nevertheless, it does not make clear how this could be funded or if the same person who undertakes the supervision should also be the coach and what qualifications and skills they require. The reality, as highlighted within the UK case study, is that often there are not the resources to provide adequate coaching and mentoring for all staff. Moreover, in reality coaching and mentoring can sometimes become an accountability, tick-box exercise that does little to enhance professional development or lay to rest some of the complex dilemmas practitioners face on a daily basis. As Edwards and Nuttall (2009) assert, we are living in complex and changing landscapes of practice, and this has led to more complex ethical and equity dilemmas which require a continual critical approach and professionalization when engaging with the issues and finding innovative and creative ways of adapting practice. This is where coaching and mentoring have a vital role to play.

Chapters 1 and 7 clearly demonstrate that where coaching and mentoring is well resourced and funded there are immense benefits for not only for the coachees but also ultimately for children and families. The willingness of governments to fund this, particularly in times of austerity, is questionable. The current undervaluing of Early Years does not readily provide a context where coaching and mentoring would be viewed as a priority, despite economists highlighting the fiscal benefits to society in investing in our youngest children. It seems that so much of the provision in Early Years relies on the goodwill of the staff. However, we are delighted to see that delegates at the recent G20 summit in Buenos Aires have signed a declaration that Early Childhood sustainability and quality enhancement will be prioritized as a means to 'build human capital to break the cycle of intergenerational and structural poverty, and of reducing inequalities, specially where young children are most vulnerable' (G20 Policy Paper, 2018). It is hoped that such an aspiration includes coaching and mentoring as integral to this in order to maximize the ability of practitioners to deliver robust services. Practitioners and leaders will require quality coaching and mentoring in order to deliver this agenda. How this might be provided is discussed within the chapters and examples of different models given within the case studies. Critical and reflective questions have been asked within each chapter in order to see how models of practice might be adapted to your particular settings.

As we have seen, there is a tension about how coaching and mentoring is used and how it is set up within differing organizations and countries. Are they, as Chapter 4 and the case studies from Singapore discuss, mainly used as an induction into systems and processes, or are they part of a broader-based approach in enabling practitioners to gain expertise in their field? Is coaching and mentoring just for inexperienced practitioners or do leaders also require this? As argued in the chapters, in a rapidly changing arena such as Early Years there is a need for all practitioners to acquire skills that enable them to manage changes in policy and practice and to contribute to the delivery of high quality Early Years services. This is done by gaining new knowledge, applying self-reflection and setting self-sustaining practices and goals. However, there are particular issues within the UK, for example, about whether the Early Years have a level playing field in relation to starting points. In schools, all staff are qualified to a defined level, such as teachers and teaching assistants. In the Early Years, there are often not the same defined qualifications and coaching and mentoring providers need to be aware of the potential need to undertake basic skills with those they are coaching and mentoring. In contrast, Singapore has a highly developed career pathway, but mentoring is only offered to the most inexperienced staff. This has implications for maintaining quality and retention of more experienced staff.

In order to foster an environment in which successful coaching and mentoring take place, the development of a culture of inquiry and curiosity within organizations in joining a 'competent system' of promoting learning and critical reflection is key (Early Education and Care (CoRe, 2011: 21)). Chapters within the book highlight the need for this culture to be developed so that a Community of Practice, where this is valued and promoted, is fostered to support the framework of coaching and mentoring. Within this, coaching and mentoring offers practitioners the opportunity to engage in learning how to think, work with others, communicate effectively and deliver ethical practice. Coaching and mentoring are important means of enabling practitioners to gain a belief in themselves and to develop the ability to take responsibility and control over events that affect their lives as part of a Community of Practice. This is elucidated in several chapters and case studies in which examples of practice within an international arena showcase the impact of carefully designed coaching and mentoring. 'Coming to know oneself within and through the changing personal and professional landscapes, having a strong value base and reflecting on the wider issues for practice, lifelong learning and the building of communities of practice are a strong basis for success' (Walker, 2017: 419; see also Opengart and Short 2002). Such skills afforded by coaching and mentoring are key in managing adversity, challenges and inequalities which are ever-present in professional life in Early Years. As Chapter 10 explores, an individualized yet standardized approach to this is helpful as it enables evidence-based practice to underpin an approach which prioritizes individual developmental needs.

The chapters and case studies show that, in order to be effective, this process needs to be set up as two-way and that the relationship between the coach/mentor and coachee/mentee is crucial in developing trust. Here the culture of the organization has an important part to play. As Chapter 3 highlights, a motivated and supported culture will offer the best environment within which for coaching and mentoring to take place. This includes the consideration of potential power imbalances between the two parties involved. There is a tension between the coaches and mentors needing to be experienced and skilled and to understand the wider socio-economic agenda of Early Years and the need to build trusting relationships based on mutual respect. Where there is a recognition that both are learning from the process and value is placed on a culture of respectful relationships where issues can be debated in safety within acceptable boundaries, effective coaching and mentoring is likely to flourish. Here a strengths-based approach is useful, both as a starting point for the coachee and mentee and as confidence and skills develop. Such an approach is discussed in Chapter 6, where the concept of pedagogic mediation is explored as a democratic approach to professional development. Here a safe space is provided for practitioners to discuss and reflect on working practice.

The importance of a provision of a safe emotional and physical space for practitioners to reflect on practice is highlighted throughout the book. Practitioners are working with children and families daily with potentially complex issues that may require prompt responses and attention. This is particularly highlighted as an issue in Chapter 5, where safeguarding is considered in some depth. Coaching and mentoring not only provide the opportunity to look back and think about the responses that have been made, but also give the chance to look forward to using the learning that has arisen from this and consider the implications for future action. Ensuring that Early Years practitioners have the confidence to become powerful and skilful advocates for children is essential so that their professional voice is heard and recognized by other professionals – this is a cornerstone of successful coaching and mentoring in this arena. However, a distinction needs to be made between intensive mentoring and counselling, as there can be a fine line between the two. Counselling involves a trained professional who is able to diagnose and work with emotional problems and is generally intended to be short-term. Once the mentor finds that mentoring sessions are slipping into the realm of psychological and personal problems, it is time to refer the mentee to a trained counsellor.

As Chapter 4 highlights, it is as important for all practitioners, whether inexperienced or leaders, to have access to high quality mentoring and coaching in order to encourage retention of staff. Becky Poulter Jewson in her case study in Chapter 13 alludes to this and the difficulties of having to finance her own mentoring as this is not provided by her organization. Similarly, Chapter 4 highlights the importance of a trusting relationship, which is similar to having a critical friend with whom to work. However, there is a need for this to be balanced with fostering the coachee's independence. This all takes time to evolve as possible philosophy clashes and insecure processes in supporting the coaching and mentoring can undermine the potential for a successful relationship. Thus, the setting up of national frameworks for coaching and mentoring is an issue requiring attention for all countries as they respond to Early Years as having 'the compelling and developing evidence base which indicates its potential to achieve, social, economic, political and economic progress' (Pascal and Bertram 2019: 183). The quote from Pascal and Bertram highlights leadership as key within settings in 'enabling learning, pedagogy, participation, distributed power, voice, challenge, stimulation, social equity, democracy, community and achievement to flourish in a positive and purposeful climate'.

This concept is supported in Chapter 3 where Josephine Bleach introduces a framework of first, second and third person practice, as espoused by Torbert (2001), which is necessary in transforming practice. It is within this model that the leader has a key contribution to make as a coach or mentor. Knowing when it is relevant to use supervision, coaching or mentoring and understanding their staff, context and service are skills used in maximizing the potential of practitioners to deliver high quality services for children and families. The tension experienced by leaders of settings who provide mentoring and coaching is explored in Chapter 4. Combining an authoritative role with the requirements of being a coach or mentor can, at times, prove difficult, and the need for leaders themselves to have appropriate training within these roles is not always considered a high priority as it may be implicitly expected that leaders already possess these skills.

Mentoring and coaching require time, space, patience, deep listening and a willingness to find and build on the strengths of those who are mentored or coached. The effects are not always immediately apparent: mentors and coaches do not have magic wands. Mentees and coachees may be reluctant to contemplate change, while mentors and coaches coax them to trust the processes involved in change. The examples provided in both parts of this book share best practice. They underline the need for mentors and coaches to be open and non-judgemental, while evaluating what they hear and see. They also illustrate the importance of shared understanding and celebrate what can be achieved with trust over time.

Mentoring and coaching are shown by this book to be capable of providing powerful and empowering support. Striving for the best outcomes for children and families is of the highest priority for society. Having had the privilege of compiling this book, we have no doubt that mentoring and coaching is a powerful way forward in enabling practitioners to address the future global challenges which we face. This is particularly apparent when mentoring and coaching are seen as equal partnerships where those who are supported are encouraged to 'own' the process and outcome.

References

CoRE (2011) *Competence requirements in early childhood education and care. European Commission, Directorate General for Education and Culture, final report.* University of East London, Cass School of Education and University of Ghent, Department for Social Welfare Studies. Available online: https://download.ei-ie.org/Docs/WebDepot/CoReResearchDocuments2011.pdf (Accessed 28 December 2018).

Edwards, S. and Nuttall, J. (2009) *Professional learning in early childhood settings.* Rotterdam, Sense Publications. Available online: https://www.sensepublishers.com/media/801-professional-learning-in-early-childhood-settings.pdf (Accessed 28 December 2018).

G20 Policy Paper (2018) *G20 Summit recommendations G7/G20.* Buenos Aires, Argentina, Advocacy Alliance (US). Available online: https://www.icrw.org/wp-content/uploads/2018/04/G20-Policy-Paper-2018.pdf (Accessed 28 December 2018).

Opengart, R. and Short, D. C. (2002) Free agent learners: the new career model and its impact on human resource development. *International Journal of Lifelong Education*, 21: 220–233.

Torbert, W. R. (2001) The practice of action inquiry. In Reason, P. and Bradbury, H. (eds) *Handbook of action research, participative inquiry and practice.* London, Sage, pp. 250–261.

Pascal, C. and Bertram, T. (2019) Pedagogic system leadership within complex and changing ECEC systems. In Cheeseman, S. and Walker, R. (eds) *Thinking about pedagogy in early education: pedagogies for leading practice.* Oxford, Routledge, pp. 182–205.

Walker, R. (2017) Learning is like a lava lamp: the student journey to critical thinking. Research in post-compulsory education. Available online: https://doi.org/10.1080/13596748.2017.1381293 (Accessed 28 December 2018).

Index

abstract thinking 102-5, 150, 159-60
abuse of children 49, 52, 54
action research 32
action steps 148
action zones 8
Adler, Alfred 12
advocacy 49
Alder, H. 30
alignment within systems 23
'analytical observers' 102, 104
Anderson, W. 49
Ang, L. 19
Aotearoa 115, 118
Appreciative Inquiry 2, 116-18, 121, 180
Argyris, C. 75, 121
Aristotle 10
Aro Arataki Children's Centre 115-16, 118, 121
art
   in the curriculum 171-2
     growth through the medium of 172-6
attitudes of in-service teachers 189-92
Australia 90
authoritarian leaders 28
autonomy 146-7

Bachkirova, T. 11
Balduzzi, L. 69
Bandura, A. 131, 159-60
'banking model' of education 61
Bass, B. 69, 75
behavioural competency model 96
Belgium 163-77
benefits from mentoring and coaching 195
Bertram, Tony 17, 22, 59, 82, 181, 198

best practice
   reflection on 142
   sharing of 118, 198
bicultural curriculum 118-21
Bishop, R. 121
Blanchard, K. 29
Bleach, Josephine 198
Bloom, P.J. 129
Bourdieu, Pierre 47, 50-1
Bradbury-Jones, C. 54
brain development 1
British Columbia Early Learning Framework 132
Britto, P. 23
'buddies' 95
'burn out' 140

Callan, S. 70
Canada 125-6
capacity-building 23
Cape Peninsula University 83
case studies 63, 195-6
change agents 21, 28
child-centred education 81, 136, 147
children, traditional conceptions of 82
children's centres 8, 181
Chitwood, S. 49
Chu, M. 40
classroom management strategies 156-8
closing of mentoring and coaching sessions 73, 186
Clutterbuck, D. 8, 10-11, 24, 186
coach-mentors 8, 100-4, 146-51, 156-60
coach-teacher interactions 100, 103-6, 150-2, 156, 160
coaching 5, 7-11, 14-15, 152

dangers inherent in 12
definition of 8-11, 29, 48-9, 69
goals of 102-3
value of 79
cognitive coaching 79-86, 192
cohesiveness of teams 119
collaborative relationships 31, 41, 145, 147, 150
collegial relationships 150
Common Assessment Scoring System (CLASS) 146, 151, 154, 156
common features of mentoring and coaching 14
communities of practice 39, 61, 74, 142, 180-1, 196
competency-based training 68
competent managers 28
competent systems 22-3, 196
confidentiality 183
consciousness 82, 85
Conservative Party 8
constructivism 169
contracts 41, 183
control, sense of 30
cooperation between agencies 181
counselling seen as distinct from mentoring and coaching 184
Cox, E. 11
Craw, J. 121
critical reflection 22, 34, 75, 174, 195-6
cross-agency approaches 20-1
Cubey, P. 119
cultural awareness 164
cultural education 176
cultural maps 173
culturally-responsive teaching (CRT) 148
curiosity, culture of 196
curriculum implementation 94

decision-making processes 28-9
'deficit' thinking 80, 121
democratic leaders 28
dependency 13
developmental psychology 164

Dewey, John 101
differences between mentoring and coaching 18, 197
'discussion before issue' 142
diversity and 'diversattude' 163-4, 175-7
documentation, pedagogic 63
domestic violence 52, 54
Douglas, H. 52
Drake, D.B. 166, 170
Duhn, I. 121

Early Childhood Care and Education (ECEC) 1, 7-8, 12, 19-23, 32, 34, 37-42, 91
   leadership in 21
Early Childhood Project Approach Fidelity Form (ECPAF) 147, 155
Early Childhood systems and policies 17-22
Early Learning Initiative (ELI), Irish 5, 27, 31-3
Early Years Foundation Stage (EYFS) 136, 194
Early Years Initial Teacher Training (EYITT) programmes 68, 70
Early Years Teacher (EYT) status 68
Ebrahim, H.B. 80
Edwards, S. 195
efficacy 82, 131; *see also* self-efficacy
email, use of 73
emotional component of safeguarding and protecting children 9, 54-6
empowerment 140, 145, 194, 199
'encountering' phase of pedagogic mediation 62-5
engagement of children in education 106; *see also* participation by children in education
ethical issues 29, 65
Eun, B. 60
Eurofound 164
European Union Quality Framework for Early Childhood Development and Care 38

evidence-based practice 102, 106, 196
experiential learning theory 42, 101, 158

face-to-face contact 73
feedback 72, 188
Ferguson, H. 54
Fernandez, C. 23
first person practice 27, 30-4, 198
followers 120
Formosinho, J. 63
Freire, P. 61-2, 101
Froebel, F.W.A. 69-70
Fullan, M. 30, 32
funding 195

Gallagher, S. 51
Gardiner, W. 95
Garvey, B. 10-11
Gasper, Michael 18
Geertz, C. 11
Georgenson, J. 19
Gibson, H. 120
Glickman, C.D. 101, 104, 159
goal-setting 69, 102-3
Goodard, C. 52, 54
Gopnik, Allison 172
government policies 20
'Grade R' 80-5, 188, 190
Greenwich University 68, 70
Grey, A. 120
ground rules 13
'GROW' model 71, 185
G20 group of countries 195

habitus 47, 51
'handholding' 93
Hargrove, R. 164
Harlow, E. 49
Hawkins, P. 40
Hayden, D. 49
Hayden, J. 120
Head Start programmes 100, 103, 154
Helm, D. 49-50
Henshall, A. 75

here-and-now focus 170
human capital 195
Hunt, S. 52, 54

identity 170, 174
  personal and *professional* 165
indigenous knowledge 119
induction to an orgaization or role 93-4
induction support 126, 130
integrated systems approach 19-22, 33, 194
intercultural dialogue 175
intrapersonal intelligence and skills 31, 33
Ireland 5, 27, 31-3
Isaacs, S. 15
isomorphism, pedagogical 63

Jewson, Becky Poulter 197-8
job satisfaction 131
John, Karen 12, 15
journals, personal 186
judgemental attitudes 14

Katz, L. 131
knowledge, construction of 59, 70, 83
Kolb, D.A. 42, 101, 158-9

Lacey, Josh 174-5
laissez-faire leaders 28
Laming, Lord 49
language barriers 158, 160
language learning 119
Law, H. 165
Lazzarri, A. 69
leaders' need for their own mentoring and coaching 22
leadership 21-2, 27-31, 198
  strength of 120
  styles of 28-9
  tasks of 31
  theories of 28-9
learning communities 32-3
learning culture 22

learning environments 146, 151
learning experiences 86, 155, 158
learning from mistakes and failure 172, 181
Leedham, M. 8
Lewin, K. 63
liberating approaches 62
life-course approaches 20-1, 194
life experiences 51
lifelong learning 164
listening 62, 64
  active 173
location of mentoring and coaching sessions 13
logs of coaching 147-8, 159
Lyndon, H. 64

MacBeath, J. 30
McMahon, C. 9
McNamee, S. 118
management
  demanding nature of 28
  in relation to leadership 28-9
Māori culture 115-17
Meadors, P. 54
Megginson, D. 8, 10, 186
mental health problems 12
mentoring 5-10, 13-15, 18-22, 37-9, 42, 69-70, 73-6, 90-5
  characteristic features of 10-11
  conditions for success of 32
  cross-sectional 19
  dangers inherent in 12
  definition of 8-11, 29, 48-9, 69
  distinctiveness of 10
  inside and *outside* types of 95
  main purpose of 93
  perceptions and practice of 93-5
  stages of 74
  training and preparation for 38-9
mentoring for mentors 38, 50
metacognition 81-2
Metzger, D. 171
Molla, T. 73

Montessori approach to education 84
Moos, L. 30
motivation of individuals 13
multi-perspectivity 177
mutuality 11

narration, pedagogical 132
narrative coaching 165-7
narrative imagination 174
narrative space 166-7
National College of Ireland 5, 27
National Professional Qualification in Integrated Centre Leadership (NPQICL) 8, 12, 15, 181
Netherlands, the 163
New Zealand 115-19
Nolan, A. 73
Nores, M. 23
note-taking 183, 186
Nussbaum, Martha 174
Nuttall, J. 195

Oliviera-Formosinho, J. 80-1; *see also* Formosinho, J.
ongoing process of mentoring and coaching 21
open-ended questions 42
openness to a whole setting 62, 64
organizational culture 47, 51, 197
'outsiders' as catalysts 6
'ownership' of process and outcome 120-1, 199

Parsloe, E. 8
participation by children in education 80-6, 189-92
participatory research 63
Pascal, Chris 17, 22, 59, 82, 181, 198
Payler, J. 19
pedagogic mediation 6, 58-66, 197
  advantages and limitations of 65-6
  ethical and participatory nature of 65
  four elements of 61-2
  recent research findings on 64-5

underlying theory of 60-1
pedagogic system leadership 22
Pedagogy-in-Participation 59
peer groups and peer-observations 39, 138
peer mentoring 126-8, 131-2
peer reflection, facilitation of 139-40
person-centred experience 18
Peshkin, A. 50, 55
Piaget, Jean 101
play 174
Portugal 59
positive psychology 12
positives, focus on 12
post-traumatic stress 54
power relations 9, 14, 23, 34, 41, 63, 197
practicum experience 188-91
preparedness for formal schooling 154
prior knowledge, accessing of 83-4
'professional conversations' 136-42
  impact of 140
  misunderstanding of the purpose of 139
professional development 18, 21-2, 29, 37-9, 42, 101, 125, 154, 195
  continuing (CPD) 22, 39, 58, 74
  participatory approach to 63
'professional' teachers 150
professionalization 164, 166
Project Approach 104-5, 147-50, 155-7, 160
protection
  of children 47-50, 54-6
  of practitioners 54
psychology of mentoring and coaching 12

qualification mentoring 68
qualifications of school staff 196
Rau, C. 119
reciprocal relationships 74-5
reflection
  on action 184
  Pershkin approach to 55
  single-loop and *double-loop* strands of 75
reflective conversations 151
reflective narrative 189-92
reflective perspective on coaching 165
reflective practice 1, 5, 18, 30, 39-42, 48, 50
reflective practitioners 54-5
Reggio Emilia approach to education 84
Reid, R. 120
relationships, criticality to mentoring of 182-7, 196-8
resources 118-19, 194-5
Richards, C.M. 49, 51
Riley, K.A. 30
Ritchie, J. 119
role models 14
Rosen, R. 21
Rouse, E. 40
Ruch, G. 50
Rutgers University 99

safeguarding of children 6, 47-9, 54-6, 139, 141, 197
Schön, D. 75, 121, 184
second person practice 27, 30-4, 198
secondary transformation syndrome (STS) 54
secondary trauma 55
self-belief 196
self-efficacy 39, 131, 159
self-knowledge 31
self-starting teachers 105
Seligman, Martin 12
Sergiovanni, T.J. 120
Shabani, K. 60-1
Shier, H. 190-2
Shohet, R. 40
silencing 50
Singapore 6, 89-96, 195-6
  Childcare Masterplan 89-90
  Early Childhood Development Authority (ECDA) 96-7
  Principal Matters programme 96

Skills Framework 91
Síolta 32
situational leadership 29
skills involved in mentoring and coaching 14
social construction 83, 169
social nature of human existence 12
Socrates and Socratic questioning 10, 42, 185
South Africa 79-81, 188
SPARK quality rating scale 92
spiral of learning 101
Starr, J. 10, 13
states of mind 81-5
Stelter, R. 165-6, 169
Stokes, P. 10
story-telling 166-7, 171-3
Stover, S. 120
strengths-based approaches 197
supervision 9, 12, 14-15, 24, 40-2, 48-50, 54-5, 136, 147, 150, 160, 194
    functions of 41
    reflective 40-2
suspension of one's own pedagogical beliefs 62, 64
systems of Early Childhood education 17-22, 40, 42

tacit knowledge 166
targeted coaching 101-3
teacher-child interactions 155, 160
teacher development 101-5; *see also* professional development
teacher-directed activities 81, 84-5
teacher-experts 150, 152
teachers' strategies 116
team teaching 119-20
template for the monitoring of coaching 137

Te Whāriki curriculum 115
theory, *espoused* and *in use* 121
'thick' description 11
third person practice 27, 30, 33-4, 198
Thorpe, Sheila 181
tick-box exercises 195
Torbert, W.R. 198
training programmes 68, 139, 185
transformational leadership 68
transformative practice 22, 34
transmissive practice 80, 85
Trodd, L. 15
trust 11, 13, 18, 150, 166-7, 184, 186, 197-8
Tuohy, D. 28
types of mentoring and coaching 23-4

United States 6, 99-106
    National Institute for Early Education Research 99
Urban, M. 22

values 166, 169-70
Van Heusden, B. 175
vicarious experience 180
Vygotsky, L.S. 60-1, 101

Walker, Rosie 196
Walsh, T. 52
Weisling, N. 95
Wenger, E. 61, 180-1
Wertsch, J.G. 60
workforce of Early Years education 60, 99-101
working environments and workplace culture 50, 55-6, 130

Zigarmi, P. and D. 29
zone of proximal development 60-1

Milton Keynes UK
Ingram Content Group UK Ltd.
UKHW051100260624
444756UK00005B/78